THE ULTIMATE GUIDE TO
MOTOR BOATS

THE ULTIMATE GUIDE TO
MOTOR BOATS

Barry Pickthall

CHARTWELL
BOOKS, INC.

Published in 2004 by
Chartwell Books, Inc.
A division of Book Sales, Inc.
Raritan Center
114 Northfield Avenue
Edison. NJ 08837 USA

ISBN 0-7858-1822-7

Printed in China

Acknowledgements
This book would not have been produced without the reintroduction to the pleasures of powerboating given to me by the Earl of Normanton, chairman of the historic Harmsworth Trophy race series and his co-driver Barry Appleby, who took me for a spin on the bows of their *Premier Crew* race boat. I was on board to photograph the pair preparing for the annual Cowes-Torquay-Cowes classic, and as we powered down the Solent, in England, the sheer exhilaration of bouncing across waves at 100mph far outweighed the jarring after-effects the experience had on my back later that day!

Previously, I had been a strict 'rag 'n' sticks' man, viewing 'stink boats' simply as a means to an end; as photo boats to get in among the action at yachting regattas around the world, or to carry me from A to B in the shortest possible time. His Lordship's total emersion in the sport was catching. Before long, I was not only photographing these growling beasts racing across Tor Bay, but discovering the pleasures of fishing trips, enjoying some extended cruising and soaking up the sheer luxury aboard some of the world's great superyachts.

Thanks must also go to Ros Nott and her Sports Reports crew for much of the historic information and contacts they provided, Brian and Annabel Trodd at Regency House Publishing, for their unstinting patience and support during the production stages, and Ed Boldero and Tasha Wakefield at PPL for their untiring efforts on picture research. I am also grateful to Bill Shakespeare for allowing us to quote from his book *Powerboat Racing*, J. Lee Barrett's race commentary published in *Speedboat Kings: 25 Years of International Speed Boating*, and Leslie Field for his compilation of record achievements. Also Kevin Desmond for allowing us to publish some of his remarkable collection of historic pictures.

Finally, grateful thanks are also extended to the many boat companies and individuals who provided vital information on the vessels featured in this book.

CONTENTS

CHAPTER ONE
DESIGN CRITERIA

What type of boat do I buy? The first-time purchaser is faced with a bewildering array of shapes and sizes, some of them very specialized and all intended for varying conditions and applications. If your interest is fishing on shallow rivers or lakes, then a small flat- bottomed boat that is light, stable and easy to transport could well be the boat for you, since it carries little draft and has a good clear bow area for casting.

Duck hunters have similar requirements, except that their boats and its engines need camouflaging to blend in with the environment. They also need a large area uncluttered by seats so that they can lie down, hidden from sight, with only their guns protruding over the gunwale.

Fishing offshore requires a more rugged design with a greater freeboard and a hull shape that will slice through seas rather than bounce uncomfortably over them. The deep-V hull is the most popular, but catamaran

A Zodiac inflatable boat with Evinrude outboard motor.

designs can be just as seaworthy and offer greater stability when drifting with waves and currents.

Ski-boats are now also highly developed, and there are flat-bottomed designs for competition use to maximize acceleration and give precise turning characteristics; but these are meant for flat water conditions and are not the type in which to take to sea.

High-speed racing-type boats are invariably eye-catching and attractive, but piloting a boat at 100mph (161km/h) plus takes a great deal more skill and experience than driving a car at these speeds. They are also very much more thirsty on fuel and need a thick wallet to run them. Earplugs may also be a useful accessory.

There are a large number of general-purpose designs around that you can ski behind, fish from and generally have a good time. If you are a first-time buyer, don't allow your enthusiasm to overrule your head by buying the first boat that comes along. If you have friends who have a boat, ask to go out with them first and see if you like it. Ask their advice, and if you are visiting a reputable dealership, tell them that you are looking for a first boat and what you intend to use it for. They will be looking to keep you as a customer and are unlikely to sell you anything unsuitable. The best advice is to buy a popular marque – one that will keep its re-sale value and is easy to trade in should your initial experiences afloat point you in the direction of a different type of boat.

Another important consideration when buying a boat to tow is whether or not your car is suitable. The old expression 'putting the cart before the horse' could not be more apt when trying to tow a boat that outweighs your car, four-wheel-drive or not. The best rule of thumb is that the laden weight of the trailer should not exceed 85 per cent of the vehicle weight. Exceed this, and the trailer may begin to zig-zag uncontrollably when the car is freewheeling down an incline and lead to it either collapsing or pulling the car off the road. In some U.S. states there is also a maximum width restriction of 8ft 6in (2.6m). Then there is the problem or whether or not the tow vehicle has enough power and traction to pull the boat back out of the water and up the slipway. Again, your local dealer is best placed to advise.

Any boat with a powerful engine can be dangerous in the hands of a beginner. Many dealerships run or can recommend courses that teach the finer points of powerboating, in other words, 'Get boat-smart from the start'. Enrol the whole family in a safety course and get a free vessel safety check each year. In the U.S., you can contact the U.S. Coastguard Auxiliary on 800-368-5647 or via the web at www.cgaux.org. The U.S. Power Squadrons provide similar courses and can be contacted nationally on 1-888-FOR-USPS or at www.usps.org.

Hull design has certainly come a long way over the past half-century, but when compared with dolphins, which can swim at speeds of up to 50mph (80km/h), with a muscle power equivalent to just 4

horsepower, our designers still have a long way to go. There is a great deal still to be learned from nature when it comes to reducing friction, and a lot more can be done about streamlining boats, as well as looking for more seaworthy solutions to the shapes of hulls. Construction also plays an important part. Modern composites are now much more advanced over the standard fibreglass, while woven materials such as carbon and Kevlar, specialist sandwich-core materials and advanced epoxy and polyester resin systems, can make for both stronger and lighter hulls.

There is pressure on the industry not only to make boats look sleeker, but also to provide a smoother more comfortable ride. The benefits are obvious: if boats are able to cut through waves with less effort, then they require less engine power, which in turn leads to lower fuel consumption and fewer emissions. While fuel prices remain so cheap in the U.S., Americans have no incentive to curb their gas-guzzling habits, but elsewhere in the world, where fuel carries a 600 per cent tax loading, the pressure to improve fuel consumption is as strong from consumers as it is from ecologists. This explains why Europe is looking for various ways to improve both ride and fuel economy with Very Slender Vessels (VSVs) – foil-assisted wave-piercers and delta-wing-shaped boats. There are also the wave-piercing catamaran designs from Tasmania and New Zealand.

When serving my time as a boat-building apprentice back in the late 1960s, woodworking skills were one thing and

measurements quite another! I learned that while engineers measured to the nearest 1/100,000th of an inch and electricians worked to the nearest millimetre, boat builders, a law unto themselves, worked to the nearest boat. Take a close look at any Concours d'Elégance entry at a classic wooden boat rally and you will see what I mean. Often, there will be more planks on one side, and more often than not there is a marked difference in hull shape between one side and the other.

Today, most manufacturers use the latest computer-aided manufacturing techniques and equipment to ensure that their boats are designed and produced to tolerances so exacting that our forefathers would have been astonished. Advanced AutoCAD and Digitizer systems not only enable us to produce virtually full-sized models of new designs before production commences, but also to utilize these same computer codes to steer CNC-milling equipment and laser cutters to produce exact three-dimensional shapes at the tooling stage, to ensure that all component parts fit exactly every time. This, in turn, leads to stronger, fairer boats moulded from modern materials that have a life expectancy as long as our own and retain their value into the bargain.

Hull forms can be divided largely into two broad categories: displacement and planing. Planing hulls obtain dynamic lift from a combination of hull shape and the speed at which they move through the water. A planing hull is designed so that, at speed, hydrodynamic forces are used to lift

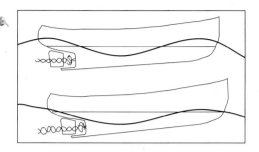

the hull almost out of the water, reducing drag and wave-making resistance to allow relatively high speeds.

Traditional shapes for non-planing boats are described as displacement hulls. They follow Archimedes' principle that any floating object displaces its own weight of water, at rest as well as at speed. As they move, these hull shapes are constantly pushing aside their own weight of water, which sets up a wave pattern which moves along with the boat. As speed increases, the length and height of these waves also increase to the point where the hull is supported by one wave generated by the

OPPOSITE
Mariah DX213 bowrider.

ABOVE
Top, the wave pattern around a displacement hull. Below, the wave pattern around a displacement hull when the boat is forced to travel more than her 'hull speed'.

RIGHT
A Grand Banks semi-displacement motor cruiser travelling at speed.

bows and another at the stern. At this point, the boat has then reached what is termed its maximum displacement speed, because the only way it can go faster is to climb up over its own bow wave. This maximum speed relates directly to the waterline length of the hull. The longer the hull, the faster it will travel. This figure can be calculated by taking the square root of the length of the boat's waterline, multiplied by a factor of 1.4. Thus, a displacement hull with a waterline length of 25ft (7.6m) has an

effective top speed of 7 knots. This, of course, depends on the engine and propeller being matched to these speed expectations. If the boat is underpowered, then it will not reach its theoretical design speed. If it is overpowered, then the boat will try to climb over its own bow wave and her stern will sink right down in the trough, creating a great deal of inefficient wash and a wasteful consumption of fuel. Any further increase in speed can only be achieved by an inordinate and inefficient use of extra power.

A semi-displacement hull is a hybrid of these two types, combining round or V-shaped sections forward and flat-bottomed sections in the aft run. When pushed above hull speed, this design type operates partially as a planing hull, but at the expense of increased fuel consumption. This type of design offer a comfortable (though wet) ride through heavy seas, though it will wallow badly when stationary and have a tendency to broach when running with the seas.

THE DEEP-V HULL

Conceived by Ray Hunt in 1963, the high deadrise or deep-V hull offers speed, comfort and safety in rough water. The sharp entry of the bow sections minimizes pounding and with no deep forefoot the boat will keep to a straight course without the tendency to broach. The V-shaped bottom is carried all the way aft to the transom, which results in an evenly-distributed displacement and lateral plane. These factors combine to urge the hull to travel through or over swells with little steering effort, even in quartering or following seas.

A rising chine forward and the addition of multiple spray rails knock down the spray and add lift. A widely-flared bow also adds considerable buoyancy and makes the design less prone to bury its nose when running through following seas or taking solid water onboard.

The high deadrise V-shape is inherently stable, and this stability increases further once the boat is on the plane. The V-shape also allows the hull to bank into turns rather than lean outward, as do round- or flat-bottomed boats. At slow speeds, the deep V-hull has more draft than a flat planing hull and behaves much more like a displacement

OPPOSITE
Bertram 510, showing deep V-hull.

Charles Raymond Hunt (1908–78), father of deep-vee and cathedral hull forms. *Ray Hunt is one of the legendary figures in*

American powerboat history. Born into a sailing family based on the water's edge at Boston, Hunt was a natural world-class sailor – a rag-n-sticks man first and powerboat man second. He won the Sears Cup twice, the first time when he was only 15 years old, and both he and his designs dominated the 5.5-m class, one of his boats winning a Gold Medal at the 1960 Olympic Games, while he captured the 1963 world championship in another.

Hunt had no formal education in yacht design or engineering but knew instinctively what made boats, both power and sail, go fast. He went to work for the naval architect Frank C. Payne, where he met Waldo Howland in 1932 and with him formed Concordia Yachts to design and build yawls. During this time, he also designed the 110 and later the 210 flat-bottomed double-ended powerboats, which were among the first to make use of marine plywood.

In 1958, he built a 23-ft (7-m) wooden deep-vee prototype open powerboat for himself and it was while watching the

America's Cup trials off Newport, Rhode Island, that yacht charter business owner Dick Bertram spotted the boat in among the spectator fleet.

Bertram was so impressed by her performance and manoeuvrability in the spectator chop out on Rhode Island Sound that he commissioned Hunt to design a 30-ft (9-m) version for himself.

Bertram raced this open boat in the 1960 Miami/Nassau race and won it with ease in record time, despite it being one of the roughest races on record; the rest is history. Bertram formed a boat company to build the boats in fibreglass under licence from Hunt, and in less than a decade the business had grown into one of the largest pleasure boat builders in the world.

Ray Hunt went on to develop the cathedral hull shape that made Boston

LEFT
Charles Raymond Hunt.

BELOW
The deep-V viewed from the stern.

Whaler a household name and also drew the very distinctive lines for the Huntress and Huntsman power cruisers built by Fairey Marine in England.

*His company, C. Raymond Hunt & Associates, founded in 1966, provided custom designs for well-respected builders like Alden, Boston Whaler, Chris*Craft, Grady-White, Grand Banks and Hinckley. After his death in 1978, Ray Hunt was inducted into the National Marine Manufacturers Hall of Fame and honoured with the Ole Evinrude award for his contributions to powerboating.*

hull, though some can prove hard to manoeuvre. The amount of V in a hull is denoted by its angle of deadrise, which often varies between 18° and 25°. The greater the angle, the better the performance in rough weather but with the trade-off of lesser speed than flatter hulls in calmer conditions.

A recent innovation to improve the handling and performance of all V-hulls is the Spray Rail, invented by Ocke Mannerfelt. These 3-ft (1-m) long aluminium profiles fit along existing running strakes and are designed to deflect the water downwards away from the hull to improve both direction and lift, and thus enhance speed and/or fuel economy.

ABOVE
Ocke Mannerfelt's 'Bat boat' delta-shaped racing design, showing twin steps and wings.

LEFT
The advantage of a deep-V hull in heavy seas.

OPPOSITE
Bertram 510, showing stepped hull.

STEPPED HULL

The form of the stepped hull was first utilized successfully in the 1920s to suck air under the aft sections of the hull to minimize wetted area and planing resistance. The bubbles of air this produces act like ball bearings to reduce friction and produce a smoother surface for the boat to run on. Stepped hulls were used very effectively by Harmsworth and Gold Cup winners like John Hacker and Gar Wood, whose successive Miss America designs all had this development. These boats were not always easy to handle, however, having a tendency to spin out during turns, whenever the aft sections were angled over too far, and lose their grip. In the 1930s, racing hulls like that of the 1934 Gold Cup winner *Delphine IV*, carried multi-steps or 'shingles' along a much greater length of the hull. Nowadays, designers have a much greater understanding of stepped hulls and how to limit their shortcomings. During the Second World War many Allied patrol boats had stepped hull configurations with an almost flat run aft. These were very fast in calm conditions but had appalling ride and handling problems in force 4/5 conditions and above, when the German E-boats, with their semi-displacement hulls, ran rings around them. Typical of these 'vented' hulls were the high-speed stepped hull launches designed to run in pairs ahead of flying boats, which allowed the plane to ride their wash and assist it over its 'hump' speed and get on the plane. These boats operated only in sheltered waters and were not tested sufficiently in rough conditions before the

DESIGN CRITERIA

Renato 'Sonny' Levi

(Born 1926), European design genius.
*Renato Levi, the son of a shipyard
owner, was born in Karachi, Pakistan.
He was schooled in France and
England and served as a pilot officer in
Britain's Royal Air Force during the
Second World War. He later studied
aeronautical engineering in England
before going to Bombay to head up the
design office at his father's shipyard. It
was while in India that he began to
experiment with deep-vee hull designs
as early as 1958.*

In 1961, a year after Ray Hunt's

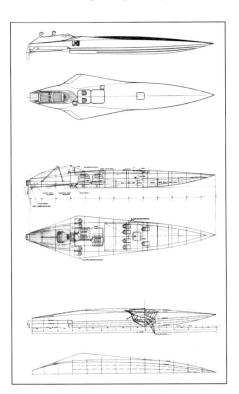

radical deep-vee design, Blue Moppie,
had won the Miami/Nassau race in record
time, Sonny moved to Italy to manage the
Cantiere Navaltecnica yard and it was
here that Levi's creative instincts were
given full rein. Sonny drove one of these
designs, the 30-ft (9-m) A. Speranziella
(which had a deadrise at her transom of
20° and was one of the first designs to
have spray rails along the entire length of
the hull) to victory in the 1963
Cowes/Torquay classic.

In 1965, Sonny set up his own design
agency to concentrate on the increasing
demand for his racing boats. One of the
most important was the delta-shaped 36-ft
(11-m) Surfury, built for the powerboat
racing brothers Charles and Jimmy
Gardner. This had a near-constant

deadrise of 25° and was powered by twin
turbocharged Daytona 1050-hp petrol
engines, harnessed in tandem to a single
propeller – a novel arrangement that
saved the equivalent of 200hp in reducing
the drag of a second propeller and shaft.
The boat had a top speed of 58 knots and
won the 1967 Cowes/Torquay Race, three
years after her launch.

Other notable designs during that

ABOVE

Surfury, designed by Sonny Levi,
winner of the 1967 Cowes-Torquay
powerboat race.

LEFT

The delta-design, *Dart*, circa 1972,
designed by Sonny Levi.

period included Ultima Dea, *a 34-ft, 46-
knot flyer built for Fiat chief Giovanni
Agnelli and powered by three 430-hp
Maserati engines,* G. Clinquanto, *a 35.6-
ft powerboat equipped with four 320-hp
engines that gave her a top speed of 55
knots, and* G. Whiz, *an 108-ft (33-m)
luxury superyacht designed with Jon
Bannenberg for American Ben Le Bow,
powered by twin 3,500-hp MTU diesels to
give her a speed of 48 knots.*

*Levi's distinctive delta boats were
shaped like elongated triangles in vertical
and horizontal planes, with maximum
beam at the transom. They had a cut-
away forefoot, high chine and deep
deadrise or deep-vee hull sections to
improve performance into head seas.
They also had little or no flare in the
bows to minimize resistance when
piercing through waves, as well as the
flying characteristics generated by
widely-flared bows. His boats were also
drawn with a marked reverse sheer,
designed to reduce the bow profile and
move the boat's aerodynamic centre of lift
further aft to reduce the windward list
phenomenon exhibited by most deep-vee
hulls. All sections were convex in shape to
maximize panel strength and the topside
sections were raked outboard throughout
the length of the hull to better absorb
impact should the boat land heavily on its
side.*

*This delta concept was proved at the
1964 Paris Six Hour Race when two*

prototype circuit racing boats, the Levi 16 Thunderbolt, driven by Len Melly and John Merryfield, won the race outright, and Fi-Fi, a Levi 17-ft design driven by Don Shead, won its class.

Levi has turned his genius to developing many unique concepts. These include the wave-piercer, or forward ram, which he first experimented with in 1968 by fitting a 9-ft extension to an existing Delta 28 hull. Another first was the 'ram wing' effect in 1966 to improve the aerodynamics on racing catamarans. In 1972, Levi patented a surface-piercing step-drive propeller system that was used successfully on famous European racing craft like Alto Volante, Dart *and* Acidiavolo. *This Levi drive system was developed over the years to improve reverse thrust and steerage at slow speed and was fitted to Richard Branson's Atlantic record-breaker,* Virgin Atlantic II, *which Levi also designed. Despite losing more than ten hours after loading contaminated fuel during a scheduled rendezvous with a fuel barge in mid-Atlantic, this 72ft 3-in (22-m) powerboat, fitted with twin MTU 2000-hp diesels which gave her a top speed of 50 knots, beat the previous record from New York to Bishop Rock off England's coast, held by the liner* United States, *by 2 hours 8 minutes, having averaged 35.69 knots.*

In 1987, the Royal Society of Arts honoured Sonny Levi with its ultimate accolade – Royal Designer for Industry.

stepped hull concept was extended to wartime applications.

One of the principal reasons for the spinout was the fact that the forward step was positioned too close to the boat's centre of gravity. Another was that the aft run was too flat to provide sufficient lateral resistance. It was only after the advent of Ray Hunt's deep-V hull concept that the step could offer advantages to mainstream production designs. American designer Harry Schoell incorporated 12° deadrise in the aft sections, coupled to a planing flat, and sometime a concave-shaped pad at the top of the V, which improved performance and handling characteristics over a wide speed range.

Other designers have incorporated the 'vented chine', which also sucks air down through channels within the hull to reduce friction but without changing the underwater shape.

More recently, the Swedish-based Ocke Mannerfelt design team has taken the stepped hull configuration several levels further, with its successful 'Bat boats', which have won world offshore championships both in America and Europe. These boats have two transverse steps; the first is more of a chine vent, and sets the angle of attack and guides the hull, while the second smooths out the water flow over the last part of the hull, which carries the load. This has a slight concavity in the V and carries much flatter sections at the apex to encourage lift.

DELTA HULL

The Delta-shaped racing hulls were conceived originally by Sonny Levi back in the 1970s and are a development of the deep-V hull. His boats are best described as elongated triangles in vertical and horizontal planes, with maximum beam at the transom. They have a cut-away forefoot, high chine and deep deadrise or deep-V hull sections to improve performance into head seas. They also have little or no flare in the bows to minimize resistance when piercing through waves or the 'flying' characteristics that widely-flared bows generate. Levi's boats are also drawn with a marked reverse sheer designed to reduce the bow profile and move the boat's aerodynamic centre of lift further aft to reduce the windward list phenomenon exhibited by most deep-V hulls. All sections are convex in shape to maximize panel strength and the topside sections are raked outboard throughout the length of the hull to better absorb impact should the boat land heavily on its side.

Compare Levi's drawings for the *Dart* (opposite) with the Ocke Mannerfelt Bat boats. Both share the same long, narrow hull form, incorporating steps, and share the wings that make the Bat boats so distinctive. These 7.9-m D-24 and 8.65-m B-28 boats which race as APBA One Design classes in America, can top 100mph (161km/h) and between them have won nine world titles on both sides of the Atlantic.

The wings have proved extremely successful in improving stability at speed. Working on the ground effect principle, the wings force air downwards, which then rebounds back off the water to provide lift. This, in turn, produces transverse stability at speed, counteracting any inclination to 'chine walk' – a side-on phenomenon that can affect hard chine boats at speed. These wings work particularly well in rough water, helping to maintain the level of the angle of attack even when the boat is airborne. If the angle of attack increases too much, then wings stall out, dropping the bows and preventing the boat from flipping over backwards. As the hull lands back on the water the wings compress the air to soften the landing. The boat does not land on its side and when returning to the water the wings compress the air underneath, cushioning the landing.

WAVE-PIERCING HULLS

It was the early Polynesians who first discovered that long, narrow hull shapes slice easily and efficiently through, rather than over, waves. This concept was developed extensively during the 1980s and '90s to produce a series of hybrid designs. One of these was *Elan Voyager*, produced by British multihull designer Nigel Irens. This was based on a slender monohull with transverse stability provided by smaller outer hulls to give exceptional fuel economy, speed and comfort, even in very rough conditions. The original boat, which is now used as a

fast inter-island passenger ferry in the Cape Verdes, has an overall length of 21.3m, a maximum speed of 32mph (50km/h) and seating capacity for 12 passengers. Powered by a single 180-kW engine, she set a record-breaking unrefuelled voyage around Britain, completing the 1,568-mile (2523-km) trip in 72 hours at an average of 24.725mph (39.79km/h) and used just 440 gallons (2,000 litres) of fuel. The success of this prototype led to the design and construction of the 35-m *Cable & Wireless Adventurer*, which went on to set a powered circumnavigation of the world in a record time of less than 75 days.

Adrian Thompson, another British multihull designer, then came up with his VSV or Very Slender Vessel wave-piercing powerboat concept. The essential design element is a narrow elliptical-sectioned

OPPOSITE
SWATH catamaran being used as a camera platform in the America's Cup. The underwater torpedo-style buoyancy tubes supporting the catamaran are clearly visible.

LEFT
Halmatic 22-m VSV (Very Slender Vessel), designed by Paragon Mann and built by Vosper Thornycroft. Its wave-piercing design allows it to travel at 70mph (113km/h) with up to 26 passengers.

BELOW
Elan Voyager: the prototype powered trimaran designed by Nigel Irens.

DESIGN CRITERIA

BELOW
Cutaway of a 170-mph (275-km/h) Class 1 offshore racing catamaran, powered by twin Lamborghini V12 engines.

RIGHT
The Glacier Bay Ocean Runner 3470 catamaran.

OPPOSITE
The 2003 UIM world champion, *Miss Norway*, a Class 1 offshore racing catamaran capable of 170mph.

canoe body with a beam to length ratio in excess of 6:1, which offers several advantages over the traditional deep-V hull form. Instead of bouncing over the waves, the VSV cuts straight through to offer a much better ride and a much reduced fuel consumption. The wide chines provide roll stability when stationary and dynamic lift at speed, as well as control heel in tight turns. The design also exhibits a very low RADAR print and has obvious military uses as a fast troop carrier.

CATAMARANS

The wave-piercing concept has seen the greatest development in catamaran design. The idea of a semi-submerged hull goes

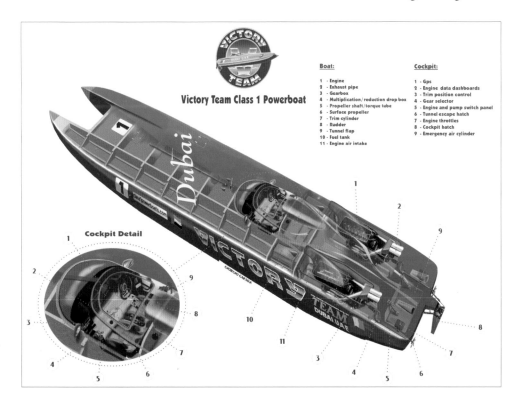

Victory Team Class 1 Powerboat

Boat:
1 - Engine
2 - Exhaust pipe
3 - Gearbox
4 - Multiplication/reduction drop box
5 - Propeller shaft/torque tube
6 - Surface propeller
7 - Trim cylinder
8 - Rudder
9 - Tunnel flap
10 - Fuel tank
11 - Engine air intake

Cockpit:
1 - Gps
2 - Engine data dashboards
3 - Trim position control
4 - Gear selector
5 - Engine and pump switch panel
6 - Tunnel escape hatch
7 - Engine throttles
8 - Cockpit hatch
9 - Emergency air cylinder

Cockpit Detail

back to the 1880s when C.G. Lundborg was awarded the first patent for a single-hulled semi-submerged ship. The first SWATH or small-water plane-area twin-hull vessel, the Duplus was seen in 1968. It was a 120-ft (37-m) self-propelled oil exploration support vessel designed by the Dutch naval architect J.J. Stenger, who based his design on the fact that submarines lying at periscope depth experience little wave motion. America's Cup skipper Dennis Conner used a similar catamaran with long ballasted underwater tubes and ultra-fine waterline sections as his support vessel for successive America's Cup campaigns in the U.S.A. and New Zealand, and this concept has since been carried forward by Lockheed Martin with the development of the IX-529 'Stealth' ship, *Sea Shadow*. This 160-ft long, 70-ft wide craft was designed as a test

platform to research advanced technologies in propulsion, automation, sea-keeping abilities and reduced radar signature. The angled sides of the craft extend below the waterline to torpedo-shaped hulls, which provide the vessel with exceptional stability in heavy weather. Although the craft performs well in the open sea, its 14-ft (4.3-m) draft limits its manoeuvrability in and access to many harbours. Top speed is around 13 knots.

The Stealth boat in the James Bond film, *Tomorrow Never Dies*, came not from the ideas developed by the U.S. military in San Francisco Bay, but from the pioneering catamaran builders Incat, based in Tasmania, which applied the wave-piercing principles to modern high-speed ferries with great success. Long, slender waterborne hulls characterize their design, each subdivided into multiple water-tight compartments, with very little buoyancy at the bow. As each hull encounters a wave it tends to 'pierce' through rather than ride over it. The first of these wave-piercing catamarans was used as a press boat at the 1986–87 America's Cup, where its speed and stability over 6–10-ft Indian Ocean swells off Perth, Australia, was most impressive. These ideas were later carried forward to produce large car ferries, three of which since won the Hales Trophy for the fastest crossing of the Atlantic by a commercial passenger ship. These Incat-

CATHEDRAL HULL

The Cathedral hull was another first for deep-V designer Ray Hunt. His triple-V planing monohull concept first developed by Boston Whaler, offers a wide rectangular full-length cockpit, coupled with tremendous stability and load-carrying capabilities. The original 13-ft (4-m) Boston Whaler gave a notoriously wet and bumpy ride when speeding upwind, but this was overcome with later models, which carried the central V-shaped hull well forward of the two side pods and cut through the water much better. The concept has since been followed by other builders, like Hurricane, whose line of deckboats takes full advantage of Hunt's original concept to maximize cockpit space.

OPPOSITE LEFT
Spirit, a 24-m wave-piercer.

OPPOSITE RIGHT
The 'Stealth' ship *Sea Shadow*.

LEFT
Orkney dory, with a cathedral hull design originated by Ray Hunt and Boston Whaler. Later versions have a deeper central V-hull, which improved their performance and limited slamming when running against head seas.

BELOW
A Boston Whaler used by the U.S. Coastguard.

built ferries also caught the attention of the U.S. military, which has leased the HSV-X1 for evaluation. The vessel can transport more than 400 tons of equipment and troops over great distances at speeds of up to 45 mph (72km/h) – a load that by comparison would take 14 aircraft to transport over a two-week programme at considerably great cost. In New Zealand, the Craig Loomes design group produced a series of luxurious pleasure and sports fishing boats from 40–70ft (12– 21m), using the same concept, which offer enormous internal space for their overall length while exhibiting smooth, fast running and great stability.

On a smaller scale, American companies such as Glacier Bay, Pro Sports and SeaCat, produce a series of fast sports fishing boats, which combine wide cockpit area with excellent sea-keeping qualities. Glacier Bay has proved that these boats are capable of cruising open oceans: they have made passages across the Pacific, across to Bermuda and around the west and east coasts of the U.S.A.

Catamarans have also come of age in the offshore racing world on both sides of the Atlantic, with Class 1 cats powered by twin V-12 Lamborghini or Lycoming T55-L7 gas turbines achieving speeds of between 170 and 200mph to out-perform the monohull racers in all but the very worst conditions, when racing is invariably cancelled anyway.

CHAPTER TWO
PROPULSION SYSTEMS

We rely on the screw propeller in one form or another to provide the thrust for all water propulsion systems. Its origins date back to before 950 BC, when the Egyptians used an auger-type device to move water for irrigation purposes. Archimedes used the same principle to bail out flooded ships around 250 BC, while Leonardo da Vinci also worked on refining the propeller for pumping water and for supporting his famous helicopter design.

But the concept did not become a reality to propel waterborne craft until the advent of steam power and the invention by Smith and Eriksson, who patented the first screw propeller design in 1835. They came across the answer to making an efficient water propeller after their wooden prototype lost half the length of its blades after

grounding on the bottom and finding that, suddenly, their boat went faster! Smith capitalized on this stroke of luck by increasing the number of blades and cutting down their length and width to finish up with a design that is comparable to the propellers we use today

In 1870, C. Sharp from Philadelphia, patented the first partially submerged propeller for shallow-draft vessels, while in Britain John Thornycroft was starting to produce fast torpedo boats that could achieve 16mph (26km/h) with his screw propeller designs. As speeds climbed, so did the problems of cavitation or aeration around the blade tips, which Sir Charles Parsons overcame in 1897 by fitting three propellers to each shaft of his 39-mph (63-km/h) steam-powered fast patrol boat, *Turbinia*.

The *Encyclopedia Britannica* describes the screw propeller as a device with a central hub and radiating blades placed so that each forms part of a helical (spiral) surface. By its rotation in water, a propeller produces thrust, owing to fluid forces acting

upon the blades, and gives forward motion. A propeller's thrust is proportional to the product of the mass of water that it is acting on and the accelerating rate; for the most efficient propulsion, the mass should be large and the acceleration small.

Large-bladed propellers with less pitch are more efficient than smaller props with

deeper pitch but, in reality, the practical constraints on tip clearance from the hull, and the limitations of shaft angle and overall draft, conspire to limit the prop diameter to something smaller than optimal size. The screw propeller moves though the water in a similar manner to a mechanical auger moving through a piece of wood. The distance or forward motion depends principally on the area and pitch of the blades. The latter is measured by the theoretical amount the propeller would move forward with each complete turn if it had no additional drag from the boat and drive. Hence, a 13-in (33-cm) pitch propeller will move that amount of water with each revolution.

In practice, propellers perform well below their theoretical pitch figure, and this decreases further the faster it spins when cavitation sets in. Hence the need to match the propeller blade diameter and pitch to the size and expected performance of the boat it is going to propel. Most engine manufacturers have a computer programme to calculate the optimum prop size for a boat and predict its performance. If you are looking for independent advice, then the software PropWorks2 propeller selection and speed prediction package is available over the World Wide Web for around $40.00.

Cavitation is caused when the pressure on one part of the blade falls below ambient pressure (atmospheric + hydrostatic head) and a vacuum is formed. This is most prevalent during fast acceleration and sharp cornering. The tell-tale signs are a sudden increase in revs and loss of power, strong vibration and a stream of bubbles running from the tip of the blades, which can be a major source of propeller damage.

Propeller design has certainly improved in recent years with the introduction of Volvo Penta's dual-bladed Duoprop, which with some applications can improve torque by 15 per cent, and the latest 4- and 5-bladed supercavitation propellers for high-end applications when minimal slip is required during acceleration.

OUTBOARDS

It was Ole Evinrude who came up with the first successful outboard engine back in 1909. Today, they are the most common form of propulsion within the marine leisure world, providing compact, weatherproof units from 1.5–300hp that are infinitely more reliable than they were even a decade ago. At one end of the market are the light, simple battery- powered electric auxiliaries used to power a tender or provide super-quiet manoeuvrablity when fishing. At the other are the sophisticated two- and three-litre compact models with electronic engine management systems and race-bred performance. In between is an enormous choice of engines, including two- and four-strokes, prop or jet power, that carry the well known brand names of Evinrude, Johnson, Honda, Mariner, Mercury, Suzuki and Yamaha. Some of these, like Evinrude and Johnson, Mariner and Mercury, offer the same engines under different badges. Evinrude and Johnson are now owned by the Canadian company, Bombardier, while

Mercury, which was started by American Carl Kiekhaefer back in 1939, and its sister brand Mariner, are controlled by the Brunswick Corporation.

Two- and four-stroke engines have very different characteristics and it is as well to weigh up their pros and cons before choosing an engine for your boat. The two-stroke has a better power-to-weight ratio and superior low-down torque than a four-stroke, making it a better choice for waterskiing and other applications where fast acceleration is required. The downside is that they use more fuel than four-strokes

LEFT and BELOW
Cutaways of Evinrude outboards.

and produce greater emissions, though this has been addressed with the latest models fitted with direct-injection and electronic engine management systems. Where the four-stroke really scores is with its greater torque at the top end of its rev range, and quieter running without the smoky exhaust that is the trademark of all two-strokes.

Ole Evinrude (1877–1934), father of the outboard motor.

Born in Norway, Ole Evinrude emigrated to America with his parents when he was five and was brought up in Cambridge Wisconsin. He learned his engineering trade in the industrial heartlands of Pittsburgh and Chicago before returning to Wisconsin at the age of 23 to start his own machine shop.

He got the idea for his outboard motor after taking friends out in a rowing boat for a picnic. By the time they had reached a nearby island, the ice cream they were carrying had all melted, leading Ole to think how much quicker they would have got there had their small boat been equipped with an engine.

Evinrude began work on his outboard in 1906 and by 1909 had developed a one-cylinder power detachable motor for rowing boats, rated at 1.5hp. There had been earlier outboard designs, but Ole's invention was the first to enjoy commercial success. Subsequent outboard motors all followed his transmission design, with the engine mounted over a vertical shaft driving 90° bevel gears that turned the propeller.

In 1910 he founded Evinrude Motors in Milwaukee, with partner Chris Meyer, to build and market his invention. The continued ill-health of his wife, Bess, eventually led him to sell the company to Meyer so that he could look after her, and they and their son, Ralph, spent from 1914 to 1919 travelling America. On their return, Ole proposed to Meyer that they build a twin-cylinder version, but he showed little interest in renewing their old partnership. So Evinrude started a second company, ELTO (Evinrude Light Twin Outboard) to manufacture his new design. In 1929, just prior to the Great Depression, he bought back his old company and merged the two businesses under the name of OMC (Outboard Motor Corporation). Bess died in 1933 and Ole a year later, and the family business passed to Ralph, who merged with the Johnson Motor Company in 1936 to form the Outboard Marine Corporation – the first conglomerate in the U.S. marine industry. The company became one of the leading world manufacturers of outboard and inboard/outboard engines, and also owned a stable of boat manufacturers. In 2000, the corporation went into liquidation and the engine manufacturing business was taken over and restructured by the Canadian company, Bombardier.

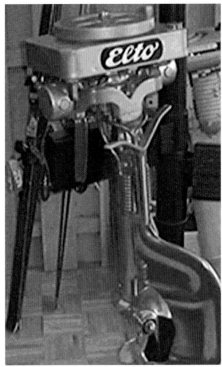

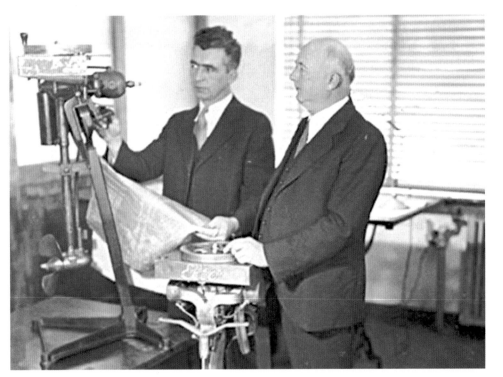

ABOVE FAR LEFT
Ole Evinrude, producer of the Evinrude and Johnson outboard range of motors.

ABOVE
The ELTO (Evinrude light twin outboard), Evinrude's first twin-cylinder outboard motor.

LEFT
Ole Evinrude and his ELTO motor.

INBOARDS

Most marine inboard engines are adapted car and truck motors, though some, like Volvo Penta, Mercruiser and Yanmar, are purpose-made for a marine environment. Inboard installations offer the ability to place the engine weight to greatest advantage and connect it via a reduction gearbox directly to the prop shaft or via a V-drive. On large superyachts, a further option of diesel-electric power has its advantages. Here, diesel generators, which can be mounted well forward to optimize trim, drive electric motors coupled directly to the shafts, which cuts down considerably on the noise and vibration within the hull.

However, the exposed shafts, struts, P-brackets and rudders all contribute to parasitic drag. The greater the incline of the shaft, the less efficient the forward thrust becomes. The exposed shafts not only produce form and frictional drag as well as vibration, but also lose a surprising amount of power from friction generated by the shaft rotating in the water.

INBOARD/OUTDRIVES

The drag problems associated with standard inboard installations are largely overcome by the hybrid inboard/outboard configuration first considered by Jim Wynne, who made a prototype steerable outdrive leg using old outboard parts, and licenced the idea to Volvo Penta. The advantages of the inboard/outdrive are simple installation, lower noise and vibration levels, and the ability to raise the

Rudolf Diesel (1858–1913), father of the diesel engine.

For the son of itinerant German immigrants forced to live first in France, before being deported to England during the Franco-German War, Rudolf Diesel was lucky to have had any education at all, let alone be sent to some of the best learning centres in Europe. Born in Paris on 18 March 1858, he moved to England with his parents at the age of 12. From London, he was sent to Augsburg in Germany, his father's home town, to finish his schooling. His brilliance was quickly recognized and he became the protégé of Carl von Linde, a pioneer of refrigeration who sent him to a technical school in Munich, where he graduated with a degree in thermal engineering.

Diesel's dream, even in those formative years, was to develop an internal-combustion engine that would approach the theoretical efficiency of the Carnot cycle. He first experimented with an expansion engine, often with explosive results, using ammonia and coal dust, but in 1890, while working at Linde's firm in Berlin, he conceived the idea for his engine, using oil as the propellant compressed with air to atomize it.

ABOVE
Rudolf Diesel.

A German development patent was registered in 1892 and the following year he published a first description of his engine. This consisted of a 10-ft (3-m) high single cylinder driving a flywheel at its base. With financial support from the Maschinenfabrik Augsburg and the Krupp steel firms, he produced a series of increasingly successful models, culminating in 1897 with an advanced 25-hp, four-stroke, single vertical cylinder compression engine. Its high efficiency, coupled with the engine's comparative simplicity, made it an immediate commercial success. The first vessel equipped with a diesel engine was launched in 1903, and two years later the Swiss company, Sulzer, manufactured the first reversible marine diesel engine.

Rudolf Diesel was honoured with doctorates and awards, but disappeared in mysterious circumstances in 1913 from the deck of the mail steamer, Dresden, *en route to London to meet an admiral in Britain's Royal Navy shortly before the outbreak of the First World War.*

Diesel's enduring legacy is a highly reliable, economical and hard-wearing internal-combustion engine, in which air is compressed to a temperature sufficiently high to ignite fuel injected into the cylinder, and where combustion and expansion actuate a piston engine – thus converting the chemical energy of the fuel into mechanical propulsion. A century on, his invention remains the most widely used motive power in the marine environment.

leg like an outboard when navigating in shallow waters, to clear weed, rope or plastic, and allow the boat to take to the ground on a falling tide. Their disadvantage is that engine weight is centred well aft, which can cause some boats that have not been designed specifically for inboard/outdrive installation to bounce badly when heading into rough seas.

WATERJETS

Waterjet units, like the Hamilton Jet and Castoldi range, generate propulsive thrust through the reaction created when water is forced in a rearward direction. Following Newton's Third Law of Motion, in which 'every action has an equal and opposite reaction', they work in the same way that backward thrust is felt when holding a powerful fire hose. The discharge of a high-velocity stream of water from the jet unit generates a reaction force in the opposite direction, which is then transferred through to the boat to propel it forward.

The one-piece jet unit is mounted inboard at the back of the boat with the nozzle cut through the transom and the water intake fitted flush in a flat section of the hull bottom. Water enters the jet unit intake at the bottom of the hull. This flow is accelerated through the narrowing diameter of the unit by an impeller and discharged at high velocity through the nozzle in the transom. Steerage is achieved with twin rudders positioned either side of the nozzle deflecting the jet stream. Directing the stream one way forces the stern of the boat

CLASSICS AT TAHOE

'I'd give a thousand bucks for that,' the man sighed, pointing at a perfectly restored Chris*Craft runabout gleaming in the afternoon sun.

'You're crazy!' exclaimed a bystander. 'That boat's worth $50,000.'

'I don't mean the boat,' said the first man, his gaze still wistful. 'I mean that gas cap. I have a boat identical to this, and that gas cap is the only thing I need to complete an original restoration.'

In the field of human endeavour there are obsessions and then there are magnificent obsessions. Someone who lovingly restores classic speedboats can easily succumb to the latter. Consider, for example, the man who wanted that gas cap. A gas cap that merely fits could be found at any auto supply store for a couple of dollars. But a 1929 gas cap, chrome-

BELOW LEFT
This two-cockpit runabout is unusual for the enclosed forward cockpit, making the boat usable in all weathers.

OPPOSITE
So Rare III is an award-winning, typical 1940s Chris*Craft runabout, with barrel stern, extreme tumblehome aft, and fish-shaped lines to the deck.

PAGE 28
This Chris*Craft Cobra marked the end of the classic wooden runabout, since the 1950s-era tailfin was made from a new-fangled material called fibreglass, that would soon become the material of choice. Cobras traditionally had gold-painted tails and large Cadillac engines.

PAGE 29
This Chris*Craft two-cockpit launch has a cabriolet top, much like cars of the 1920s, with varnished wooden bows and a windscreen that can be hinged up to allow the breeze to enter the cockpit.

plated bronze with the Chris*Craft name in flowing script – that's his Holy Grail. Indeed, for more than a year, this conservative stockbroker has spent weekends pawing through greasy boxes in the shadowy corners of old boatyards. To what end? The answer is the annual Tahoe Yacht Club Concours d'Elégance, which takes place at the height of each summer.

Lake Tahoe, nestled in the High Sierras straddling the California/ Nevada border, might seem an unlikely spot for a gathering of antique and classic boats, since it is far from where most of these mahogany craft were built. But the 125 or more boats entered each year clearly establishes the resort's reputation as the finest repository of classic boats in the world. Lake Tahoe, a mere 25-miles (40-km) long, reputedly has more than 500 wooden runabouts and cruisers, and some say twice as many may be hidden away in dusty boathouses or garages. The Sierra Boat Company, a leading restorer of vintage wooden boats, alone stores more than 200 classics during the winter.

What magnetic force attracts these craft to a lake in the far West? There are two explanations: money and a perfect climate. Lake Tahoe is a summer playground for the wealthy, and the lake-front homes belong to well-heeled captains of industry.

More importantly, however, the

climate is perfect for preserving old wooden craft. The boating season is extremely short, so many years can pass before a boat begins to show its age. The air is crisp, clean and dry, and the lake waters are chill on even the hottest days of summer. Wood rot – the curse of antique boats which thrives on warmth and dampness – simply doesn't stand a chance at Lake Tahoe. Not that the boats entered in the Concours would be allowed to associate with stray fungus spores, anyway. These boats are far too cosseted.

Early on the first morning of the Concours, owners, family and friends descend upon each boat for last-minute cosmetics. Stray droplets of water are removed so that nothing can distract the judges from the flawless hand-rubbed varnish; thick Turkish towels and furniture wax are used to polish the metalwork; even the docklines are carefully coiled. No detail is too small to overlook.

This is all in preparation for the judges who, with only their clipboards to distinguish them from mere mortals, wield immense power. Their passing is marked by silence where once had been the murmur of conversation or the squeak of polishing cloths upon glistening brass and varnish. Their departure leaves a wake of audible sighs and the faint sheen of moisture

on owners' foreheads. The slightest imperfection – a tiny flaw in the expanse of varnish or even the wrong gas cap – can bring pencils down onto the dreaded scoring sheets to note a demerit.

Each engine must be started for the judges, and woe betide any owner whose engine hiccups a single drop of oil onto paint that is surgically clean. Never mind that these boats have engines seven or

CF 1432 JR

OPPOSITE
Launches of the early 1900s usually had open cockpits, allowing owners to furnish them how they liked, which might include a set of wicker armchairs or a woven rug laid on the cockpit floor.

LEFT
This is the classic launch, with folding windshield, long foredeck, and open cockpit with aft seat. In this case, the black hull colour is striking but was probably white when new.

more decades old. It is just not possible to call up your local auto parts store and order a set of connecting rods for an engine that came out of a First World War biplane. But this obsession for detail is what separates the entrants in the Tahoe Yacht Club Concours d'Elégance from mere boat-owners. It takes time, talent, and a hefty bankroll just to maintain one of these wooden classics. To restore it to and keep it in Concours condition raises the cost appreciably. It also requires the

perseverance of a bloodhound, the patience of a martyr and a cunning that borders on the illegal.

Take Bob Boldt as an example of supreme dedication. When he bought Big Sky, *his five-decades-old 21-ft Stancraft Torpedo runabout, it was in nearly flawless condition, apart from having the wrong engine. To make the restoration perfect, he needed an original engine, but that 1946 Challenger 8 engine proved as elusive as Bigfoot. Boldt scoured the country for years without success then, hearing a rumour, tracked down his engine, covered with dust in a Montana barn.*

What kind of boats arrive for the Concours? Just about anything you may have dreamed about, ranging from lean pre-war runabouts to a Thunderbird, a 55-footer powered by a pair of Allison fighter plane engines. Sedan cruisers share space with meticulously restored outboard skiffs in which youngsters went fishing in the 1930s, and haughty racing runabouts have a dock to themselves. Wherever you look there is perfectly finished wood and metal and acres of varnish agleam in the late afternoon sun. It is midsummer in the new millennium, but it seems like the Roaring Twenties, when we were too naive to number our wars and before fibreglass turned boats into cookie-cutter lookalikes.

Afterwards, the winners gather up their silver and the losers toy idly with the judges' scoring sheets, silently planning winter-long campaigns to have windshield brackets rechromed to perfection or to find that gas cap and to hell with the cost. It is a nostalgic time, prompting memories of other golden afternoons, perhaps as a youngster, when summer vacation meant lakes and waterskiing, the warmth of varnished mahogany and the tingle of spray on the skin.

One by one, the engines come to life, some with thunderous roars, others with gentle burbles that reflect a more elegant age. As the boats head out onto the smooth lake, the sun drifts behind the pine-covered mountains, leaving an afterglow that makes one think that maybe, just maybe, it is still 1927 for a few magic hours on this very special afternoon.

OPPOSITE TOP LEFT
This is Thunderbird, a 55-ft Huskins yacht once owned by Bill Harrah of casino fame. Powered by twin 12-cylinder PT-Boat engines, it has a stainless steel cabin and is capable of speeds over 50mph (80km/h).

OPPOSITE BELOW LEFT
Ornate figureheads were common on many runabouts, such as this winged mermaid with flowing hair.

OPPOSITE TOP RIGHT
This Chris*Craft speedboat from the 1920s has a classic steering wheel that includes a throttle lever for speed control. Just below and left of the wheel is a chrome shift lever from the floor.

OPPOSITE BELOW RIGHT
Early Chris*Craft runabouts were noted for their planked mahogany decking with striking white caulking.

LEFT
A row of Chris*Craft runabouts show off their American flags while waiting for judging at the annual Lake Tahoe Concours d'Elégance. Each has their engine compartment open for inspection and the chrome hull trim is polished to perfection.

in the opposite direction. Reverse thrust is gained by lowering a deflector or bucket over the jet stream as it leaves the nozzle. This reverses the direction of the force forward under the boat or directly downwards, depending on how far the deflector is pulled down over the flow, to propel the boat astern or maintain a stationary position. The waterjet is infinitely more controllable than any propeller system; the reverse bucket can be used to stop the boat in an emergency, often within its own length. The units also offer complete safety to swimmers and wildlife, for there are no moving external parts. Draft is also minimized, and boats powered by jet units can operate in little more than their own depth of water.

One major disadvantage is that weed, plastic bags and other flotsam can severely restrict or block the intake. The units are fitted with weed deflectors, but to clear them invariably entails stopping the engine. Jet units are not recommended in areas where there are high levels of weed or rubbish floating on the surface.

SURFACE-PIERCING PROPELLER DRIVES

Racing, they say, improves the breed. Well, surface-piercing propeller drives, like trim tabs, have come straight off the back of high-performance race boats and are now beginning to emerge on faster production models. Three race proponents, Sonny Levi, Howard Arneson in the U.S.A. and Italian Fabio Buzzi, as well as the U.S.-based firm, Power-Vent, have each

Charles William Feilden Hamilton (1899–1978), father of the waterjet propulsion system.

William Hamilton was a self-taught engineer and inventor from Ashwick Station on New Zealand's South Island. Born into a wealthy farming family, he set up the Hamilton Group of companies in 1921 to manufacture agricultural machinery and earth-moving equipment, before turning his attention to perfecting the waterjet principle in the later 1940s.

ABOVE
The first Hamilton waterjet unit, circa 1954. Called the 'Quinnat', it consisted of a vertical-shaft centrifugal unit, driven through a right-angle gearbox.

LEFT and BELOW
Bill Hamilton.

ABOVE
The 'Rainbow' series of jet units, circa 1956. A small direct-drive centrifugal type of unit, the Rainbow gave a good performance in suitable light craft without the noise of a gearbox. About 125 were manufactured and marketed in New Zealand.

Primitive waterjet units, like the Hanley Hydrojet, were already in being, but these were low-powered devices operating under water. Hamilton believed that the concept had many benefits over propeller drives and the big breakthrough came in 1953 when he fitted his own design through the transom of a riverboat to output just above the waterline. Expelling

the jet of water into the air rather than into the water provided a marked improvement in performance, and by adding twin rudders to direct the water and a 'reverse bucket' that could be swung over the output nozzle to redirect the flow back under the boat, offered incredible directional stability, iwhich also applied when the boat was stationary. This first model, named the

Quinnat, increased the speed of its test-bed boat to 17 knots and eliminated the need for underwater appendages. In 1956, Hamilton introduced the first production unit – The Rainbow jet – a small direct-drive centrifugal-type unit that gave good performance when fitted in small, light speedboats. One hundred and twenty-five of these were manufactured and sold in New Zealand. The next breakthrough came a year later with the introduction of the 'Chinook' model, with its straight-through flow and two- and three-stage axial flow turbine, which increased performance considerably.

Hamilton's company also developed a range of speedboats, all powered with his Hamilton jet units, and in 1960, Sir William's son, John, pulled off a massive publicity coup by leading the first boat expedition up the fiercely-flowing Colorado river. It was the vivid image of these boats jumping the rapids, avoiding boulders and other underwater obstacles that would have destroyed any propeller-driven boat, that 'sold' the concept around the world.

The Beuhler Corporation based in Indianapolis now manufactures the Hamilton jet units.

ABOVE LEFT
An early Hamilton jet boat.

LEFT
A Hamilton 212 waterjet unit.

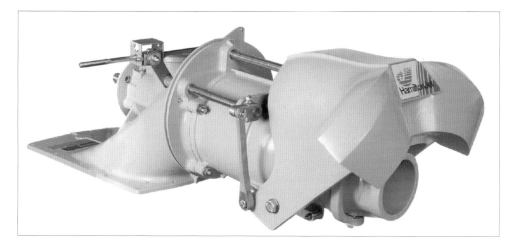

developed their own drive systems to minimize propeller-shaft inclination and reduce mechanical friction and cavitation.

The idea of having the propellers running half out of the water may at first sight seem to be somewhat inefficient. But traditional propellers produce considerable cavitation when under load, witnessed by the amount of air bubbles leaving the propeller tips. Surface-piercing props, on the other hand, ventilate this air to the surface, making them move water more efficiently and faster. By having the prop shaft parallel with the boat's waterline trim, the thrust component is pushing at the optimum angle. Another plus over inboard/outdrives, which lose 15–17 per cent efficiency through their complex geared drive arrangement, is their minimal bearing friction which cuts the loss down to 1–2 per cent. They are also much lighter, offering a 75 per cent weight-saving over an outdrive, and can handle much greater power. Another significant advantage over all other propeller propulsion configurations is that there is virtually no limit to the size of the propeller, allowing for a a larger, lighter-loaded, more efficient design. Steering is achieved either by a rudder blade set immediately behind the specially-designed four-, five- or six-bladed surface-piercing propeller, or in the case of the Arneson Drive, effected by moving the entire propeller shaft (which rotates on a ball joint) from left to right using an hydraulic ram attached to the outer support bracket.

The downside to surface propellers is

PROPULSION SYSTEMS

their poor performance in reverse. This is
caused partially by the 'cleaver'-style
propellers with their thick trailing edges
and the very fact that the water flow is
directed back onto the transom. One
answer is to fix baffle plates between the
transom and propeller, which swing out to
deflect the flow down under the transom
when reverse gear is selected.

Another problem comes at low speed
when the surface propeller is fully
submerged and the top half is operating in
the turbulence set up by the transom. It
then requires more torque to drive the
propeller at a given rpm, which the
engine may not be able to deliver, so that
the boat never climbs over its hump speed
and gets on the plane. The Levi drive
overcomes this by directing the engine
exhaust into the water in front of the
propeller. Other installations, like the
Power Vent, utilize passive 'aeration
pipes' leading air down from above the

waterline to the forward side of the
propeller to achieve the same effect. A
third solution, used by Fabio Buzzi, is to
install two-speed gearboxes to deliver the
required torque.

POWER VENT INSTALLATION

Surface-piercing propulsion systems are
now common in most race craft but have
also been proven on much bigger boats.
Richard Branson's 72ft (22-m) *Virgin
Atlantic Challenger II*, which weighed 37
tons, had a pair of Levi drives delivering
the power from her twin 2000-hp MTU
diesels to give the boat a top speed of
57mph (92km/h) during her record
transatlantic crossing in 1987.

In 2000, Fabio Buzzi designed the
80-ft (24-m) *Record* to become the fastest
powerboat in the world. However, a
downturn in the economic climate put an
end to that attempt, but the boat, fitted
with four 2,000-hp MTU diesels and
driving four Trimax surface drives, giving
the boat a top speed of 70 knots, did set
new records from Monaco to London and
in the Round Britain.

MULTI-SPEED GEARBOXES

Two-, four- and even six-speed drives are
another development from the race circuit
and are designed to help a craft, even
with a heavy payload, to get up on the
plane quickly. A 38-footer powered by

two 420-hp diesel engines can, with the
aid of a two-speed drive, accelerate onto
the plane within 3 seconds and reach 52
knots at 3,300rpm in 8 seconds. Then, as
in a car, the driver, simply by flicking a
switch and without throttling back, can
shift up to second gear and the boat will
continue to accelerate dramatically to 70
knots.

These electronically-operated
gearboxes are likely to become far more
commonplace on production powerboats,
especially those that carry a heavy
payload in terms of accommodation or
fuel. They not only offer better
acceleration, but also improved economy
and less power to drive the boats.

CHAPTER THREE
SPEED

Water speed records have improved considerably since official timings began at the turn of the 20th century. In the first Harmsworth Trophy race in 1903, for instance, the 75-hp-powered *Napier*, owned by Selwyn Francis Edge and driven by his chauffeur, Miss Dorothy Levitt, averaged 19.5mph (31.4km/h). A century later the world water speed record stood at 319.627mph (514.375km/h).

Garfield 'Gar' Wood was first to break through the 100-mph barrier with his *Miss America IX* in 1931. A year later, Kaye Don's *Miss England III* was clocked at 119.81mph (192.81km/h) on Loch Lomond, Scotland. Sir Malcolm Campbell pushed this to 129.5mph (208.4km/h) in 1937 and raised it to 130.93mph (210.7km/h) a year later, before his hydroplane *Bluebird II* set a speed of 141.74mph (228.1km/h) on Lake Coniston, England in 1939. This benchmark

LEFT
Napier, winner of the first British International Harmsworth Trophy in about 1903.

OPPOSITE ABOVE LEFT
Selwyn Edge's chauffeur, Miss Dorothy Levitt, takes the helm of *Napier* in the Harmsworth Trophy race, circa 1903.

OPPOSITE BELOW LEFT
Miss Dorothy Levitt, the owner's chauffeur, may have been at the helm of the winning boat in the trophy's inaugural year.

OPPOSITE ABOVE RIGHT
The Harmsworth Trophy.

stood until 1950 when the American hydroplane, *Slo-Mo-Shun IV*, was timed at 160.323mph (258km/h) in Seattle, Washington.

In 1955 Sir Malcolm Campbell's son, Donald, driving the jet-propelled boat *Bluebird K7*, broke the 200-mph barrier with a speed over a measured mile of 202.32mph (325.59km/h) on Lake Ullswater, England. This was increased to 216mph in an attempt on Lake Mead later that year. Campbell improved this speed on five other occasions between 1956 and '58 when the boat was clocked at 248mph on

Lake Coniston. A year later, he pushed this to 260.35mph before reaching 276.34mph (444.71km/h) on Lake Dumbleyung, Australia in 1964. In 1967, Campbell and his *Bluebird K7* were clocked at 328mph (527.85km/h) moments before the boat somersaulted into the air, killing its driver.

The American boat, *Hustler*, raised the official record to 285.213mph (458.99km/h) at Guntersville later that year and the record has been held since by Australian Ken Warby, whose *Spirit of Australia* set the current record of 319.627mph (514.376km/h) in 1978.

Outboard-powered craft have always lagged significantly behind inboard-engined boats and it was not until 1954 that Italian Massimo Leto di Priolo finally broke the 100-mph barrier with a speed of 100.36mph (161.5km/h) over a measured mile. In 1960, Bert Ross, Jr. raised this to 115.547mph in Seattle and by the end of 1998, even low-powered hydroplanes like J. Sean McKean's 500-cc outboard-powered boat were being timed at 126.076mph. But the outright record has stood since 1989, when American B. Wartinger set a speed of 176.55mph (284.12km/h). This compares to the outright propeller-driven record of 205.494mph (330.7km/h) set by fellow American Russ Wicks in 2000. The outright record for a diesel-powered boat stands at 156.49mph (251.84km/h), set in 1992 by Fabio Buzzi's FB 55 design *La Gran Argentina*.

Two trophies, the Gold Cup and the British International Harmsworth Trophy, have probably had the most influence on the speed and design of powerboats during the 21st century. The Harmsworth Trophy, a magnificent solid-bronze sculpture of two boats powering through rough seas, was commissioned by Sir Alfred Harmsworth, the British newspaper baron, in 1903 – the same year that the Wright brothers took their first flight. It was donated as an international trophy to encourage the development of the sport and has since become the powerboating world's equivalent to yachting's America's Cup.

The first event was held in Cork, Ireland, and was won by an Englishman by

Sir Malcolm Campbell (1885–1948) and **Donald Campbell, CBE** (1921–67), Speed Kings of the 20th century.
The Campbell name is synonymous with

speed with a succession of cars and hydroplanes all named Bluebird *after Maurice Maeterlinck's play* L'Oiseau Bleu. *Malcolm was a British auto-racing driver who set world speed records on*

land and water. A pilot in the Royal Flying Corps during the First World War, Campbell relished speed above all else. In 1924 he attained a world land speed record of 146.16mph (235.21km/h) and continued to raise the ultimate speed benchmark during eight further attempts, culminating with a speed of 301.1292mph (484.6km/h) on a run across Bonneville Salt Flats on 3 Sept.ember 1935 – the first land speed performance to break the 300-mph barrier.

Two years later, Malcolm, who was knighted for his achievements in 1931, captured the world water speed record at 129.5mph. In 1938, he raised the record to 130.93mph, and finally, on 19 August 1939, on Coniston Water, England, set the record of 141.74mph (228.102km/h) that was to remain unbroken until after his death in 1948.

Donald Malcolm Campbell was born to follow in his father's footsteps. His father had made a business out of these record-breaking feats and his son inherited both his father's thirst for speed and his success in attracting sponsors. After Sir Malcolm's death, Donald bought the hydroplane, Bluebird K4, to defend his Father's record against the American Henry Kaiser. After numerous attempts and modifications, the campaign ended

Sir Donald Campbell, holder of the World Speed Record.

with a 170-mph crash in 1951. The accident prompted Campbell to develop a brand-new gas turbine-propelled three-pointer Bluebird K7. This hydroplane design was much more successful, setting 7 world records between 1955 and 1964. In the first attempt, on 23 July 1955, on a run across Lake Ullswater, England, Campbell broke the 200-mph barrier with a speed of 202.32mph. This was increased to 216mph (347.6km/h) during an attempt on Lake Mead later that year. Campbell improved this speed on five other occasions between 1956 and '58 when the boat was clocked at 248mph (399.1km/h) on Lake Coniston. He was awarded the Commander of the British Empire medal in 1957.

Campbell then turned his attention to reclaiming the land speed record, but during an attempt at Utah in 1960, his car crashed heavily and he was forced to take a two-year break from the business of record-breaking in order to convalesce. His accident led some commentators to compare him with his father and questions were raised as to his ability. These doubts had a serious psychological effect on Campbell, but it did not stop him from continuing. Possibly spurred to greater efforts by his critics, Donald's greatest achievements came in 1964. when, driving his gas turbine-powered Bluebird on Lake Eyre Salt Flats, Australia, he broke through the 400-mph barrier for the first time with a speed of 403.1mph (648.7km/h) on 17 July. He then set about improving the world water speed record and was finally rewarded on New Year's Eve with a top speed of 276.34mph on Lake Dumbleyung, also in Australia. This made him the first man to hold both world land and water speed records in the same year.

Returning to England, Donald set his sights on breaking through the 300-mph water speed barrier, and during the winter of 1966-67 set up camp on Coniston Water, England, to prepare for the attempt. On 4 January, the day his new company, Bluebird Marine, launched a waterjet-propelled speedboat at the London International Boat Show, he made his attempt. On his first run across the glassy lake, he set a speed of 297mph. Keen to improve on this, he turned the boat round without refuelling or waiting for the surface of the lake to settle, and was clocked at 328mph (527.85km/h), moments before the three-pointer hydroplane hit the backward ripples from the previous run. The bows rose upwards and Bluebird was flipped backwards through the air before nose-diving back into the water at a 45° angle.

All that was found of Campbell was his shoes, the boat having presumably disintegrated into thousands of pieces on impact. But three decades later, in March 2001, Bluebird K7 was recovered, still in a recognizable state, from the bottom of the lake and is now to be restored. Two months later, Donald Campbell's body, along with the St. Christopher medallion that his father had given him as a lucky charm, was also recovered from the waters, 35 years after his fatal crash.

ABOVE
The Harmsworth Trophy, circa 1905: the twin 72-hp-engined *Napier II*, which achieved a speed of 29.93mph.

BELOW
The Harmsworth Trophy, circa 1903: *Napier* (outside boat), winner of the first British International Harmsworth Trophy.

the name of Selwyn Francis Edge, whose steel-hulled *Napier* averaged 19.5 knots. The trophy assumed international significance the following year when entries from France and the U.S.A. joined the fray in the Solent. Selwyn Edge again dominated the race and twice rounded the Royal yacht, acknowledged by the king and queen at the finish. But it was a short-lived victory, for the committee ruled that his Napier Minor had failed to comply with the qualifications and the trophy went instead to the second-placed Henri Brasier of France.

As a result, the next race in 1905 was held at Arcachon, France, which resulted in a walkover for the British boat driven by Lionel Rothschild and the Hon, John Scott Montagu after the French boycotted the event and the Americans withdrew. The latter successfully defended the trophy in 1906; however, the American, Edward J. Schroeder, had his record-breaking powerboat *Dixie* shipped over to compete and she won, captained by Barclay Pearce, at an average of 31.85mph (51.26km/h).

Schroeder's *Dixie 11*, *Dixie 111* and *Dixie IV* held sway in all-American contests in 1908, 1910 and 1911, and it was not until T.O.M. Sopwith, the British aircraft manufacturer, crossed the Atlantic in his *Maple Leaf IV* that the trophy returned to Britain. *Maple Leaf IV* averaged 43.1mph (69.36km/h) in the race off Huntingdon

OPPOSITE
Fabio Buzzi's FB 55 design, *La Gran Argentina*.

Garfield Arthur Wood (1880–1971),

King of Speed in the pre-war era.

The son of a ferry boat captain in Iowa, Gar Wood was raised in a marine environment. One of 12 children, his interest in all things mechanical and his father's ferry boat in particular, led the young Wood to study at a technical college in Chicago, where he gained a diploma in engineering science.

He made his fortune when he invented the hydraulic hoist used in the truck industry, which allowed him the luxury of indulging his first passion – powerboat racing. Picking up Chris Smith's 1915 Gold Cup winner Miss Detroit, *at a forced auction, got him onto the front line, and by shrewdly making Smith a partner in his race team, Wood received the technical back-up he needed. With* Miss Detroit II, *the two won the Gold Cup together in 1917 and kept a firm hold of the trophy for a further five years.*

Wood then turned his attention to the other side of the Atlantic and to winning the Harmsworth Trophy, the powerboat world's oldest and grandest prize. He won

it at his first attempt in 1920 with Miss America *and fought off the cream of British and European competition to keep a tight grip on this world title until 1933 with nine more boats all carrying the same patriotic name. With* Miss America IX, *he also secured the world water speed record, breaking through the 100-mph barrier for the first time on 20 March 1931.*

With Orlin Johnson as his mechanic, the two formed one of the most successful racing combinations of all time. Wood handled the steering while Orlin acted as throttle man. Since there was no way that they could talk to each other above the din of the massive unsilenced aero engines, they developed a series of hand signals to communicate with one another. The one most often used by Wood was the hand thrust forward with the palm down which, in simple terms meant, 'Give it all you've got!'

The Smith/Wood building partnership foundered in 1922 on the rocks of

conflicting interests. While Smith was looking to use their racing successes as a foundation for mass-producing boats, Wood simply wanted to use them as springboards to the next great challenge. Chris Smith went on to form Chris*Craft, and perhaps encouraged by this success, Woods later launched his own manufacturing yard at Marysville, Michigan. He concentrated on the high end of the market, producing the Liberty line of luxury powerboats powered by 500-hp adapted war surplus engines. The firm also produced a highly successful line of open speedboats, building some 3,300 units between 1922 and 1947.

ABOVE LEFT
The Harmsworth Trophy, circa 1921: Colonel A.W. Tate (left) talks to American legend, Gar Wood.

BELOW
1915 Gold Cup winner, *Miss Detroit*.

Bay N.J., then won again the following year in a series of races in Osborne Bay off the Isle of Wight with a much-improved speed of 56.4 mph (90.76km/h). This record prevailed until the outbreak of the First World War and the cessation of competition.

During those dark days the trophy came close to being lost when the Admiralty

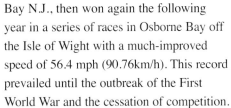

ABOVE
Circa 1926: 'Jo' Carstairs competing for the Harmsworth Trophy, powerboat racing's oldest honour.

ABOVE RIGHT
Circa 1926: Jo Carstairs racing *Estelle II* in the Harmsworth Trophy race.

yacht, *Enchantress*, where the Harmsworth bronze had been stored, was bombed during a Zeppelin raid. All the records were lost, but miraculously all that was damaged on the trophy was its wooden plinth. This was eventually restored in 1920 by Gar Wood, using a piece of mahogany from his successful challenger, *Miss America 1*.

Wood dominated the competition throughout the 1920s and early '30s, winning the Harmsworth title a record nine times, though he was challenged by the British oil millionaires, Betty 'Jo' Carstairs who, in her quest for victory, sponsored a series of aero-engined hydroplanes over a four-year period, each costing $30,000.

Bill Shakespeare, in his book

Powerboat Racing, gives this colourful account of Betty Carstairs' determined attempt at regaining the trophy from Wood in 1928.

'In 1928 the British International Trophy, last won by the United States in 1920 by Gar Wood, was challenged for by the wealthy yachtswoman Betty Carstairs, who commissioned S.E. Saunders Ltd. of East Cowes, Isle of Wight, to build two challengers, *Estelle I* and *Estelle II*, both single-step hydroplanes, to designs by F.P. Hyde-Beadle.

'The rules of this race, which was intended to be to motorboat racing what the America's Cup was to sail racing, limited the overall length (like the

International Cowes-Torquay race today) to 40ft, but Betty Carstairs' challengers were much smaller than this. Estelle I, 26ft with a beam of 5 ft 6 in, was designed for a potential of 100mph and was powered by a single 900-hp Napier aircraft engine such as powered the S5 Schneider Trophy winner of Flight Lieutenant N. Webster in September 1927. *Estelle II* was 21ft, beam 6ft, but her single step was of vee-section as against the flat step of her sister. The highest speed ever attained on water at that time was 80mph so the two challengers aroused great interest.

'The race itself was to be held at Detroit, and thus in fresh water, so all British trials had to be held in this medium

THE ULTIMATE GUIDE TO MOTOR BOATS

and all design requirements could be fulfilled without consideration of the effect of salt water on the engine cooling systems or the hull fastenings. The idea was that the two Estelles would race against each other on Lake Windermere in the Lake District, the largest sheet of inland water in Britain, and as a result of these trials a third challenger would be built to incorporate all that was best in the first two. This is an indication not only of the wide design and building potential in those days but also of the availability of money to pay for it. It makes me more than a little envious.

'The result of the Windermere trials was so disappointing that at one stage Betty Carstairs called the whole thing off, but on second thoughts, and no doubt under pressure from those intent upon retrieving lost honours, she decided to enter *Estelle II*. Betty Carstairs was a short, rather dumpy little thing, but, by golly, she must have had the heart of a lion.

'The defence was overpowering. Gar Wood entered his reconditioned *Miss America* with which he had taken the trophy in 1920, re-engined with two Liberty motors of 500hp apiece. He also built *Miss America VI*, powered also by twin Libertys, and *Miss America VII*, a new conception powered by two of the new Packard automotive engines of 800hp apiece.

'Not content with this he also built *Miss America VIII* with a single Packard 800hp motor, while in addition, a Mr. Talbot entered a boat to the design of John L. Hacker powered by a Miller motor of 620-cu inch capacity with a potential of

700hp. It was obvious, therefore, that America not only feared the challenge but was also properly taking all precautions to see that it would not succeed by "packing the sidelines".

'The result was inevitable, and Goliath beat David. *Estelle II* capsized in the first race injuring Betty Carstairs' ribs and damaging her mechanic Joe Harris even more seriously, and Gar Wood went on to win in *Miss America VII* at a speed of 92.838mph. The uneven contest sounded the death knell of the Liberty aircraft engine, which, up to that time, had held supreme in the field of big time motorboat racing. From then on it was Packard all the way, right on up to World War II when they powered many of the British Admiralty's motor gunboats.'

Woods' *Miss America I* had raised the average speed record for the event to 61.4mph in the 1920 event off Osborne Bay, and kept his hand on the bronze with a succession of Miss Americas on the Detroit river in 1921, 1926, 1928, 1930, 1931, 1932 and 1933, raising the record first to 75.2mph in 1929, 77.1mph a year later, 78.4mph on Lake St. Clair, and 86.8mph (139.68km/h) with *Miss America X* in 1933. One of the most dramatic and controversial confrontations came in 1931 when Kaye Don, a racing-car driver and flying ace from the First World War, took *Miss England II* to challenge Wood on his own waters on the Detroit river. Don got a one-second lead on Wood's *Miss America IX* at the start, and to the excitement of some 600,000 spectators, carried this lead all the

way to the finish. It was Wood's one and only failure in the Harmsworth competition.

Reporting the event, J. Lee Barrett set the scene for this remarkable race in his book, *Speedboat Kings: 25 Years of International Speed Boating*.

'At 4:45 pm, fifteen minutes before the starting gun, the river had quieted down. It was like a sheet of glass. The *Miss England II* moved out slowly from its moorings at the Edsel Ford boathouse on the mainland side. It was being towed across the river to the judges' stand amid a deafening clamour of horns, sirens, whistles and bombs, and the incessant whirl of a dozen aeroplanes overhead.

'Kaye Don and his two mechanics, all fitted out in spotlessly white overalls strapped in by steel-ribbed life preservers, stood on the deck of their white speedboat – stalwart, healthy, fearless young Britons, ready to ride to their death, challenging the master for speedboat honours. They were just kids.

'There was a catch in the throat to see them standing there on the bow of their beautiful boat as it moved across the river. It was momentous testimony of England's wish to be supreme on the water. England had thrown that responsibility on the shoulders of these youngsters. The ruddy glow of the river coloured their faces in the light of an already departing sun.

'The hearts of these young Britons must have ticked a little faster. America had poured out 600,000 people in a tribute to their courage. It was a sight they had never seen in England, a sight they may never see

in the world again. The stage was set for a great spectacle. It was like a Roman amphitheatre fifty times enlarged, with the big sunset ball of the sun throwing its sharply bladed fires across the water.

'We stood with Mrs. Gar Wood on the deck of Charles F. Kettering's beautiful yacht, the Olive K. Wood's Miss Americas weren't in sight. In one minute the five-minute time signal would be cannoned from the judges' stand, the signal for Wood and Don to get ready. Wood's Grayhaven home is up there beyond the easterly turn of the course. We strained our eyes to see the wake of his Miss Americas way out there. But we couldn't. Wood hadn't come out yet.

'We had our eyes riveted on Mrs. Wood. She was a little pale. And nervous. Her right hand was twitching on the deck rail, her left fingering a locket on her breast. She had her eyes fixed in the distance, on that thin slip of water that runs beside her home at Grayhaven. It was from that point that she expected to see the Miss Americas dash out, tracing four lines of white wake behind them. You wouldn't see the boats. It's too far away. You see the wake first – thin little white lines in the water.

'The gun from the judges' stand cannoned the five-minute time signal. That's the signal for Wood and Don to get ready, to get their engines warm, to position for the flying start to the line.

'We could hear the two 2,000 horsepower engines in Miss England II roar to a start. We couldn't see the boat. It was

SPEED

anchored near the judges' stand. But we could hear the thunder of those engines. You could hear that far up the river, like distant cannons booming.

'Five minutes were left. The five huge time discs were poised there high above the yacht club dock. One of these discs drops each minute.

'Another disc dropped. Four minutes were left. Miss England II thundered past the yacht on which we were standing and speeded toward the higher waters of the river for position and the flying start to the line. Still Wood couldn't be seen.

'Mrs. Wood grew increasingly nervous. "Where are they?" I heard her ask. She didn't want an answer. No one knew anyway. Only Gar Wood. Wood was timing his start to a split second.

'I knew Wood would be on time. He always is.

'Mrs. Wood put the field glasses to her eyes. Even yet she couldn't see the wake of the American boats.

'The second disc dropped. Three minutes left. A million eyes were turned now in the direction of Wood's home. I began to wonder myself. Wood had three minutes to get to the line from his home.

'Packed humanity was silent – only the distant drone of Miss England II could be heard above the whir of aeroplanes flying overhead. She was circling above the intake power station, throwing a beautiful stream of mist on each side of her.

'The third disc dropped. Then the fourth. Only one disc was left. Wood had only one minute. He must get his boat to the

line before the last disc dropped or Don would beat him across.

'And Don was set on beating Wood across. He had told him a few days before. "If I'm going to win this race, Mr. Wood, I've got to be first across that line."

'Wood knew why this was true. Even Don didn't believe his boat could take Miss America's wash. And it couldn't. Wood knew that too. He had even said to Steele and several others a few days before the race that he did not think Miss England II could finish. And Wood is an excellent judge of speedboats. He can stand on the dock watching these boats in trials and often tell exactly what's wrong with the boat. He'd often done that with his Miss Americas and Miss Detroits.

'It was a question of who would lead the other across the line. Don was determined he would lead Wood; Wood was just as determined he would lead Don.

'Don was so intent on leading Wood across that he had previously asked the officials for a lane so that he wouldn't be interfered with by the two American boats.

'"How much of a lane do you want?" Edenburn asked him.

'"About four hundred yards. It will take me at least that far to get my boat up on the step and planing at the line."

'Edenburn conferred with Chapman, Harry Greening and Otto Barthel. This request of Don's was without precedent. But they agreed to grant Don's wish.

'Nothing in all sport can match the picture of the flying start in a boat race. It's a beautiful sight to watch. But it needs steel

nerve, fine judgment for the men in the boats to get their bow across just at the spark of gun-fire. That's where the drama is – in that dash to the line. The crowd knows, Wood knows, Don knows. These men must judge every second accurately from a distance far above the line. If you go over more than five seconds too soon you're out of the race, disqualified. If you go over too late you've got to take the wash of the other boat. And that's dangerous. At 100 miles an hour.

'And now race time was almost at the stroke of zero. One disc remained.

'The faint drone of the engines in the two Miss Americas came to us. We looked, saw the two twin lines of wake. Wood was coming, heading straight for the line, his Miss America IX leading. They came down the stretch like mad bulls. But Don, too, was ready.

'We could see him straighten his boat out of the white arc he had made in the water. He was heading toward the start. The roar was getting terrific. Three thundering torpedoes were opening up their throttles, straightening out, charging to the judges' stand.

'Wood's boat, the Miss America IX, seemed to porpoise a little. I had never seen that in any of his boats before. His boats were always as steady, as true, as straight as a die. They always planed out so beautifully.

'But Wood kept coming. So did Don – Don leading. That too was a strange sight to this immense throng. Wood had always gone across first. But Miss England II was up on her step, and was charging, throttles

open, down the stretch, at over 100 miles an hour.

'I knew Wood had his throttles open, too. He always does, across the line. But somehow he couldn't get the speed he needed. Don kept pulling away from him. When they crossed the line the timer's ticker tape showed that Don had crossed just three-quarters of a second ahead of Wood, on the inside, on the buoy track. That's how close these boats were together.

'Don had done two things in those swift seconds; he had beaten Wood across and he had seized the coveted track, the inside. If Wood was ever to pass Don, he'd have to cross Don's wash.

'Wood never passed him. Don sped his boat around the course to a new Harmsworth heat record of 89:913 miles per hour. It meant that on the straightaway Don had to travel well over 100 miles an hour to achieve that speed.

'Wood was much better at the buoys than Don. Miss England, rounding the first buoy on the west, scudded dangerously. Wood followed. It was beautiful to see the America IX spin around those buoys. To do that Wood uses two propellers. Just before Wood turns the wheel, Johnson, who handles the throttles, checks the starboard (inside) propeller, while the port (outside) propeller turns at high speed.

'How these two men can synchronize so well is a mystery. They act as one. They have to.

'Miss England has only one propeller. But it has two rudders, bow and aft. Don depends chiefly on his rudders to make the

buoys. But he has difficulty straightening his boat after the turns. Everyone could see that. Once, his giant hydroplane, coming out of the easterly bend just before completing the fourth lap, was bearing down on the dock of the yacht club. The spectators near the front of the dock, those who could see what was happening, pushed back, frightened. *Miss England* was out of control. But suddenly the strong arm of England's war ace straightened her and averted tragedy.

'Even though Wood moved up on Don at the buoys he didn't seem to have enough speed in his boat. It was porpoising badly in Don's wash. And the leaping was getting worse.

'Those who knew the dangers of a porpoising boat were afraid for the life of Wood and Johnson. They knew the trouble Johnson was having with those propellers. Sometimes the America IX was completely out of water because even in the face of Wood's troubles they were travelling down the straightaways at over 100 miles an hour. At that speed the slightest mishandling of the throttle controls means almost certain tragedy. Every time the boat came back to the water Johnson had to be careful not to shut down the throttle too quickly. If he did the propellers would put on a drag, draw the bow down, throw the stern into the air. The centre of resistance then moves up into the bow and a complete turtle will result – and possible death.

'Johnson had to be dead sure that the engines were running just slightly faster than the speed of the boat each time the boat came back to the water.

'Not only that. He had to check the water, the oil, watch the tachometer readings, throttle the inside propeller just at the correct moment near the buoys, while keeping the outside propeller just at the correct speed.

'And besides he had to watch the buoys. "I always keep my eyes on those buoys," Johnson said.

'He used uncanny judgment in everything he did. The America IX averaged 87.027 miles per hour. That was a Harmsworth record for Wood.

'The America VIII finished last, far behind the other two boats.

'It was the first time in Harmsworth history that Wood had been beaten. The impossible had happened.'

His next boat, *Miss America X*, successfully defended the trophy against challenges from Kaye Don's world speed record holder, *Miss England III*, and a 25-ft single-engined challenger driven by Hubert Scott-Paine.

ABOVE
The Harmsworth Trophy, circa 1912: *Baby Reliance III*, 26-ft long and powered by a single Sterling 150-hp engine.

SPEED

culminating in the Cowes/Torquay/Cowes classic. Now the trustees, led by powerboat enthusiast the Earl of Normanton, are intent on expanding the series to include other events around the world and so encourage greater international competition.

The Gold Cup was first presented in 1904, a year after the Harmsworth, but with the almost identical goal of encouraging powerboat design and speed developments in the U.S.A. Unlike its British equivalent, the Gold Cup has always been competed for on home waters. It is now the premier trophy within the Unlimited Hydroplane Class, and is fought for in gas turbine- and piston engine-powered boats that can exceed 200mph.

The first Gold Cup race, held over a 32-mile course on the Hudson river, was won by C.C. Riotte of the Columbia Yacht Club, driving the 60-ft 110-hp auto boat *Standard* at an average of 23.6mph (37.97km/h). The cup was held twice that year, and on the second running Willis Sharpe Kilmer driving *Vingt et Un II*, a 38ft 9-in (11.8-m) Clinton H. Crane design,

Competition was suspended until the end of the Second World War when R. Stanley Dollar, Jr. from San Francisco, whose family owned the famous Dollar Steam Ship Line, retained the trophy for America until Bob Hayward captured it for Canada in 1959 with his *Miss Supertest III*, and retained it for two years on Lake Ontario.

The Harmsworth Trophy then ceased as an event for more than a decade until Mike Doxford's offshore powerboat *Limit Up* won it back from Britain in 1977. Australia reigned in 1978 when Doug Brinker's *Taurus* took the bronze 'down-under', which sparked fresh enthusiasm for the challenge in America. Bill Elswick and then Bill Clauser won it back in their entries *Longshot* and *Satisfaction* in 1980 and '81 and Al Copeland took it the

following year with his *Popeyes*, keeping the trophy until fellow-American George Morales claimed it after the Cowes/ Torquay classic with his boat *Fugua Shoes* in 1983. The last American winner was Mike Seabold, and his son won it in 1986 with a Class 1 catamaran.

In recent times, the trophy has become the ultimate prize for endurance-class racing, centred on a series of offshore races

ABOVE LEFT
The *Daily Mail* International Harmsworth Trophy 2003: *Wettpunkt* skipper, Hannes Bohinc.

OPPOSITE
Wettpunkt. com, current holder of the Harmsworth trophy, driven by Hannes Bohinc.

powered by a 75-hp engine, showed that size was not everything by increasing the speed record to 25.3mph (40.71km/h). For the next five years, the trophy remained in the hands of Jonathan Wainwright from Chippewa Bay with his smaller, low-powered *Chip* and *Chip II* boats that failed to match the early speed records. It was not until E.J. Schroeder came onto the scene in 1908 with his mighty Clinton H. Crane-designed *Dixie II*, powered by a 220-hp engine driven by Wainwright, that speeds begin to climb above 30mph.

From 1909 to 1913, the Gold Cup was held at Alexandria Bay, N.Y. In 1910, Alfred Graham Miles achieved a breakthrough in design with his 20-ft *PDQ II*, powered by a 60-hp engine to push the speed record to 36.8mph (59.22km/h). But this win also marked the end of boating on a budget in events like this, for the following year speed increased to 44.5mph (71.61km/h), achieved by Casimir S. Mankowski's 32-ft *Ankle Deep*, powered by a mighty 300-hp motor.

1914 saw the emergence of Christopher Columbus Smith, the founder of Chris*Craft, when the event moved for one year to Lake George, N.Y. His 200hp-powered 20-ft design, *Baby Speed Demon II*, driven by Robert Edgren and owner Jim Blackton, Jr., broke the 50-mph barrier for the first time. His next design, *Miss Detroit*, won the following year in New York and though Smith and his team carried the Gold Cup back to Detroit, where it remained until 1925, the effort broke him financially and the boat was auctioned off in a fire sale. Every cloud has a silver lining, however,

Christopher Columbus Smith

(1861–1939), creator of the Chris*Craft legend.

Christopher Columbus Smith left school at 14 to become a duck hunter and in between helped his brother Henry build small boats at Algonac on the St. Clair river in Michigan. Despite the lack of any formal training in design, engineering or woodworking, the young Chris soon revealed the intuitive skills that were to make him an expert in all three. The two formed the company, Smith Brothers, but when Henry left to follow other pursuits, Chris continued in the business and became more and more interested in performance boats. The Dart *was his first commercial break, for when it began to accumulate performance records, clients*

turned to Smith to build boats for them to race on local circuits. One of these was John J. Ryan, for whom Smith developed the hydroplane-stepped hull which led to the Reliance series of speciality race boats built by the Smith-Ryan Boat & Engine Company.

The partnership foundered after Smith persuaded local citizens to invest in a new design – Miss Detroit – *which won the 1915 Gold Cup but failed as a commercial enterprise. The two partners defaulted on their loans and the boat was sold at auction to the industrialist Garfield Wood. But every cloud has a silver lining and, just when things were at their darkest, Wood decided to enlist Smith as a partner in his team and gave him the opportunity*

of continuing to build high-performance race boats. Together, they achieved tremendous success. One of the most notable was Miss Minneapolis – *the first boat to break the 60-mph barrier in 1916. By 1921, Smith had launched his first production boat – a 26-footer powered by a 100-hp Hall Scott engine, but while he dreamed of applying Henry Ford's mass-production philosophy to water, Woods' focus of attention was on the winning rostrum. This eventually led to the break-up of their partnership and the formation of a new company, Chris Smith & Sons Boat Company, in 1922.*

During the first year of operation, the company built 24 boats and had a turnover of $52,000. Within seven years,

production had leapt to 946 boats and a turnover of $3,200,000, with the Chris*Craft brand becoming a household name. During the Second World War, the company built the wooden landing craft that were to carry American troops ashore in the D-Day Normandy landings in 1944.

Chris Smith died in 1939, but his son, Jay W. Smith, continued the family firm until 1958 when the company was sold on his retirement. A succession of owners failed to return the company to its former glory and by the mid-1980s it was saved from bankruptcy by the giant engine-makers, OMC. When the Evinrude/Johnson corporation in turn went out of business in 2000, all looked lost for Chris*Craft until Steven Julius decided to take the helm, managing to revive the company fortunes by returning to Chris Smith's founding principles of concentrating on quality and performance, and mixing these ingredients with the modern demand for retro-styling; in fact, the latest models show the distinct 1950s looks of their illustrious forebears.

OPPOSITE ABOVE LEFT
Christopher Columbus Smith, founder of Chris*Craft.

OPPOSITE LEFT
Chris*Craft troop carriers used in the D-Day landings in Normandy.

and the man to pick up the pieces, and Smith, was the industrialist and keen powerboat racer, Gar Wood.

As a result, *Miss Detroit* defended the trophy on her home waters in 1916, but it almost turned into an unmitigated disaster for all concerned. Wood failed to show up on the morning of the start and Smith had to appeal to the public to find a substitute driver for the single-stepped hydroplane. A young man by the name of Johnny Milot from Algonac, Michigan, stepped forward, and with no time to put on overalls jumped into the cockpit besides Wood's mechanic, Jack Beebe, and headed off for the start. Milot was unfamiliar with the course and the 250-hp Sterling-engined *Miss Detroit*; he followed in the wake of the fleet for the first few laps until he succumbed to seasickness. Beebe then took over the wheel and, remarkably, went on to take the winner's flag with the ashen-faced Milot slumped beside him.

Undaunted, Smith and his new partner, Wood, dominated the Gold Cup for the next eight years with *Miss Minneapolis*, *Miss Detroit II*, *III*, *IV* (which took the record to 70mph) and the mighty 900-hp- powered *Miss America*, while Smith's first 25-ft Packard Chris*Craft, owned by Jesse G. Vincent, won the race in 1924 and '25.

Speeds did not exceed the 70-mph barrier again until after the Second World War when the Gold Cup returned to Detroit for one year in 1946 and was won by Guy Lombardo's *Temp VI* with a speed of 70.878mph (114km/h). The next design breakthrough came with the emergence of

stepped hydroplane hulls with *Miss Sweetie* in 1949, which set a speed of 78.6mph (126.49km/h) around the Detroit course, followed by a series of Ted Jones- designed Slo-Mo-Chun boats. Racing for the cup in 1951, *Slo-Mo-Chun IV*, driven by Lou Fageol, took the record to 90.871mph (146.23km/h). The cup has remained in the domain of the Unlimited Hydroplane Class ever since.

In 1957, another Ted Jones design, *Miss Thriftway*, driven by Bill Muncey, crossed the 100-mph barrier with a speed of 101.787mph (163.8km/h) at Seattle. Back in Detroit, *Atlas Van Lines*, owned by Fran Muncey and driven by Chip Hanauer, marked the start of a winning partnership from 1982 to 1987 with a speed of 120mph (193.1km/h).

1989 saw Bernie Little's first successful *Miss Budweiser*, driven by Tom D'Eath, push the barrier once more, first to 131.209 at San Diego, then to 143.176mph (230.41km/h) the following year back at Detroit, where the Gold Cup has remained ever since. Chip Hanauer was first to smash the 150-mph mark with a speed of 152.591mph (245.56km/h) with the gas turbine-powered *Miss PICO* in 1999.

European and world racing records are ratified by the Union of International Motorboating (UIM), a club founded in 1922. The major divisions within powerboat racing are between the various types of inboard and outboard craft. Each division has a number of classes, depending on the type and cubic capacity of their engines. Most major events are run by the

national authority in each country, often over closed courses. Some famous events, such as the Mississippi Marathon and the Paris Six Hours, are endurance races. Under UIM rules, points towards a world championship are awarded to the first six finishers of each race. The Class 1 World Offshore Championship is made up of races held in favoured Mediterranean venues such as Anzio, Istanbul, St.-Tropez and Trieste, with Middle-Eastern locations like Dubai and the Arab Emirates. Races are also held in the Norwegian capital of Oslo, and in Plymouth or Guernsey in the U.K.

Other world championships, like the Unlimited Hydroplane Class, are run on a much more local basis only in North American waters, with American racers the only competitors. In other sports, including sailing, world championship status requires entries from at least six countries, so not all world titles won in American waters have quite the right ring about them.

Offshore racing became popular during the second half of the 20th century as designs made powerboats more seaworthy. A major event is the Miami/Nassau Race from Florida to the Bahamas, first held in 1959. This was followed in 1961 by the Cowes/Torquay classic in England, The Round Britain race, inaugurated in 1969, the London to Monte Carlo on the Mediterranean in 1972 and the Cannonball Race from Miami to New York in 1994.

Sadly for the sport, American and European/Middle Eastern race boats rarely compete together. The American Powerboat Association (APBA), which

Bernard Leroy Little

(1925–2003), nicknamed the 'King of Boats'.

Bernie Little remains one of the U.S.A.'s most successful team owners. At the time of his death at the age of 77 in the spring of 2003, his Miss Budweiser Unlimited Hydroplane *racing team had chalked up a record of 134 victories and 22 world championship titles. His racing career began shortly before the 1963 season, when August A. Busch III, then head of the Anheuser-Busch brewery giant, decided that his company should get itself in the forefront of this thrilling sport of circuit racing. As well as owning three Anheuser-Busch distributorships, Little flew and sold helicopters, and since hydroplane racing is the nearest thing to 'flying by the seat of one's pants' he seemed the ideal candidate to mastermind Budweiser's campaign. This Budweiser partnership endured for four decades – the longest continuous sponsorship programme in the history of motor sports.*

Little was one of just 36 sailors to survive the sinking of the USS Marathon *in 1945 when the troopship, moored off Okinawa, was rammed by a Japanese suicide submarine. Recalling that incident when questioned about the dangers of hydroplane racing, Little's favourite riposte was always: 'Man – when you scramble out onto a burning deck and jump into the water, into smoke, oil and flames in the middle of the night – that's fear.'*

The first Anheuser-Busch boat, the Beer Waggon, *as she was dubbed, was launched in 1965. She wasn't the fastest on the circuit, but being equipped with four*

seats instead of two, the boat won the publicity stakes wherever she ran. Astronauts, movie stars and politicians vied with the media to beg a ride in this 150-mph machine, which continued to run under the Budweiser flag until the end of the 1965 season. Little's first victory came in 1966 when a new Miss Budweiser, *hurriedly brought into service in mid-season after her predecessor had been destroyed during a race in Washington, D.C., won the Tri-Cities Atomic Cup and San Diego Cup with Bill Brow at the wheel.*

Brow was killed the following year while competing in the Tampa Suncoast Cup, and Little faced a double tragedy when Mike Thomas, Brow's replacement within the team which won the British Columbia Cup at Kelowna, was killed in a construction accident during the latter part of that year.

Undaunted, Little commissioned Ed Karelsen to design a new Miss Budweiser for the 1968 season and after overcoming a series of bugs, the team picked up the World High Points Championship in 1969, '70 and '71. By this time, horsepower was king, but not even the 1,200hp produced by the Rolls-Royce Merlin-engined Miss Budweisers from 1975 to '76 could re-create the early glory days. Indeed, it was not until the first of three Miss Budweiser hulls, fitted with a Roll-Royce Griffon engine and producing 1,000 more horsepower than the earlier Merlin motor, that the team got back to its winning ways, with 1980 the most successful to date. With Dean Chenoweth driving, the team chalked up 20 heat victories and an outright lap record of 138.249mph (222.48km/h) en route to their fourth world championship title. The next year, it won the title again after clinching victory in six of the eight races and raised the lap record to 140.187mph (225.6km/h). The 1982 season seemed to be going the same way until tragedy struck the team once more when it was leading the world championship mid-way through the season. Its boat flipped during qualification for the Tri-Cities Atomic Columbia Cup and Dean Chenoweth was killed.

The boat was re-built and continued to dominate the Unlimited Hydroplane scene

for three more years to bag Little's seventh world title in 1984. Chenoweth's death troubled Little greatly and he realized that something had to be done to make the sport 'safer and safer, not just faster and faster'. By 1985, he and his crew chief, Jeff Neff, introduced the Bubble Bud to

seat the driver 'indoors' and cocoon him in the event of a flip. A year later, he and designer, Ron Jones, Sr., installed the cockpit canopy from an F-16 fighter plane on the first of their gas turbine-powered boats, which won three races outright and took the championship at the end of the

season. It was the canopy, however, that caught the attention of the rule-makers, and from the 1987 season onwards it was a mandatory requirement on all new unlimited hydroplanes. Since then, the F-16 canopy has undoubtedly saved the lives of many drivers who have quite literally

walked away from what would have been fatal accidents. 'Safety has always been first in my mind,' said Little of his idea. 'I'm not a very good loser, but I don't believe in winning at any cost, especially when it is a matter of a driver's life.'

Little's gas turbine-powered *Miss Budweisers* continued to dominate the hydroplane world for another two decades, pushing the lap record beyond the 170-mph barrier and winning the championship record 22 times, the last time in 2002, when the famous trophy was renamed in his honour: The Bernie Little World High Point Championship Trophy.

OPPOSITE LEFT
Bernie Little and his *Miss Budweiser* team with the Gold Cup in 2002.

OPPOSITE RIGHT
The air intake on the original *Miss Budweiser* unlimited hydroplane.

LEFT
The original gas turbine-powered *Miss Budweiser* unlimited hydroplane, with her compact jet engine on the quayside.

PAGE 54
Miss Budweiser, powered by a Lycoming gas turbine aero engine capable of 200mph (320km/h).

controls both inshore and offshore racing across the U.S., has different class parameters to those set by the UIM, which ratifies all world records for powerboats and controls racing elsewhere in the world. When the two groups did race together on

the offshore circuit during the 1970s and '80s, it led to some great international competition and it can only be hoped that, one day, trophies like the Harmsworth, Class 1 and Endurance World Championships will bring the disparate

groups back together once more.

Endurance records have captured the imagination just as much as speed records, and the Atlantic has always been the greatest theatre of operation. Jim Wynne cut his teeth this way, long before going on to

Virgin Atlantic Challenger II crosses the Bishop Rock finish in 1986 to win the Blue Riband, after crossing the Atlantic from New York in 3 days 8hrs and 32 mins – an average for the 2,874 miles (4625km) of 35.69 knots.

dominate offshore powerboat racing on both sides of the pond by becoming the first to cross the Atlantic in a 22-ft outboard-powered boat back in 1958. The wackiest was in 1990, when ex-British paratrooper, Tom McClean, who had already claimed crossings in the smallest boat, made the 3,000-mile crossing from New York to Falmouth in a 37-ft (11.3-m) powered 'bottle'. Despite its looks, his *Typhoo* Atlantic challenger was quite sophisticated and included the latest navigation equipment as well as a four-poster bed!

By the early 1980s, engine design and propulsion units for superyachts had advanced to the point where powerboats could challenge outright records across oceans. Richard Branson, the pop music and airline millionaire, was the first to look at challenging the transatlantic record that had been held by the liner *United States*, which had set a time of 3 days 10 hours on her maiden voyage in 1952. He was particularly interested in reviving the Hales Trophy, a gaudy gilded prize first awarded in 1838 to the Blue Riband holder, which had been gathering dust in the American Merchant Marine Museum for four decades. He had the 64-ft (19.5-m) catamaran, *Virgin Atlantic Challenger*, built by Class 1 specialists Cougar Marine in 1985, and after waiting in New York for the right weather conditions, set out with a team of acknowledged endurance specialists that included round-the-world yachtsman Chay Blyth and powerboat champion Ted Toleman to beat the time set by the *United States*. After a fuel leak forced them to seek fresh supplies

James R. Wynne (1929–90), World Offshore Powerboat Champion and father of the stern drive.

Jim Wynne remains one of America's most successful powerboat champions and one of those fortunate few whose work and passions seem perfectly matched. Wynne began racing powerboats as a hobby during his schooldays and merged hobby and career after gaining a degree in mechanical engineering from the University of Florida and a master's from MIT, by becoming chief test engineer at the Kiekhaefer Corporation. This, his first job, was to supervise the testing of Mercury outboard motors at Wisconsin and Florida which he continued to do until 1958, when he took part in the first transatlantic crossing by an outboard-powered craft, crossing from Copenhagen to New York in a 22-ft (6.7-m) boat.

This Atlantic crossing was one of many firsts in Wynne's career. He designed the first turbine-powered Thunderbird, the first production boat for Don Aronow, the first Formula, the first

Magnum, and in 1968, the first commercially-successful stern-drive propulsion system. Working in his parents' garage with old outboard motor parts, he constructed and patented a working model of the stern-drive unit and saw it into production with Volvo Penta.

By casting an engineering perspective on the sport of powerboat racing, Wynne became a prominent figure in offshore racing. He held several world powerboat records and won the World Offshore Championship in 1964 and 1966 in boats of his own design, during a period when world titles meant something and were not limited to local events. In 1966, his 30-ft (9.1-m) Ghost Rider withstood the pounding seas better than its engineer, who suffered two broken legs during the race.

*His race-boat experience and engineering background eventually led him to work as a consultant. In 1965 he established Wynne Marine, Inc., a firm specializing in the design of powerboats, yachts and commercial vessels, which designed models for more than 30 manufacturers, including Carver, Chris*Craft, Cobalt, Cruisers, Inc., Donzi, Grady-White, Hatteras, Larson, Stamas and Trojan.*

Ghost Rider, in which Wynne won the 1966 Cowes-Torquay race, the Miami to Nassau, the Miami to Key West and the St. Petersburg Hurricane Classic 200 to take the world title that year, remains one of his most enduring legacies. Almost 40 years on,

this extreme deep-V wooden cold-moulded wooden race boat, powered by twin 750-hp turbocharged Daytona engines, is still racing. Current owners, Capt. Barry F. Cohen and Cmdr. Alen Sands York, entered her in the 2004 Miami-New York Race. Wynne co-designed the boat with Waltman Walters and she became the exemplar for those first Formula, Donzi and Cigarette designs produced for Don Aronow

Another of Wynne's milestone designs was Maui Kai, one of the first catamarans to race in offshore competition. Owned by Hugh Doyle of Treasure Island, Florida, this too was a cold-moulded wooden hull and raced only three times, but she won two of those events and proved that, when conditions were right, offshore cats could compete on better than equal terms with their monohull rivals. This success led to many Class 1 teams fielding both monohull and catamaran racers at the big events and deciding on the day of the race which boat to use. Four decades on, the catamaran concept that Wynne championed has been taken to such a level that these 180-mph (290-km/h) craft are raced successfully in all weathers.

ABOVE LEFT
Ghost Rider, designed and driven by Jim Wynne.

from a passing ship in mid-Atlantic, the boat hit a submerged object (probably a ship's container) and sank just 138 miles (222km) from the Bishop Rock Lighthouse off the Scilly Isles, which marks the start of the western approaches and has been the traditional 'finish line' for these passage records since the great days of clipper ships and before. Her crew lived to tell the tale and Branson looked to Sony Levi to design a second challenger.

Virgin Atlantic II was a 72-ft (22-m) monohull powered by twin 2,000-hp MTU diesel engines displacing 37 tons, which had a top speed of 55mph (88.5km/h). Branson and his crew set out from the Ambrose Light, New York, on 27 June 1986 and covered the first 526 miles at 52.82mph. The team had set up a rendezvous with refuelling ships at three points along the course, and it was at the second of these, 1,236-miles (1990-km) across, when *Virgin Atlantic II* was two hours ahead of the record, that things began to unravel. For some reason, a third of the 2,500 gallons (11365 litres), transferred from the bowser, turned out to be water. The crew consequently lost valuable time clearing the tanks and replacing them with clean diesel. The tanks, however, were filled with an anti-surge material which kept releasing

A SeaCat catamaran car ferry seen against the New York skyline at the start of a transatlantic record attempt. The vessel broke the record for commercial shipping to win the Hales Trophy and Blue Riband.

water every time the hull hit a large wave, rather like shaking a sponge. This water then caused the paper filters in the system to swell and restrict the supply of fuel to the engines, necessitating frequent stops to change the cartridges. Soon, the supply of filters ran out and it was only the Royal Air Force that saved the day by air-dropping a fresh supply to the boat. These delays cost dearly, for a depression sweeping across the Atlantic behind them eventually caught up with the boat, turning the last stage into something of a nightmare. At the finish, Branson and his crew took the record with just 2 hours 8 minutes to spare, after averaging 41mph (66km/h) over the 3,000-mile distance.

The Trustees at the American Merchant Marine Museum were not impressed, and the thought of losing their trophy to a speedboat appalled them. Citing the 147-year deed of gift, they claimed that commercial passenger- carrying vessels could only claim the Hales Trophy. Branson's suggestion that Chay Blyth had been their paying passenger on

LEFT
The Aga Khan's gas turbine-powered *Destriero*, the current holder of the Blue Riband.

OPPOSITE
The 112-ft (34-m) long, 11,500-hp *Gentry Eagle*, which recorded a transatlantic crossing of 62hrs 7mins in 1989. Top speed was 73mph (117.5km/h).

ABOVE
The Hales Trophy.

ABOVE RIGHT
David Scott-Cowper, standing on pack ice alongside his 30-year-old converted lifeboat, *Mabel E. Holland*, in 1990. His solo circumnavigation took three years via the Canadian North-west Passage. He was awarded the YJA Yachtsman of the Year title for the achievement.

OPPOSITE
David Scott-Cowper leaving Cape Town.

board *Virgin Atlantic Challenger II*, cut little ice.

Undaunted, Branson put up his own Virgin trophy – a silver model of the Bishop Rock Lighthouse, and the first to step up to the plate was Hawaiian property tycoon and powerboat enthusiast, Tom Gentry. In 1989 he had launched the 112-ft, 11,500-hp *Gentry Eagle* and after setting records from Miami to Nassau and back (5hrs 20mins) and then from Miami to New York (19hrs 17mins), shattered the transatlantic crossing record with a time of 2 days 14 hrs 7 mins – a 23 per cent improvement on the time set by Branson who was at the finish to present Gentry with his trophy!

By now, the Blue Riband might have been back in American hands, but the trustees of the American Merchant Marine Museum refused even to entertain handing the Hales Trophy to Gentry's powerboat. They remained just as adamant even when a commercial passenger vessel did manage the feat in 1990. The SeaCat, a surface-piercing catamaran car ferry, built by Incat in Tasmania, claimed the trophy after making the Atlantic crossing in 3 days 7 hrs. The trustees now claimed that a catamaran, however large, was not a steam-powered ocean liner, but SeaCat's owners, Hoverspeed Great Britain, took the matter to court, claiming that the original deed allowed for the trophy to be awarded to the fastest vessel making a surface transatlantic crossing, whether it was powered by steam or oil and had one hull or two. It was successful, and the Hales Trophy was grudgingly handed back across the Atlantic.

SeaCat's commercial record lasted until 1998, when it was broken twice by Incat-built catamarans. The current holder, Cat-Link V, is a 183-ft (55.8-m) Spanish car and passenger catamaran ferry and her attempt was eventful: barely hours after departing from New York she was diverted to a search mission off the coast of Canada, delaying her by two hours. Even so, she crossed the Atlantic in 2 days, 20 hours – the first such transatlantic voyage by a commercial vessel in under three days – and the first to average over 40 knots (46mph/74.03km).

The current outright power record stands at 2 days 10 hrs 34 mins, set in 1992 by the Aga Khan's gas turbine-powered 223-ft (68-m) *Destriero*, at an average of 52.55mph (84.6km/h). It is this boat that holds the Blue Riband.

After these Atlantic runs, the last great challenge was to circle the globe. The first to do so in a powerboat was British solo adventurer, David Scott-Cowper, who took three years to complete the voyage via the Canadian North-west Passage in a 30-year-old converted lifeboat, *Mabel E. Holland*, still fitted with her original Gardiner diesel

Tom Gentry (1930–98), World Offshore Powerboat champion.

Tom Gentry was certainly a go-getter, both in business and boating. The self-made multi-millionaire from Hawaii began to deal in real estate at an early age by risking all on the back of a pension policy he pledged against his first deposit. His colourful life was effectively ended in 1994 when the 40-ft (12.2-m) Class 1 Skater catamaran, Team Gentry, *flipped as he gambled on cutting inside a back marker at the third turn during the Key West race. Speeding in at close to 100mph, he quickly ran out of space, was forced to move out to the right, then execute a quick left turn to maintain course. As the boat came around it hooked and flipped over.*

Gentry and his throttle man, Rickie Powers, found themselves trapped inside their respective cockpits without oxygen which, according to Powers, was 'an extremely panicky situation'. 'When that thing went over, there was no oxygen. It was just instant submersion. One minute you're breathing and talking and the next thing you're under water. I didn't even have a chance to gasp for breath.'

Harnessed to their seats, upside-down and disoriented, both men used all their previous training to get themselves out of the F-16 cockpit canopies. 'I opened the hatch, undid my seat belt and that's when all hell broke loose,' said Powers. 'The life jacket I was wearing just pinned me to the floor of the boat. So I'm floundering around and got tangled up underneath the dash. Then I got my wits and realized I had to grab some oxygen, because I wasn't going to get out.' To survive in these situations, Team Gentry, *and other canopy-equipped race boats carry emergency oxygen. Gentry's boat had two sources for each crew member, including a built-in system with a scuba regulator and a small back-up air cylinder. However, the system is not linked up for automatic feed to the pilots in the event of an emergency. Powers grabbed the spare back-up air and tried to put it in his mouth, but found that the protective dust cover was still on. Still floundering, he discarded the cylinder and again attempted to get out, but could not counteract the life jacket's buoyancy, which kept him pinned to the floor of the boat, now above him. 'I had to breathe,' he said. 'I took one breath of salt water. I thought to myself it's unbelievable, I'm breathing underwater.'*

With hands and arms flailing, Powers suddenly felt something that seemed familiar. 'It's like God handed me the regulator, and with my last breath I cleared the regulator and just sat there. Suddenly, everything was fine.'

Gentry, then 64, was not as fortunate. When the paramedics eventually got to him, the American ace was unconscious. He was rushed to hospital in a critical condition but never recovered, and remained in a coma until his death in 1998. 'Tom must have experienced the same things I did,' said Powers. 'For some reason, he didn't have the mind to go for the regulator. He tried to get out, and I guess he ran out of time.' Gentry did not suffer any impact-oriented injuries but the accident serves to highlight the ever-present dangers of powerboat racing.

It was the end of a remarkable career. Just a month before, Gentry had set a world speed record for his class by driving the same boat at an average speed of 157.4mph (252.3km/h) across San Diego Bay.

In 1989, he had set an outright record across the Atlantic to take the Blue Riband with his powerboat, Gentry Eagle, *with a time of 62 hours 7 minutes. He had also won the UIM offshore world championship in 1976 and 1987 and received that organization's highest award, the Gold Medal of Honor in 1993.*

'My dad was the original "self-made man",' Gentry's son, Norman, who had raced with him across the Atlantic said. 'He was unique. He was dynamic. He took and overcame risks, both in business and in sports. He loved the pulse of business and the intensity of competition.'

It was that love of speed and the constant gamble against risk that was to cost him so dear.

LEFT
Tom Gentry and Richard Branson after Gentry's *Gentry Eagle* broke the transatlantic record in 1989.

OPPOSITE
Tom Gentry's *Team Gentry* catamaran.

engines. It took Cowper three seasons simply to break through the North-west Passage. He decided to leave the boat, beached in the ice, and return to England each winter until the following spring. After one winter he found that the ice had expanded the boat's wooden propeller tunnels and breached the hull. She was completely flooded, but after bailing out the bilges and changing the oil and filters, remarkably, the engines fired up without problems. He was also attacked by polar bears but finally completed the round-the-world voyage in 1990 and won the YJA Yachtsman of the Year award.

In 1998, Nigel Irens designed the 105-ft (32-m) *Cable & Wireless Adventurer*, and based his slender concept hull with transverse stability provided by small outer hulls. The idea, first proven with his prototype, *Elan Voyager*, offers exceptional fuel economy for a given load, together with speed and comfort. *Cable & Wireless Adventurer* was built as a commercial passenger ferry, and taking paying passengers around the world,

LEFT
Nigel Iren's *Cable & Wireless Adventurer*.

OPPOSITE
The unlimited hydroplane, *Winston Eagle*, leaving a huge plume of spray behind her during a hydroplane race in the U.S.A. These craft are capable of speeds in excess of 200mph (320km/h).

completed a record-breaking circum-navigation in 1998. Departing from and returning to Gibraltar, the vessel covered the 24,500 nautical miles in 74 days 20 hours, spending some 62 days at sea. The average speed achieved was 18.975mph (30.54km/h) and the average fuel consumption about 1mpg

Many yacht clubs hold predicted log races which test navigational skill rather than outright speed. The skipper must predict the exact time his or her boat will pass specified points on a predetermined course, which they make without a watch, adjusting their boat speed to overcome variations in wind, tide and current. The skipper coming closest to their prediction wins.

The speed and sea-keeping capability of boats also play a major role in fishing championships. The ability to get to the fishing grounds first, then ride the swells comfortably, are major plus factors to bringing home the best catch, and manufacturers make sure their boats get as much of the limelight as the guys manning the rods.

Tom McClean and his Atlantic challenger bottle boat, *Typhoo*, in which he successfully crossed the Atlantic alone from New York to Falmouth in 1990.

WORLD WATER SPEED RECORDS

YEAR	SPEED (mph)	BOAT	DRIVER	LOCATION
14 April 1874	24.6	Sir Arthur Cotton	Felix Thackery Haig	Chiswick Reach, England
1885	26.2	Stiletto	Nathaniel Herreshoff	
1887	30.0	Ariete		
1895	33.75	Boxer		
April 1897	37.71	Turbinia	Charles Parsons	River Tyne, England
June 1897	39.1	Turbinia	Charles Parsons	Portsmouth, England
June 1897	9.73	Elaine	--	Long Reach, Greenwich, England
July 1900	42.73	Viper	--	
1902	22.36	Mercedes	--	Nice, France
Spring 1903	45.06	Arrow	Charles R. Flint	Hudson River, N.Y.
12 July 1903	24.9	Napier	Campbell Muir	Queenstown
Spring 1904	25.1	Trèfle-à-Quatre-Feuilles	M. Théry	Monte Carlo, Monaco
1904	26.65	Trèfle-à-Quatre-Feuilles	M. Théry	Paris, France
29 October 1904	28.36	Onontio	Harrison B. Moore	Hudson River, N.Y.
3 February 1905	29.3	Challenger	A.D. Proctor Smith	Palm Beach, Florida
1905	29.93	Napier II	Mr. Tucker	Long Reach, Greenwich, England
1905	32.45	Dubonnet	Emile Dubonnet	Monte Carlo, Monaco
1905	33.80	Dubonnet	Emile Dubonnet	Juvisy, France
1 February 1906	34.17	Legru-Hotchkiss		Paris, France
5 August 1908	36.6	Dixie II	Clinton Hoadley Crane	Hempstead Harbor, Bayonne, N.Y.
April 1910	43.6	Ursula	Noel M. Robbins	Monte Carlo, Monaco
9 September 1911	45.21	Dixie IV	Fred K. Burnham	Huntington Bay, Long Island Sound, N.Y.
July 1912	46.51	Maple Leaf IV	T.O.M ('Tommy') Sopwith	England
September 1912	58.26	Tech, Jr.	Coleman du Pont	Huntington Bay, N.Y.
1914	59.964	Santos-Despujols	Victor Despujols	Monte Carlo, Monaco
1915	66.66	Miss Minneapolis	Christopher Columbus Smith	Put-in-Bay, OH
9 September 1919	70.86	Hydrodome IV	Casey Baldwin	Beinn Bhreagh, Bras d'Or Lake, Nova Scotia
15 September 1920	74.97	Miss America	Gar Wood	Detroit, MI
September 1920	77.85	Miss America	Gar Wood	Lake George
6 September 1921	80.57	Miss America II	George B. Wood	Detroit, MI
10 November 1924	87.392	Farman Hydroglider	Jules Fischer	Sartrouville, Seine river, Paris, FR
5 September 1928	92.83	Miss America VII	George B. Wood	Detroit, MI
23 March 1929	93.12	Miss America VII	Gar Wood	Miami Beach, FL
13 June 1930	98.76	Miss England II	Henry Segrave	Lake Windermere, England
20 March 1931	102.16	Miss America IX	Gar Wood	Miami Beach, FL
16 April 1931	103.069	Miss America IX	Gar Wood	Miami Beach, FL
24 April 1931	103.49	Miss England II	Kaye Don	Parana river, Argentina
9 July 1931	110.22	Miss England II	Kaye Don	Lake Garda, Italy

SPEED

Date	Speed	Boat	Driver	Location
February 5, 1932	111.71	Miss America IX	Gar Wood	Miami Beach, FL
July 18, 1932	117.43	Miss England III (K1)	Kaye Don	Loch Lomond, Scotland
July 18, 1932	119.812	Miss England III (K1)	Kaye Don	Loch Lomond, Scotland
1932	120.5	Miss England III (K1)	Kaye Don	
September 20, 1932	124.91	Miss America X	Gar Wood	Detroit (Algonac), [St Clair River] MI
September 1, 1937	126.32	Bluebird K3	Malcolm Campbell	Lake Maggiore, Locarno, Switzerland
September 2, 1937	129.5	Bluebird K3	Malcolm Campbell	Lake Maggiore, Locarno, Switzerland
September 17, 1938	130.86	Bluebird K3	Malcolm Campbell	Lake Hallwyl, Switzerland
August 19, 1939	141.74	Bluebird K4	Malcolm Campbell	Lake Coniston, England
June 26, 1950	160.32	Slo-Mo-Shun IV	Stan Sayres & Ted O. Jones	Seattle, WA (Sand Point)
July 7, 1952	178.49	Slo-Mo-Shun IV	Stan Sayres & t Elmer Leninschmid	Seattle, WA (East Channel)
July 23, 1955	202.32	Bluebird K7	Donald Campbell	Ullswater, England
November 16, 1955	216.2	Bluebird K7	Donald Campbell	Lake Mead, NV
September 20, 1956	225.63	Bluebird K7	Donald. Campbell	Lake Coniston, England
November 1, 1957	184.49	Miss Supertest II	Arthur C. Asbury	Bay of Quinte, Picton, ON, Canada
November 7, 1957	239.07	Bluebird K7	Donald Campbell	Lake Coniston, England
November 10, 1958	248.62	Bluebird K7	Donald Campbell	Lake Coniston, England
November 29, 1957	[195.331]	Hawaii Kai III	Jack Regas	Seattle, WA (Sand Point)
November 30, 1957	187.627	Hawaii Kai III	Jack Regas	Seattle, WA (Sand Point)
May 14, 1959	260.35	Bluebird K7	Donald Campbell	Lake Coniston, England
February 16, 1960	192.001	Miss Thriftway	Bill Muncey	Seattle, WA (East Channel)
April 17, 1962	200.419	Miss U.S. I	Roy Duby	Guntersville, AL
December 31, 1964	276.30	Bluebird K7	Donald Campbell	Lake Dumbleyung, Australia
June 30, 1967	285.21	Hustler	Lee A. Taylor Jr.	Lake Guntersville, AL
November 20, 1977	288.60	Spirit of Australia	Ken Warby	Blowering Dam, NSW, Australia
October 8, 1978	317.60	Spirit of Australia	Ken Warby	Blowering Dam, NSW, Australia
June 15, 2000	205.494	Miss Freei	Russ Wicks	Seattle, WA

Steam-powered, propeller driven
Internal combustion engine, propeller-driven
Jet engine, not propeller-driven
© Leslie Field, 1999

BRITISH INTERNATIONAL HARMSWORTH TROPHY RACES

YEAR	DRIVER	NATIONALLY	BOAT	RACE SITE	AV. SPEED
1913	Tommy Sopwith, Sr.	England	Maple Leaf IV	Osborne Bay, England	56.4
1914–19	No contests				
1920	Gar Wood	U.S.A.	Miss America (I)	Osborne Bay, England	61.4
1921	Gar Wood	U.S.A.	Miss America II	Detroit river, MI	59.7
1922–25	No contests				
1926	Gar Wood	U.S.A.	Miss America V	Detroit river, MI	61
1927	No contest				
1928	Gar Wood	U.S.A.	Miss America VII	Detroit river, MI	59.3
1929	Gar Wood	U.S.A.	Miss America VIII	Detroit river, MI	75.2
1930	Gar Wood	U.S.A.	Miss America IX	Detroit river, MI	77.1
1931	Kaye Don	U.K.	Miss England II	Detroit river, MI	60
1932	Gar Wood	U.S.A.	Miss America X	Lake St. Clair, MI	78.4
1933	Gar Wood	U.S.A.	Miss America X	St. Clair river, MI	86.8
1934–1948	No contests				
1949	Stan Dollar	U.S.A.	Skip-A-Long	Detroit river, MI	94.1
1950	Lou Fageol	U.S.A.	Slo-Mo-Shun IV	Detroit river, MI	100.6
1951–55	No contests				
1956	Russ Schleeh	U.S.A.	Shanty I	Detroit river, MI	90.2
1957–58	No contests				
1959	Bob Hayward	Canada	Miss Supertest III	Detroit river, MI	104.0
1960	Bob Hayward	Canada	Miss Supertest III	Lake Ontario, Can.	116.3
1961	Bob Hayward	Canada	Miss Supertest III	Lake Ontario, Canada	100.2
1962–76	No contests				
1977	Michael Doxford	England	Limit Up		
1978	Doug Bricker	Australia	Taurus		
1979	Derek Pobjoy	England	Uno Mint		
1980	Bill Elswick	U.S.A.	Longshot and Satisfaction		
1981	Bill Clauser	U.S.A.	Satisfaction		
1982	Al Copeland	U.S.A.	Popeyes	Cowes	
1983	George Morales	U.S.A.	Fayva Shoes		
1984	J. Hill, J. Jones, M. Wilson	U.K.		Bristol, England & Nassau, Bahamas	
1985	J. Hill, J. Jones, M. Wilson	U.K.		Bristol, England & Nassau, Bahamas	
1986		Mike Seebold	U.S.A.		
1987–88	No contests				
1989	Stefano Casiraghi	Monaco	Gancia dei Gancia	Atlantic City	
1990–92	No contests				
1993	Daniel Scioli	Argentina	La Nueva Argentina	Punta del Este	
1994	Andreas Ugland	Norway	BP Marine		
1995	Hannes Bohinc	Austria	Casino Tivoli		
1996–2001	No contests				
2002	Stephano Tomasso	Italy	Super Classic 40	Cowes	
2003	Hannes Bohinc	Austria	Wettpunkt.com	Cowes	

APBA GOLD CUP RACES

YEAR	LOCATION	BOAT	OWNER	DRIVER	DESIGNER	LENGTH	POWER	SPEED
1904	New York	Standard	Carl C. Riotte & Eugene Riotte	Carl C. Riotte	H. Newton Whittlesey	60.00ft	110	23.6
1904	New York	Vingt et Un II	Willis Sharpe Kilmer	Willis Sharpe Kilmer	Clinton H. Crane	38ft 9in	75	25.0
1905	Chippewa Bay, NY	Chip	Jonathan Wainwright	Jonathan Wainwright	H.J. Leighton	27ft	10.25	15.9
1906	Chippewa Bay, NY	Chip II	Jonathan Wainwright	Jonathan Wainwright	H.J. Leighton	30ft	15	20.0
1907	Chippewa Bay, NY	Chip II	Jonathan Wainwright	Jonathan Wainwright	H.J. Leighton	30ft	15	20.8
1908	Chippewa Bay, NY	Dixie II	E.J. Schroeder	Jonathan Wainwright	Clinton H. Crane	39 ft	220	30.9
1909	Alexandria Bay, NY	Dixie II	E.J. Schroeder	Jonathan Wainwright	Clinton H. Crane	39ft	220	32.9
1910	Alexandria Bay, NY	Dixie III	F.K. Burnham	F.K. Burnham	Clinton H. Crane			33.6
1911	Alexandria Bay, NY	MIT II	J.H. Hayden	J.H. Hayden				36.1
1912	Alexandria Bay, NY	PDQ II	Alfred Graham Miles	A. Graham Miles	Tams, Lemoine, Crane	20 ft	60	36.8
1913	Alexandria Bay, NY	Ankle Deep	Casimir S. Mankowski	Casimir S. Mankowski	Clinton H. Crane	32 ft	300	44.5
1914	Lake George, NY	Baby Speed Demon II	J. Stuart Blackton [16]	Robert Edgren & Jim Blackton, Jr	Chris Smith & Sons	20 ft	200	50.5
1915	New York	Miss Detroit	Miss Detroit P.B.A.	Jack Beebe & John Milot	Chris Smith & Sons	25ft 6in	250	48.5
1916	Detroit, MI	Miss Minneapolis	Miss Minneapolis Power Boat Association	Bernard Smith	Chris Smith & Sons	20 ft	250	49.7
1917	Detroit, MI	Miss Detroit II	Gar Wood	Gar Wood	Chris Smith & Sons			56.5
1918	Detroit, MI	Miss Detroit III	Gar Wood	Gar Wood	Chris Smith & Sons			52.1
1919	Detroit, MI	Miss Detroit III	Gar Wood	Gar Wood	Chris Smith & Sons			56.3
1920	Detroit, MI	Miss Detroit IV	Gar Wood	Gar Wood	Chris Smith & Sons			70.0
1921	Detroit, MI	Miss America	Gar Wood	Gar Wood	Chris Smith & Sons	26 ft	900	56.5
1922	Detroit, MI	Packard ChrisCraft	Jesse G. Vincent	Jesse G. Vincent	Chris Craft	25 ft		40.6
1923	Detroit, MI	Packard ChrisCraft	Jesse G. Vincent	Caleb Bragg	Chris Craft	25 ft		44.4

1924	Detroit, MI	Baby Bootlegger	Caleb Bragg	Caleb Bragg	George Crouch	27 ft	220	46.4
1925	Port Washington, New York	Baby Bootlegger	Caleb Bragg	Caleb Bragg	George Crouch	27 ft	220	48.4
1926	New York	Greenwich Folly	George H. Townsend	George H. Townsend				49.2
1927	New York	Greenwich Folly	George H. Townsend	George H. Townsend				50.9
1928	No contest							
1929	Red Bank, NJ	Imp III	Richard F. Hoyt	Richard. F. Hoyt	Purdy Boat Company			50.5
1930	Red Bank, NJ	Hotsy Totsy	Vic Kliesrath	Vic Kliesrath				56.1
1931	Montauk, NY	Hotsy Totsy	Vic Kliesrath	Vic Kliesrath				54.9
1932	Montauk, N.Y.	Delphine IV	Horace E. Dodge, Jr.	Bill Horn	George Crouch			59.2
1933	Detroit, MI	El Lagarto	George C. Reis	George C. Reis	John L. Hacker			60.8
1934	Lake George, N.Y.	El Lagarto	George C. Reis	George C. Reis	John L. Hacker			58.1
1935	Lake George, N.Y.	El Lagarto	George C. Reis	George C. Reis	John L. Hacker			55.0
1936	Lake George, N.Y.	Impshi	Horace E. Dodge, Jr.	Kaye Don	George Crouch			47.12
1937	Detroit, MI	Notre Dame	Herb Mendelson	Clell Perry	Clell Perry		500	68.64
1938	Detroit, MI	Alagi	Theo Rossi	Theo Rossi	Baglietto		490	66.08
1939	Detroit, MI	My Sin	Zalmon Guy Simmons, Jr.	Zalmon Guy Simmons, Jr.	Adolf Apel	24 ft		67.05
1940	Northport, N.Y.	Hotsy Totsy III	Sidney Allen	Sidney Allen				51.32
1941	Red Bank, N.J.	My Sin	Zalmon Guy Simmons, Jr.	Zalmon Guy Simmons, Jr.	Adolf Apel	24 ft		52.51
1942–45	No Contests							
1946	Detroit, MI	Tempo VI	Guy Lombardo	Guy Lombardo	Adolf Apel	24 ft		70.88
1947	Jamaica Bay, N.Y.	Miss Peps V	Roy and Walter Dossin	Dan Foster	Adolf Apel	24 ft		56.00
1948	Detroit, MI 57.45	Miss Great Lakes	Albin Fallon	Dan Foster				

APBA GOLD CUP RACES

1949	Detroit, MI	My Sweetie	Ed Gregory & Ed Schoenherr	Bill Cantrell	John L. Hacker	30 ft		78.64
1950	Detroit, MI	Slo Mo Shun IV	Stanley S. Sayres	Ted Jones	Ted Jones	28 ft		78.22
1951	Seattle, WA	Slo Mo Shun V	Stanley S. Sayres	Lou Fageol	Ted Jones			90.87
1952	Seattle, WA	Slo Mo Shun IV	Stanley S. Sayres	Stan Dollar	Ted Jones	28 ft		79.92
1953	Seattle, WA	Slo Mo Shun IV	Stanley S. Sayres	Joe Taggart & Lou Fageol	Ted Jones	28 ft		99.11
1954	Seattle, WA	Slo Mo Shun V	Stanley S. Sayres	Lou Fageol	Ted Jones			92.61
1955	Seattle, WA	Gale V	Joseph Schoenith	Lee Schoenith	Les Staudacher			99.55
1956	Detroit, MI	Miss Thriftway	Willard Rhodes	Bill Muncey	Ted Jones			96.55
1957	Seattle, WA	Miss Thriftway	Willard Rhodes	Bill Muncey	Ted Jones			101.79
1958	Seattle, WA	Hawaii Kai III	Henry Kaiser	Jack Regas	Mike Welsch			103.48
1959	Seattle, WA	Maverick	William Waggoner, Jr.	Bill Stead	Ted Jones			104.48
1960		No contest						
1961	Reno, NV	Miss Century 21	Willard Rhodes	Bill Muncey	Ted Jones			99.68
1962	Seattle, WA	Miss Century 21	Willard Rhodes	Bill Muncey	Ted Jones			100.71
1963	Detroit, MI	Miss Bardahl	Ole Bardahl	Ron Musson	Ted Jones			105.12
1964	Detroit, MI	Miss Bardahl	Ole Bardahl	Ron Musson	Ted Jones			103.43
1965	Seattle, WA	Miss Bardahl	Ole Bardahl	Ron Musson	Ted Jones			103.13
1966	Detroit, MI	Tahoe Miss	Bill Harrah	Mira Slovak				93.02
1967	Seattle, WA	Miss Bardahl	Ole Bardahl	Bill Schumacher	Ted Jones			101.48
1968	Detroit, MI	Miss Bardahl	Ole Bardahl	Bill Schumacher	Ted Jones			108.17
1969	San Diego, CA	Miss Budweiser	Bernie Little and Tom Friedkin	Bill Sterett, Sr.				98.50
1970	San Diego, CA	Miss Budweiser	Bernie Little and Tom Friedkin	Dean Chenoweth				99.56

1971	Madison, IN	Miss Madison	City of Madison	Jim McCormick				98.04
1972	Detroit, MI	Atlas Van Lines	Joe Schoenith	Bill Muncey				104.28
1973	Tri-Cities, WA	Miss Budweiser	Bernie Little & Tom Friedkin	Dean Chenoweth				99.04
1974	Seattle, WA	Pay 'n Pak	Dave Heerensperger	George Henley				104.43
1975	Tri-Cities, WA	Pay 'n Pak	Dave Heerensperger	George Henley				108.92
1976	Detroit, MI	Miss U.S.	George Simon	Tom D'Eath				100.41
1977	Tri-Cities, WA	Atlas Van Lines	Bill Muncey	Bill Muncey				111.82
1978	Owensboro, KY	Atlas Van Lines	Bill Muncey	Bill Muncey				111.41
1979	Madison, IN	Atlas Van Lines	Bill Muncey	Bill Muncey				100.76
1980	Madison, IN	Miss Budweiser	Bernie Little	Dean Chenoweth				106.93
1981	Seattle, WA	Miss Budweiser	Bernie Little	Dean Chenoweth				116.93
1982	Detroit, MI	Atlas Van Lines	Fran Muncey	Chip Hanauer				120.05
1983	Evansville, IN	Atlas Van Lines	Fran Muncey & Jim Lucero	Chip Hanauer				118.51
1984	Tri-Cities, WA	Atlas Van Lines	Fran Muncey & Jim Lucero	Chip Hanauer				130.17
1985	Seattle, WA	Miller American	Fran Muncey & Jim Lucero	Chip Hanauer				120.64
1986	Detroit, MI	Miller American	Fran Muncey	Chip Hanauer				116.52
1987	San Diego, CA	Miller American	Fran Muncey	Chip Hanauer				127.62
1988	Evansville, IN	Circus Circus	Fran Muncey	Jon Prevost/Chip Hanauer				123.76
1989	San Diego, CA	Miss Budweiser	Bernie Little	Tom D'Eath				131.21
1990	Detroit, MI	Miss Budweiser	Bernie Little	Tom D'Eath				143.18
1991	Detroit, MI	Winston Eagle	Steve Woomer	Mark Tate				137.77

APBA GOLD CUP RACES

1992	Detroit, MI	Miss Budweiser	Bernie Little	Chip Hanauer				136.28
1993	Detroit, MI	Miss Budweiser	Bernie Little	Chip Hanauer				141.30
1994	Detroit, MI	Smokin' Joes	Steve Woomer	Mark Tate				145.26
1995	Detroit, MI	Miss Budweiser	Bernie Little	Chip Hanauer				149.16
1996	Detroit, MI	PICO American Dream	Fred Leland	Dave Villwock				149.33
1997	Detroit, MI	Miss Budweiser	Bernie Little	Dave Villwock				129.37
1998	Detroit, MI	Miss Budweiser	Bernie Little	Dave Villwock				140.31
1999	Detroit, MI	Miss PICO	Fred Leland	Chip Hanauer				152.59
2000	Detroit, MI	Miss Budweiser	Bernie Little	Dave Villwock				139.42
2001	Detroit, MI	Miss Tubby's Subs	Mike & Lori Jones	Michael Hanson				140.52
2002	Detroit, MI	Miss Budweiser	Bernie Little	Dave Villwock				143.09
2003	Detroit, MI	Foxhills Chrysler/Jeep	Ed Cooper	Mitch Evans				144.15

Trophy awarded to British driver with highest points in international series of races
Trophy awarded to offshore driver with highest points in international series of races
Trophy awarded to outboard tunnel drivers in team racing format

Richard Branson's 72-ft *Virgin Atlantic Challenger II* set a modern benchmark for crossing the Atlantic in 1986.

CHAPTER FOUR
INFLATABLE BOATS & TENDERS

The origins of the inflatable boat go back to France in the late 19th century and the French balloonist, Maurice Mallet, who began flying and manufacturing hot air balloons in 1879.

By 1909, his company, the Société Française des Ballons Dirigeables (French Airship Company) had begun to exploit the idea of using airships as advertising billboards and his first collapsible Zodiac balloon, *Zodiac 1*, proved so easy to transport and dismantle that it established the firm's reputation. During the two world wars, the Zodiac factory was fully employed making barrage, bomb-carrying and observation balloons for the French military and in the early 1930s produced the first motorized captive balloons.

In 1934, Pierre Debroutelle, Zodiac's chief engineer, struck on the idea of making collapsible boats, his first design

RIGHT
Around 1937, dirigible craft were developed to transport torpedoes and bombs for the French military.

being a two-seater inflatable kayak. The French Naval Air Service followed his research with keen interest, especially when war clouds began to gather over Europe in 1937. The rudimentary craft developed by Debroutelle was the true ancestor of the modern inflatable boat. France was soon overrun by the Germans, but during the Occupation, Debroutelle continued to work in secret on his inflatable boats, using scrap balloon fabric to make up the tubes. In Britain and America, the Allied aircraft industry also produced one- and two-man inflatable rafts for airmen to clamber into when 'downed' in the sea, which undoubtedly saved many lives.

After the war, the Zodiac company diversified into making everything from manure spreaders to office furniture in order to survive, but thanks to continued defence contracts, made considerable progress in the manufacture of inflatable boats, and in particular the development of higher-performance rubberized materials. However, it was not until 1952 when Dr.

Alain Bombard crossed the Mediterranean from Monaco to Tangiers and then the Atlantic from Las Palmas to Barbados in a Zodiac Mk III inflatable dinghy, that the inflatable boat was accepted as seaworthy.

Zodiac continued to pioneer boats and life rafts for military and commercial

shipping , and in 1960 launched its first civilian boat, a small inflatable dinghy equipped with sail and oars.

The French company's products were unwittingly the origins of the rigid-bottom inflatable (RIB). Admiral Hoare, the first headmaster at Atlantic College in Wales,

ABOVE
Zodiac inflatable dinghy.

ABOVE RIGHT
Zodiac X1.

RIGHT
Zodiac *Psychedelic Surfer*, circa 1969

U.K., got his students to replace the rubber floor on a standard Zodiac dinghy with a shallow vee rigid bottom made from plywood. The X1, as it was called, proved stern-heavy and liable to flip backwards in heavy seas, but if offered greater speed and stability than the original boat and was given to Britain's Royal National Lifeboat Institute (RNLI) to test. The X2 was the first large RIB built at Atlantic College in

INFLATABLE BOATS & TENDERS

RIGHT
Zodiac inflatable.

BELOW
RNLI Zodiac X2.

BELOW RIGHT
Zodiac inflatable with Honda outboard.

close association with Avon, and was fitted with twin engines, wheel steering and a tube which ran around the rigid hull. It was a considerable improvement, but it was not until the X5 – built in 1968 by Roy Thomas, Willem de Vogel and Otto van Voorst – where the tubing was fitted on top of the deck rather than around the hull, that the concept became a practical proposition.

A year later, Atlantic College built the 21-ft (6.4-m) *Psychedelic Surfer*, which exceeded all expectations in the 1969 Round Britain Powerboat Race, where it proved itself an excellent rough-weather boat. The design was later sold to the RNLI for £1 and was developd into the Atlantic 21 rescue RIB, which became standard equipment on both sides of the Atlantic as an inshore rescue boat and spawned an entire industry for these hybrid craft.

Another development of the RIB is the flying inflatable boat (FIB). First developed in 1987, there are now more than 1,000 of these powered amphibious ultralights operating from tourist resorts around the world and as toys to entertain guests aboard superyachts. They have even seen action with Navy Seals in Singapore and with Greenpeace activists.

The two-man craft produced by Polaris can operate safely in up to force 3/4 wind and sea conditions and take around ten hours to learn to fly. The conversion from RIB to FIB takes 15 minutes of assembly time and the craft can be modified to operate on land or in snow using clip-on wheels or skis. Powered by a Rotax 582 twin-cylinder water-cooled two-stroke engine driving a three-bladed propeller, the FIB has a wingspan of 36.6ft (11.15m), a cruising air speed of 43.5mph (70km/h) and a maximum take-off weight of 895lb (406kg).

Zodiac Medline 3 RIB, powered by a Suzuki 225 four-stroke outboard.

PORTA-BOTE

Remember learning the art of origami as a child? One group to have profited from those lessons in making paper boats and planes are the guys from Porta-Bote, based at Mountain View, California. Over the past three decades they have made a mint from their folding polypropelene dinghies which start out as a 4-inch thick flat pack and pull out in seconds to an 8ft 6-in, 10ft 10-in or 12-ft dinghy that can be rowed, sailed or motored.

Weighing between 50 and 73lb, they can be packed down in moments to carry home or store on deck. Ultra stable, they can be used for fishing or carrying quite heavy loads. They have even been carried 20,000ft up Mt. Everest to provide transport across a glacial lake!

The ¹/4-in polypropylene panels, which are available in white or green, are impervious to ultra-violet light, oxidants and salt water, and Porta-Bote are so confident in the folding hinges that they provide a ten-year warranty on the hull components.

PORTA-BOTE GENESIS IV
FOLDABLE DINGHY
DIMENSIONS

Length overall:	8ft 06in (2.59m)
Beam:	4ft 08in (1.42m)
Draft:	0ft 04in/10cm
Displacement:	50lb/23kg
Carrying capacity:	2 persons/ 445lb/202kg
Engine Options:	3hp
Length overall:	10ft 10in/3.30m
Beam:	5ft 00in/1.52m
Draft:	0ft 04in/10cm
Displacement:	61lb/28kg
Carrying capacity:	3 persons/ 585lb/265kg
Engine Options:	5hp
Length overall:	12ft 00in/3.66m
Beam:	5ft 00in/1.52m
Draft:	0ft 04in/10cm
Displacement:	73lb/33kg
Carrying capacity:	3 persons/ 670lb/304kg
Engine Options:	5hp

www.porta-bote.com

ABOVE
Porta-Bote made history when it was used by the British Royal Airforce Climbing and Rescue Team in its record-setting climb of Mt. Everest.

Polaris chose RIB rather than catamaran-style floats because of the greater integrity of the single hull. The rigid bottom is designed to plane quickly and the boat is much more forgiving during take-off and landing in fairly rough seas. The boat also offers much greater protection from flying spray, keeping the pilot and passenger – and more importantly the engine – dry.

POLARIS FIB SPECIFICATIONS
FIB582

Basic unit weight: 476lb/216kg
Take-off weight: 895lb/406kg
Stall speed: 30mph/48km/h
Max speed: 50mph/80km/h
Fuel capacity: 9 gals/40 litres
Wing Span: 37.7ft/11.5m
Aspect ration: 6
Double surface: 35%
Configuration: tandem

Inflatables have come a long way since the RIB became accepted as one of the most practical forms of tender. There is a wide range of pneumatics manufactured by Avon, Cirrus, Europia, Nautica, Novurama, Wally, and Zodiac makes them to meet all requirements from the smallest 7-ft foldaway to the head-turning 45-ft, $335,000 custom-built Wally tender with a

Polaris flying inflatable boat.

speed potential close to 60mph (100km/h). These one-time utility/rescue craft are now very much up-market machines designed to impress and look the part on any superyacht. There are even those with fully-fitted forward cabins to provide full accommodation for day or weekend runs to outlying islands and estuaries.

Zodiac produces its Medline range measuring 15ft 9in, 19ft 8in and 23ft 2in. Each has a centre console with a toilet compartment in the largest model and plush seating that folds down to provide sunbeds. There is also a kitchenette complete with a sink and foldaway table for picnics on far-away beaches.

ZODIAC MEDLINE 1 RIB
DIMENSIONS
Length overall:	15ft 09in/4.80m
Beam:	7ft 03in/2.21m
Deadrise:	20°
Displacement:	793lb/360kg
Engine Options:	40–75-hp outboard
	42mph/68km/h
Design:	Zodiac

ZODIAC MEDLINE 2 RIB
DIMENSIONS
Length overall:	19ft 08in/5.99m
Beam:	8ft 02in/2.49m
Deadrise:	20°
Displacement:	1,521lb/690kg
Engine Options:	115–150-hp
	outboard
	46mph/74km/h
Design:	Zodiac

ZODIAC MEDLINE 3 RIB
DIMENSIONS
Length overall:	23ft 02in/7.06m
Beam:	9ft 10in/2.98m
Deadrise:	20°
Displacement:	2,425lb/1100kg
Engine Options:	130–250-hp
	outboard
	53mph/85km/h
Design:	Zodiac

www.zodiacmarine@zodiacusa.com

Cirrus RIBS, based in Portland, England, are unique in several respects. One is that they have been thoughtfully designed by a woman – Danielle Ceccomori – who won a competition for her ideas to improve access and seating. Available in 20- and 24-ft lengths, each has solid side steps and bows to make them easy to board and disembark. These boats

THIS PAGE and OPPOSITE
Cirrus RIBS.

have a very solid look about them and with comfortable bench seating fore and aft give a welcoming sense of security when onboard. Powered by a choice of outboard or inboard/outdrives, both boats within the Cirrus range have a top speed of 60 knots.

CIRRUS 6.3-M SPORT RIB

DIMENSIONS

Length overall:	20ft 08in/6.30m
Beam:	8ft 10in/2.69m
Draft:	0ft 10in/25cm
Deadrise:	24°
Displacement:	2,558lb/1160kg
	(3,306lb/1500kg)
Engine Options:	130-hp outboard
	60mph/96.5km/h
Design:	Danielle Ceccomori/
	John Moxham

CIRRUS 7.3-M CUSTOM RIB

DIMENSIONS

Length overall:	24ft 00in/7.31m
Beam:	8ft 10in/2.69m
Draft:	0ft 10in/25cm
Deadrise:	24°
Displacement:	Outboard -
	2,810lb/1275kg
	Inboard/outdrive -
	3,920lb/1778kg
Engine Options:	225-hp outboard
	60.0mph/96.5km/h
	Yamaha 240hp
	inboard/outdrive
	60.0mph/96.5km/h
Design:	Danielle Ceccomori/
	John Moxham

www.cirrusribs.com

THIS PAGE and OPPOSITE
Cirrus 6.3 RIBs.

THIS PAGE and OPPOSITE
Europia RIBs.

EUROPIA BOATS

Based at Vero Beach, Florida, Europia launched a plush teak-decked 39-ft RIB tender to carry aboard superyachts at the 2003 Fort Lauderdale Boat Show. Capable of transporting up to 12 people, the composite deep-V hull is powered by twin 300-hp diesel inboard/outdrives. She has a self-bailing cockpit, adjustable pneumatic suspension chairs and is fitted with a bridle so that she can be towed behind the mother ship.

EUROPIA 12-M RIB

DIMENSIONS

Length overall:	39ft 04in/11.99m
Beam:	9ft 11in/3.02m
Deadrise:	24°
Displacement:	793lb/360kg
Engine Options:	Twin 300-hp diesel inboard/outdrives
Design:	Chase

www.europiaboats.com

WALLY TENDER

This is a special import from a Monaco-based superyacht builder that does nothing by halves. Designed to present an impressive appearance at docks around the world, the hull of this 45-ft RIB is moulded from advanced composites and is built to ABS specifications for high-speed craft; it boasts 12 watertight bulkheads. With a 14-ft beam, guests can lounge on the large open teak deck, or when running at speed seek sanctuary in the seats next to the helmsman and facing aft behind. If the ride proves too exciting, there is always the stand-up head and shower room built into the console.

Fitted with twin Volvo 420-hp gas engines, she has a top speed of 57mph or 46mph with Yanmar 300 diesels.

WALLY TENDER RIB

DIMENSIONS

Length overall:	45ft 00in/13.72m
Beam:	14ft 00in/4.27m
Deadrise:	20°
Engine Options:	Twin Volvo Penta 470hp inboard/outdrives 57mph/92km/h Twin Yanmar 300-hp inboard/outdrives 46mph/74km/h
Design:	Wally Yachts

www.wally.com

THIS PAGE and OPPOSITE
The Wally tender.

CHAPTER FIVE
SPORTS & FISHING BOATS

Contender Boats, based at Homestead, Florida, have been producing sports fishing boats since 1984. Its range, which began with a classic 25-ft centre console boat, now extends from a 21-footer to a 36-ft hull. All are outboard-powered, with single, twin or triple rigs, though the Thirty-Five is offered with a twin diesel inboard option.

All the Contenders share the same proven 24.5° deep-V hull shape with reverse radius chines to provide a dryer ride in the roughest conditions. This improves lift when getting on the plane, reduces fuel consumption and improves stability when at rest.

The Twenty-One and Twenty-Three models share the same 18-inch draft deep-V hull design, cut to 21- and 23-ft lengths and come equipped with gunwale rod-

holders, live well and transom door. The 21 is powered by a single 150–250-hp Yamaha outboard, but the 23-ft model is designed to carry single or twin engines up to a total of 400hp.

The Twenty-Five is the boat that started it all. The original design has been considerably developed over the years and is now a classic among centre-console offshore sports fishing boats. Standard features include a self-bailing cockpit, a raised live fish well, large protective console, and has the option of a 240-gallon (1091-litre) fuel tank to cater for those long offshore runs.

The Twenty-Seven is fitted with twin Yamaha outboards between 200 and 250hp each and has a raised 48-gallon live well, two 56-gallon fish boxes and a further 100-gallon insulated box in the bow. The Thirty-One model is available with a forward open cockpit or with a small cuddy with a simple V-berth to rest or lock fishing gear away. Both are powered by twin Yamahas of either 225 or 250hp each.

The Thirty-One fish around, powered by the same Yamaha package, has a stylish

RIGHT and OPPOSITE
Contender Thirty-Six open fish sports fishing boat, powered by three Yamaha 300-hp 3.3-litre high-pressure, direct-injection V6 outboards.

central cuddy with a V-berth, table, galley and stand-up head to provide a level of comfort for the whole family on those weekend trips.

The Thirty-Five outboard and the Thirty-Six open fish share the same 10-ft beam hull shape. The former, which is also available with twin diesel inboards rather than the more thirsty outboards, has a forward four-berth cabin with a forward dinette, galley and head with shower facilities. A full tuna tower is also available.

The Thirty-Six is a true offshore speedster with twin or triple outboard rig that packs up to 900hp to get you to the fishing grounds first. To feed those engines, there is the option of 600-gallon (2728-litre) fuel tank capacity and with dual 50-gallon live wells, enormous fish-box capacity and storage space, this is the boat to get you out there fast and keep you fishing longer.

CONTENDER TWENTY-ONE OPEN FISH

DIMENSIONS

Length overall:	21ft 03in/6.47m
Beam:	8ft 03in/2.51m
Draft:	1ft 06in/0.46m
Deadrise:	24.5°
Displacement:	2,100lb/953kg
Max Outboard:	225hp
Design:	Contender

CONTENDER TWENTY-THREE OPEN FISH

DIMENSIONS

Length overall:	23ft 03in/7.09m
Beam:	8ft 03in/2.51m
Draft:	1ft 06in/0.46m
Deadrise:	24.5°
Displacement:	2,400lb/1089kg
Max Outboard:	400hp
Design:	Contender

CONTENDER TWENTY-FIVE OPEN FISH

DIMENSIONS

Length overall:	28ft 00in/8.53m
Beam:	8ft 10in/2.69m
Draft:	1ft 06in/0.46m
Deadrise:	24.5°
Displacement:	3,000lb/1361kg
Max Outboard:	500hp
Design:	Contender

CONTENDER TWENTY-SEVEN OPEN FISH

DIMENSIONS

Length overall:	30ft 00in/9.14m
Beam:	8ft 10in/2.69m
Draft:	1ft 06in/0.46
Deadrise:	24.5°
Displacement:	3,300lb/1497kg
Max Outboard:	500hp

CONTENDER THIRTY-ONE OPEN FISH/CUDDY/FISH AROUND

DIMENSIONS

Length overall:	32ft 06in/9.91m
Beam:	9ft 4in/2.84m
Draft:	1ft 06in/0.46m

Deadrise:	24.5°
Displacement:	3,500lb/1588kg
Max Outboard:	500hp
Design:	Contender

CONTENDER THIRTY-FIVE
OUTBOARD
DIMENSIONS

Length overall:	35ft 00in/10.67m
Beam:	10ft 00in/3.05m
Draft:	2ft 00in/0.61m
Deadrise:	24.5°
Displacement:	5,500lb/2495kg
Engine Options:	Twin outboards or diesel inboards
Max Outboard:	750hp
Design:	Contender

CONTENDER THIRTY-SIX OPEN FISH
DIMENSIONS

Length overall:	36ft 02in/11.02m
Beam:	10ft 00in/3.05m
Draft:	1ft 06in/0.46m
Deadrise:	24.5°
Displacement:	6,000lb/2722kg
Max Outboard:	900hp
Design: Contender	

www.contender.com

CENTURY & COBIA

The Century and Cobia Boat Companies, based in Panama City, Florida, are members of the Yamaha Group and specialize in sports fishing and family boats between 17 and 32ft. Though marketed under separate brand names, the smaller Century and Cobia bay boats and centre console models up to 22ft come from the same moulds and their individual models slot in neat size order within the combined range. These boats all carry a ten-year hull warranty, and of course come equipped with a Yamaha outboard.

If flat fishing is your bag, then the three bay boats in the range are worth a closer look. Shallow-drafted, with 14–15° of deadrise to cut through a light chop without losing their stability, these inshore fishing boats come in 18-, 21- and 22-ft lengths and are easily towed behind the family car. Each has a centre console, and a large uncluttered foredeck area for fishing, and comes complete with rod-holders, tackle box, storage lockers, fish boxes, cooler, and a bait well that recirculates 14 gallons (64 litres) of water through it to keep what matters fresh. The 222 bay boat comes ready-wired to take a 36-v trolling motor on the bow.

CENTURY 1901/ COBIA 191 BAY
BOAT
DIMENSIONS

Length overall:	18ft 04in/5.59m
Beam:	8ft 00in/2.44m
Draft:	0ft 10in/25cm
Deadrise:	14°
Displacement:	1,950lb/885kg

Engine Options:	150h-p outboard	Beam:	8ft 04in/2.54m
Design:	Yamaha	Draft:	11in/28cm
		Deadrise:	15°

CENTURY 2101/COBIA 211 BAY
BOAT
DIMENSIONS

		Displacement:	2,200lb/998kg
		Engine Options:	225-hp outboard
		Design:	Yamaha
Length overall:	21ft 02in/6.45m		

CENTURY 2202/COBIA 222 BAY
BOAT
DIMENSIONS

Length overall:	22ft 00in/6.71m
Beam:	8ft 06in/2.59m
Draft:	1ft 02in/0.36m
Deadrise:	15°

OPPOSITE
Contender Twenty-Seven, with twin Yamaha putboards.

BELOW
Century 2000 centre console.

SPORTS & FISHING BOATS

Displacement: 2,100lb/953kg
Engine Options: 250hp outboard
Design: Yamaha

Century and Cobia also produce a series of small centre console sports fishing boats designed to venture further out into open waters. Ranging in size from 17 to 18ft 6in, they carry the same features as the bay boats though with extra locker space and a little more luxury.

CENTURY 1700/COBIA 174 CENTRE CONSOLE

DIMENSIONS

Length overall: 17ft 00in/5.18m
Beam: 6ft 08in/2.03m
Draft: 1ft 00in/0.30m

Deadrise: 15°
Displacement: 1,450lb/658kg
Engine Options: 90-hp outboard
Design: Yamaha

CENTURY 1800/ COBIA 184 CENTRE CONSOLE

DIMENSIONS

Length overall: 17ft 10in/5.44m
Beam: 7ft 08in/2.34m
Draft: 0ft 10in/25cm
Deadrise: 15°
Displacement: 1,850lb/839kg
Engine Options: 150-hp outboard
Design: Yamaha

CENTURY 1901/ COBIA 194 CENTRE CONSOLE

DIMENSIONS

Length overall: 18ft 06in/5.64m
Beam: 8ft 00in/2.44m
Draft: 1ft 01in/0.33m
Deadrise: 20°
Displacement: 2,150lb/975kg
Engine Options: 150-hp outboard
Design: Yamaha

LEFT
Century 2202 bay boat.

OPPOSITE
Century 2200 centre console.

SPORTS & FISHING BOATS

The larger hulls within the Cobia range, from 20ft to 32ft 6in, are available with a variety of decks, from the dual and centre consoles to the walkarounds, with fully-fitted cabins that give a new meaning to family fishing. All have built-in heads and, in the 24ft and upwards, carry a distinctive 2-ft long bowsprit to stow the anchor and keep it well clear of the hull. Models up to 27-ft long all fit within the 8ft 6-in limit for towing on the roads.

CENTURY 2000 CENTRE CONSOLE
DIMENSIONS
Length overall:	20ft 02in/6.12m
Beam:	8ft 04in/2.54m
Draft:	1ft 02in/0.36m
Deadrise:	15°
Displacement:	2,300lb/1043kg
Engine Options	150-hp outboard
Design:	Yamaha

COBIA 210 WALKAROUND/215 DUAL/CENTRE CONSOLE
DIMENSIONS
Length overall:	20ft 04in/6.20m
Beam:	8ft 06in/2.59m
Draft:	1ft 02in/0.36m
Deadrise:	20°
Displacement:	3,400/2,900lb (1542/1315kg)
Engine Options:	200-hp outboard
Design	Yamaha

CENTURY 2200 CENTRE CONSOLE
DIMENSIONS
Length overall:	22ft 00in/6.71m
Beam:	8ft 06in/2.59m
Draft:	1ft 05in/0.43m
Deadrise:	20°
Displacement:	3,500lb/1588kg
Engine Options:	225-hp outboard
Design:	Yamaha

COBIA 234 CENTRE CONSOLE/230 WALKAROUND
DIMENSIONS
Length overall:	23ft 10in/7.26m
Beam:	8ft 06in/2.59m
Draft:	1ft 03in/1ft 02in (0.38m/0.36m)

LEFT
Century 2300 centre console.

OPPOSITE
Cobia 174 centre console.

SPORTS & FISHING BOATS

Deadrise: 20°
Displacement: 3,500/4,000lb
                     (1588/1814kg)
Engine Options: 250-hp outboard
Design: Yamaha

**CENTURY 2300 CENTRE
CONSOLE/WALKAROUND**

DIMENSIONS
Length overall: 24ft 07in/7.49m
Beam: 8ft 06in/2.59m
Draft: 1ft 02in/0.36m
Deadrise: 18°

Displacement: 3,200/3,700lb
                     (1452/1678kg)
Engine Options: 250-hp outboard
Design: Yamaha

**COBIA 254 CENTRE CONSOLE/250
WALKAROUND**

DIMENSIONS
Length overall: 25ft 06in/7.77m
Beam: 8ft 06in/2.59m
Draft: 1ft 04in/1ft 03in
                     (0.41/0.38m)

Deadrise:	20°
Displacement:	4,000/4,400lb
	(1814/1996kg)
Engine Options:	300-hp outboard
Design:	Yamaha

CENTURY 2600 CENTRE CONSOLE/WALKAROUND

DIMENSIONS

Length overall:	26ft 04in/8.03m
Beam:	8ft 06in/2.59m
Draft:	1ft 03in/0.38m
Deadrise:	20°
Displacement:	4,900/5,700lb
	(2223/2586kg)
Engine Options:	Single 300-hp
	outboard
	Twin 250-hp
	outboards
Design:	Yamaha

COBIA 274 CENTRE CONSOLE/270 WALKAROUND

DIMENSIONS

Length overall:	27ft 06in/8.38m
Beam:	8ft 06in/2.59m
Draft:	1ft 06in/0.46m
Deadrise:	20°
Displacement:	4,500/5,000lb
	(2041/2268kg)
Engine Options:	Twin 200-hp/225-hp
	outboards
Design:	Yamaha

CENTURY 2900 CENTRE CONSOLE

DIMENSIONS

Length overall:	29ft 04in/8.94m
Beam:	9ft 06in/2.90m

Draft:	1ft 10in/0.56m
Deadrise:	23°
Displacement:	5,900lb/2676kg
Engine Options:	Twin 300-hp
	outboards
Design:	Yamaha

COBIA 314 CENTRE CONSOLE/312 SPORT CABIN

DIMENSIONS

Length overall:	30ft 11in/9.42m
Beam:	9ft 10in/3.00m
Draft:	1ft 06in/1ft 05in
	(0.46/0.43m)
Deadrise:	20°
Displacement:	6,500/7,300lb
	(2948/3311kg)
Engine Options:	Twin 300-hp
	outboards
Design:	Yamaha

OPPOSITE
Cobia 222 bay boat.

ABOVE
Cobia 230 walkaround.

CENTURY 3200 CENTRE CONSOLE/WALKAROUND

DIMENSIONS

Length overall:	32ft 06in/9.91m
Beam:	10ft 06in/3.20m
Draft:	1ft 08in/0.51m
Deadrise:	23°
Displacement:	8,500/9,400lb
	(3856/4264kg)
Engine Options:	Twin 300-hp
	outboards
Design:	Yamaha

www.centuryboats.com
www.cobiaboats.com

RIGHT
Cobia 312 sport cabin.

OPPOSITE
Century 2200 centre console.

INTREPID BOATS

Intrepid, based at Largo, Florida, is at the high end of the centre console sports fishing boat market in more ways than one. Its range, which starts with a 34-footer, is among the most expensive – and fastest – on the market. Powered by a choice of twin- or triple-rig outboards, these boats will flash you out to the fishing grounds at 50–60mph (80–100km/h). They all have stepped deep-V hulls, designed not only to cut through the roughest swell, but also to do it economically – if you call 1.5 miles per gallon economical!

The most important aspect for most owners, however, is that all Intrepids are semi-custom-made, so they can be exactly what you want, for cruising, diving, fishing – or all three. The large centre console on the smaller model encloses a head and shower compartment with 6ft 2in (1.9m) of headroom. To help maximize this internal space, the business side of the console is designed to accept the latest flat-screen multi-function electronics. The helm seat opens up to provide an aft-facing tackle chest and there are additional lockers built into the gunwales and under the forward seats.

Moulded from fibreglass and Kevlar over a PVC core, and cured under vacuum, these hulls are engineered to withstand

RIGHT and OPPOSITE
Intrepid 300 offshore sports fishing boat.

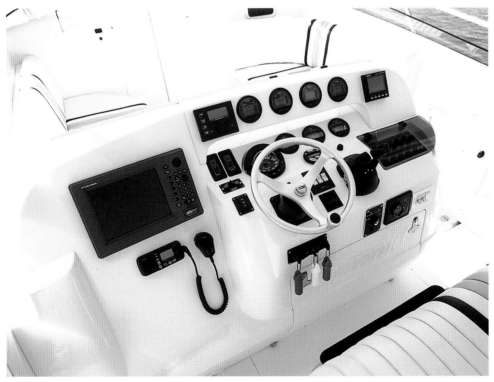

much more pounding than any crew would willingly entertain, and it is this quality that is reflected in their price.

INTREPID 348 CENTRE CONSOLE SPORTS FISHING BOAT

DIMENSIONS

Length overall:	34ft 08in/10.57m
Beam:	10ft 06in/3.20m
Draft:	2ft 00in/0.61m
Deadrise:	22.5°
Displacement:	12,000lb/5443kg
Engine Options:	Twin 300-hp
	outboards
	53mph/85km/h
Design:	Intrepid

The 37-ft model has a man-sized cuddy with 6ft 2-in (1.88-m) headroom, two berths, a head and shower unit and a small galley. The remainder of the forward cockpit is devoted to a U-shaped seating area that doubles as a sun deck. Owners have the option of ordering a side dive door cut into the starboard aft quarter of the hull to allow swimmers and divers easy access to the water, well away from the engines and props.

OPPOSITE and THIS PAGE
Intrepid 370, with views of console and V-berth cabin.

INTREPID 370 CENTRE CONSOLE/CUDDY SPORTS FISHING BOAT

DIMENSIONS

Length overall:	37ft 00in/11.28m
Beam:	10ft 06in/3.20m
Draft:	2ft 00in/0.61m
Deadrise:	22.5°
Displacement:	12,500lb/5670kg
Engine Options:	Twin or triple 300-hp outboards 65mph/105km/h
Design:	Intrepid

Intrepid's top-range 38-footer has an extra foot of beam and makes maximum use of this space to provide a forward cabin with a queen-sized bed, a settee that converts down to make a second double bed, together with a galley and separate shower/head. A wraparound screen protects

OPPOSITE and THIS PAGE
Exterior and interior views of the Intrepid 377 offshore sports fishing boat.

the U-shaped seating area ahead of the central helm position and there is the option of a transom or side dive door.

INTREPID 377 CENTRE CONSOLE/ CUDDY SPORTS FISHING BOAT

DIMENSIONS

Length overall:	38ft 03in/11.66m
Beam:	11ft 06in/3.51m
Draft:	2ft 00in/0.61m
Deadrise:	22.5°
Displacement:	15,500lb/7031kg
Engine Options:	Twin or triple outboards 60mph/96.5km/h
Design:	Intrepid

www.intrepidpowerboats.com

CHAPARRAL

The deck boat is a relatively new concept, first launched in the early 1990s to maximize space and make smaller speed boats truly multi-purpose. By utilizing the bow area for additional seating, adding enclosed heads and a simple galley, and upgrading the furnishings, suddenly, we have a boat to please all members of the family. It can still be used to fish from, sunbathe on, ski behind and explore lakes and rivers in, but with the addition of a canvas awning it is even possible to get away for a weekend. No wonder they are so popular.

These boats are not designed for rough passages, but are perfect for use on sheltered waters where their shallow V-hulls provide reassuring stability. One company to have helped to pioneer the

concept is Chaparral Boats, based in Nashville, Georgia, which has gone on to develop its range into something of an art form. It has totally open boats, others with protective walk-through windshields, and sports boats with deeper-V hulls. All are fitted out to a very high standard with fully adjustable bucket seats, sunbeds, dinette arrangements, surround-sound music systems, plenty of locker storage space, two-tier activity stern platforms and foldaway boarding ladders fore and aft. The other item they all have in common is a choice of Volvo or Mercury inboard/outdrive power units.
The SSi sports boat models are also available with enclosed foredecks, which start with a V-berth cuddy on the 22-ft model and develop into more elaborate interiors higher up the range, with a galley and microwave oven and comfortable dinette arrangement in the 29-ft variant.

The Chaparral line then leads to the Signature power cruiser range from 26 to

OPPOSITE
The Chaparral range of boats.

ABOVE
Chaparral 240 Signature cruiser, showing bathing platform.

37ft, offering full standing headroom, en suite head and shower, a galley with fridge and microwave and four berths in the 26-ft 240 model. The 270, 290, 330 and top-of-the range 350 models have accommodation for six, split between an airy forward cabin and a second double cabin aft, which becomes increasingly luxurious higher up the range with air conditioning, TV/DVD and coffee maker.

The cockpits are generously equipped with entertainment centres, sunbeds which convert into large U-shaped dinettes, walk-through transoms down to the large swim platforms and generous storage lockers under seats and built into the transoms.

CHAPARRAL 180 SSI SPORTS BOAT
DIMENSIONS

Length overall:	18ft 03in/5.56m
Beam:	7ft 02in/2.18m
Deadrise:	20°
Displacement:	2,100lb/953kg
Engine Options:	225-hp inboard/outdrive

CHAPARRAL 190 SSI SPORTS BOAT
DIMENSIONS

Length overall:	19ft 08in/5.99m
Beam:	7ft 09in/2.36m
Deadrise:	18°
Displacement:	2,900lb/1315kg
Engine Options:	225-hp inboard/outdrive

CHAPARRAL 204 SSI SPORTS BOAT
DIMENSIONS

Length overall:	21ft 03in/6.48m
Beam:	8ft 04in/2.54m
Deadrise:	20°
Displacement:	3,400lb/1542kg
Engine Options:	320-hp inboard/outdrive

OPPOSITE
Chaparral 260 Signature power cruiser.

ABOVE LEFT
The Chaparral 260's forward cabin with convertible V-berth.

LEFT
Chaparral 270 Signature power cruiser.

CHAPARRAL 210/215 SSI SPORTS BOAT

DIMENSIONS

Length overall:	22ft 00in/6.70m
Beam:	8ft 02in/2.49m
Deadrise:	20°
Displacement:	3,200/3,495lb
	(1451/1585kg)
Engine Options:	300-hp
	inboard/outdrive

CHAPARRAL 212 SUNESTA DECK BOAT

DIMENSIONS

Length overall:	22ft 08in/6.90m
Beam:	8ft 04in/2.54m
Deadrise:	16°
Displacement:	3,152lb/1430kg
Engine Options:	300-hp
	inboard/outdrive

OPPOSITE
Chaparral 290 Signature cruiser.

LEFT
Main cabin of the Chaparral 290, with galley and dinette.

CHAPARRAL 220 SSI SPORTS BOAT

DIMENSIONS

Length overall:	23ft 09in/7.24m
Beam:	8ft 06in/2.59m
Deadrise:	20°
Displacement:	3,650lb/1656kg
Engine Options:	320-hp inboard/outdrive

CHAPARRAL 230/235 SSI SPORTS BOAT

DIMENSIONS

Length overall:	24ft 11in/7.59m
Beam:	8ft 06in/2.59m
Deadrise:	22°
Displacement:	4,185/4,510lb (1898/2046kg)
Engine Options:	375-hp inboard/outdrive

CHAPARRAL 232/243/236 SUNESTA DECK BOAT

DIMENSIONS

Length overall:	24ft 03in/7.39m
Beam:	8ft 06in/2.59m
Deadrise:	16°
Displacement:	4,065/4,450lb (1844/2018kg)
Engine Options:	300-hp inboard/outdrive

OPPOSITE
Chaparral 310, showing aft deck and bathing platform.

BELOW
Chaparral 330.

OPPOSITE
Chaparral SSi sports boat.

ABOVE
Chaparral 180 SSi.

CHAPARRAL 240
SIGNATURE POWER CRUISER
DIMENSIONS
Length overall:	26ft 01in/7.95m
Beam:	8ft 06in/2.59m
Draft:	1ft 05in/0.43m
Deadrise:	18°
Displacement:	5,377lb/2439kg
Engine Options:	375-hp
	inboard/outdrive

CHAPARRAL 252/254/ SUNESTA
DECK BOAT
DIMENSIONS
Length overall:	26ft 05in/8.08m
Beam:	8ft 06in/2,59m
Draft:	1ft 05in/0.43m
Deadrise:	17°
Displacement:	4,630/4,350lb
	(2100/1973kg)
Engine Options:	375-hp
	inboard/outdrive

CHAPARRAL 256 SSi SPORTS BOAT
DIMENSIONS
Length overall:	26ft 05in/8.08m
Beam:	8ft 06in/2.59m
Deadrise:	22.5°
Displacement:	4,950lb/2245kg
Engine Options:	375-hp
	inboard/outdrive

CHAPARRAL 260 SIGNATURE POWER CRUISER

DIMENSIONS

Length overall:	27ft 07in/8.41m
Beam:	8ft 06in/2.59m
Draft:	1ft 05in/0.43m
Deadrise:	18°
Displacement:	5,977lb/2711kg
Engine Options:	375-hp inboard/outdrive

CHAPARRAL 260/265 SSi SPORTS BOAT

DIMENSIONS

Length overall:	27ft 09in/8.46m
Beam:	8ft 06in/2.59m
Deadrise:	22°
Displacement:	5,200lb/2359kg
Engine Options:	425-hp inboard/outdrive

CHAPARRAL 270 SIGNATURE POWER CRUISER

DIMENSIONS

Length overall:	29ft 03in/8.91m
Beam:	9ft 06in/2.89m
Draft:	1ft 05in/0.43m
Deadrise:	20°
Displacement:	5,977lb/2711kg
Engine Options:	375-hp inboard/outdrive

BELOW
Chaparral 210 SSi.

OPPOSITE
Chaparral 215 SSi.

OPPOSITE
Chaparral Sunesta deck boats.

ABOVE
Chaparral 212.

CHAPARRAL 274 SUNESTA DECK BOAT

DIMENSIONS

Length overall:	28ft 03in/8.61m
Beam:	8ft 06in/2.59m
Deadrise:	18°
Displacement:	4,600lb/2087kg
Engine Options:	375-hp inboard/outdrive

CHAPARRAL 290 SIGNATURE POWER CRUISER

DIMENSIONS

Length overall:	30ft 08in/9.35
Beam:	10ft 00in/3.05m

Draft: 1ft 05in/0.43m
Deadrise: 18°
Displacement: 8,500lb/3856kg
Engine Options: Twin 270-hp
inboard/outdrive

CHAPARRAL 310 SIGNATURE POWER CRUISER

DIMENSIONS

Length overall: 33ft 04in/10.16m
Beam: 10ft 07in/3.23m
Draft: 2ft 01in/0.63m
Deadrise: 17°
Displacement: 11,375lb/5160kg
Engine Options: Twin 320-hp
inboard/outdrives

CHAPARRAL 330 SIGNATURE POWER CRUISER

DIMENSIONS

Length overall: 35ft 04in/10.77m
Beam: 11ft 03in/3.43m
Draft: 2ft 01in/0.63m
Deadrise: 19°
Displacement: 13,400lb/6078kg
Engine Options: Twin 375-hp
inboard/outdrives

CHAPARRAL 350 SIGNATURE POWER CRUISER

DIMENSIONS

Length overall: 37ft 00in/11.28m
Beam: 11ft 03in/3.43m
Draft: 2ft 01in/0.63m
Deadrise: 18°
Displacement: 15,000lb/6804kg

Engine Options: Twin 375-hp
inboard/outdrives or
V-drives

www.chaparralboats.com

LEFT
Glastron DX 200 deck boat.

BELOW
DX 200 fishing-rod holders.

OPPOSITE
DX 200 helm.

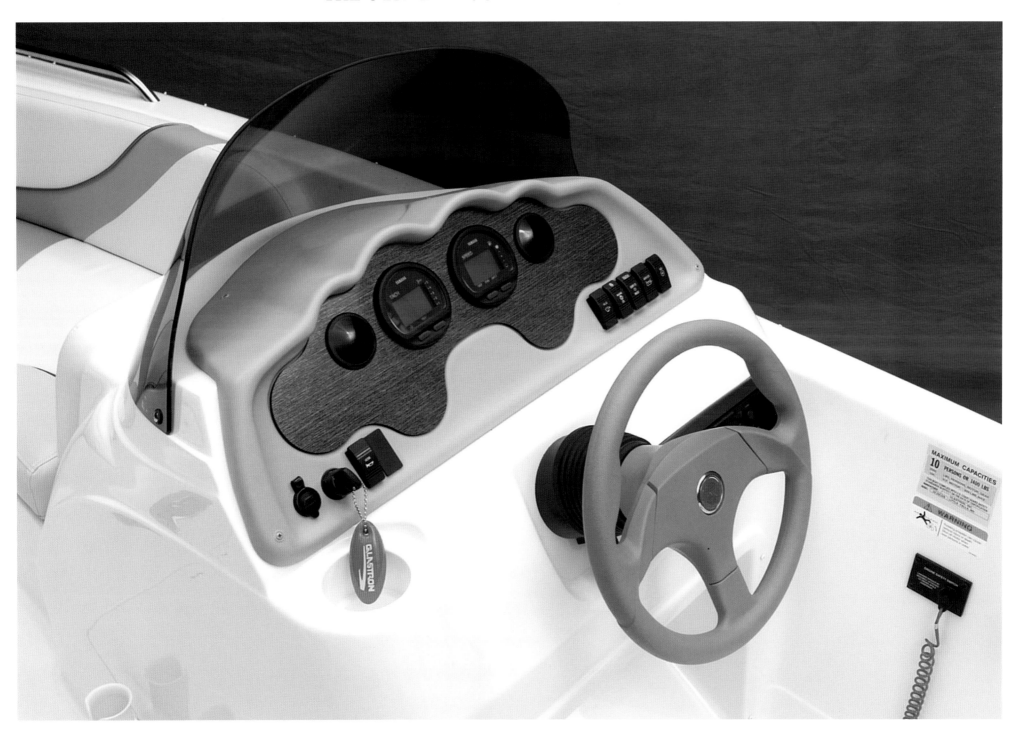

GLASTRON

Glastron is another company to have made something of a speciality out of building trailable bowrider and deck sports boats. Owned by the Genmar Group, its plant, based at Little Falls, Minnesota, is one of the largest boat-production facilities in the world, utilizing an advanced glassfibre vacuum moulding process called VEC to ensure a uniform laminate and a smooth finish on both sides. Genmar has invested heavily in this automated computerized process and is so confident in the quality of the end product that it provides a lifetime warranty on the hull and deck mouldings. Computers also control the cutting of the laminate cloth and upholstery, and robotics are used to cut and trim every edge and opening, from the dash panel to the transom cut-out for the stern drive.

With such an investment, in tooling and technology, it is understandable that Glastron offers more than one model based on each hull mould, ranging between 17- and 21-ft boats.

The GX (general sports runabout) and SX (ski and fish) models all have walk-through windshields, bow seating, swivel pilot and co-pilot bucket seats and bench seating at the rear, with a padded sunbed over the engine cover and stereo systems. All the boats are fitted with inboard/outdrives with the exception of the 17-ft 170 and 180 models, which are outboard-powered. The SX variants are supplied with such fishing essentials as an aerated live well, bow mount and connections for an electronic trolling motor,

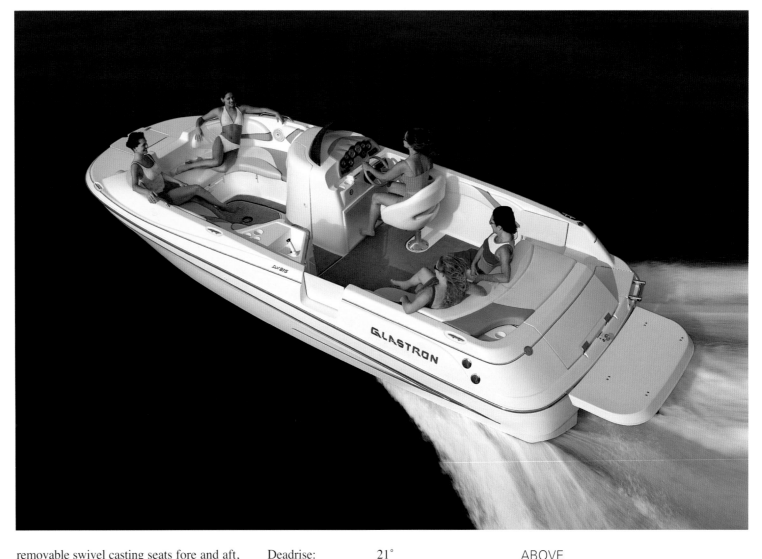

removable swivel casting seats fore and aft, and lockers for rods and skis.

GLASTRON SX 175 /SX 170 SKI & FISH SPORTS BOAT

DIMENSIONS

Length overall:	17ft 01in/5.21m
Beam:	7ft 04in/2.23m
Draft:	2ft 07in/0.79m
Deadrise:	21°
Displacement:	2,050lb/930kg
Engine Options:	3.0 GL Volvo Penta inboard/outdrive 48mph/77km/h SX 170–150-hp outboard
Design:	Glastron/Genmar

ABOVE
Glastron DX 215.

OPPOSITE
Glastron DX 235 and details.

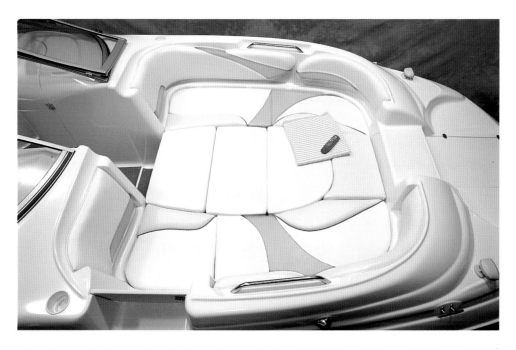

GLASTRON GX 180 BOWRIDER/SKI & FISH SPORTS BOAT

DIMENSIONS

Length overall:	17ft 10in/5.44m
Beam:	7ft 06in/2.29m
Draft:	2ft 07in/0.79m
Deadrise:	20°
Displacement:	1,710lb/776kg
Engine Options:	150-hp outboard 48mph/77km/h
Design:	Glastron/Genmar

GLASTRON GX 185 BOWRIDER/SKI & FISH SPORTS BOAT

DIMENSIONS

Length overall:	18ft 00in/5.49m
Beam:	7ft 06in/2.29m
Draft:	2ft 07in/0.79m
Deadrise:	20°
Displacement:	2,575lb/1168kg
Engine Options:	4.3L GL Volvo Penta inboard/outdrive 48mph/77km/h
Design:	Glastron/Genmar

GLASTRON SX 185/SX 195 SKI & FISH SPORTS BOAT

DIMENSIONS

Length overall:	18ft 07in/5.66m
Beam:	7ft 06in/2.29m
Draft:	2ft 07in/0,79m
Deadrise:	21°
Displacement:	2,450lb/1111kg
Engine Options:	4.3L GL Volvo Penta inboard/outdrive 48mph/77km/h
Design:	Glastron/Genmar

GLASTRON GX 205 BOWRIDER/SKI & FISH SPORTS BOAT

DIMENSIONS

Length overall:	19ft 11in/6.07m
Beam:	8ft 00in/2.44m
Draft:	2ft 10in/0.86m
Deadrise:	20°
Displacement:	2,875lb/1304kg
Engine Options:	5.0 GL Volvo Penta
inboard/outdrive	48mph/77km/h
Design:	Glastron/Genmar

Glastron GX 235 BOWRIDER SPORTS BOAT

DIMENSIONS

Length overall:	23ft 00in/7.01m
Beam:	8ft 06in/2.59m
Draft:	2ft 09in/0.84m
Deadrise:	21°
Displacement:	3,833lb/1739kg
Engine Options:	5.7L Mercury Mercruiser inboard/outdrive 48mph/77km/h
Design:	Glastron/Genmar

Glastron GX 255 BOWRIDER SPORTS BOAT

Dimensions

Length overall:	25ft 00in/7.62m
Beam:	8ft 06in/2.59m
Draft:	2ft 10in/0.86m
Deadrise:	21°
Displacement:	4,600lb/2087kg
Engine Options:	350 MAC MPI Mercury Mercruiser inboard/outdrive 48mph/77km/h
Design:	Glastron/Genmar

LEFT
Glastron GS 249 cuddy sports boat.

ABOVE
GS 249 aft cabin.

Glastron was also one of the first companies to develop the deck boat as a general-purpose family pleasure vessel. Ranging in size from 20 to 22ft 6in, these lake boats can seat a crowd, act as a giant sunbed, provide a picnic base, and with the addition of a canvas cover can be turned easily into a weekender. These lake boats have a large swim platform, toilet compartment and plenty of storage areas and can be used for just about any purpose, from fishing to water-skiing, exploring distant islands and inlets or taking the family out on a picnic.

GLASTRON DX 205/DX 200 DECK SPORTS BOAT

DIMENSIONS

Length overall:	20ft 01in/6.12m
Beam:	8ft 06in/2.59m
Draft:	2ft 04in/0.71m
Deadrise:	17°
Displacement:	2,933/1,664lb
	1330/755kg
Engine Options:	5.7 GL Volvo Penta
	inboard/outdrive
	DX 200– 150-hp
	outboard
	48mph/77km/h
Design:	Glastron/Genmar

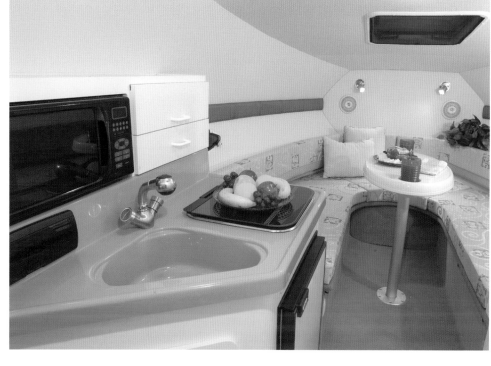

Glastron DX 210 DECK SPORTS BOAT

Dimensions

Length overall:	20ft 11in/6.37m
Beam:	8ft 06in/2.59m
Draft:	2ft 04in/0.71m
Deadrise:	17°
Displacement:	3,500/2,499lb
	1588/1133kg
Engine Options:	5.7 GL Volvo Penta
	inboard/outdrive
	DX 210 – 175-hp
	outboard
	48mph77km/h
Design:	Glastron/Genmar

GLASTRON DX 235 DECK SPORTS BOAT

DIMENSIONS

Length overall:	22ft 06in/6.86m
Beam:	8ft 06in/2.59m
Draft:	2ft 08in/0.81m
Deadrise:	15°
Displacement:	4,000lb/1814kg
Engine Options:	5.7 GL Volvo Penta
	inboard/outdrive
Design:	Glastron/Genmar

ABOVE
GS279 galley.

LEFT
GS279.

Glastron also produces two trailable sports cruisers, which pack an extraordinary amount into their 25- and 27-ft lengths. Features include a main cabin with a dinette that converts into a double berth, a galley and separate toilet compartment, together with a second double berth cabin that make an ideal bolt-hole for children.

The cockpits are arranged with L-shaped seating that folds down to make a sunbed, while a swim platform is accessed via a transom gate, shower facility and a ski tow point. Both boats are equipped with satellite stereo and surround-sound speaker systems. **www.glastron.com**

GLASTRON GS 249 CUDDY SPORTS BOAT

DIMENSIONS

Length overall:	24ft 10in/7.57m
Beam:	8ft 06in/2.59m
Draft:	2ft 08in/0.81m
Deadrise:	20°
Displacement:	4,437lb/2013kg
Engine Options:	5.7 GL Volvo Penta inboard/outdrive
Design:	Glastron/Genmar

Glastron GS 279 CUDDY SPORTS BOAT

DIMENSIONS

Length overall:	27ft 05in/8.38m
Beam:	8ft 06in/2.59m
Draft:	3ft 04in/1.02m
Deadrise:	20°
Displacement:	6,200lb/2812kg
Engine Options:	5.7 GL Volvo Penta inboard/outdrive
Design:	Glastron/Genmar

OPPOSITE
Glastron GX 180.

ABOVE
Glastron GX 180 ski and fish.

FAR RIGHT, ABOVE and BELOW
Two views of an SX 195 ski and fish.

RIGHT
Helm.

GLACIER BAY CATAMARANS

Talk to Australian fishing buffs about running out into the Pacific and Indian Ocean swells and they will tell you all about the benefits that catamarans have over monohulls. The Aussies are mad about their all-weather sports fishing catamarans, but it has taken a lot longer for the twin-hull concept to catch on in America, where there is still only a handful of builders and fewer dealers in each state. It is not surprising, therefore, that powered cats are few and far between.

Four U.S. manufacturers which do specialize in cats are Glacier Bay, Pro Sports, SeaCat and Twin Vee, and between them all they have done some extraordinary things to prove the twin-hull concept and catch our attention. One man in particular is Larry Graff, the president of Glacier Bay Catamarans, based in Monroe, Washington State. He and his colleagues, running two 26-ft trailable Glacier Bay cats on a 1,500-mile (2400-km) 10-day coastal trip from Seattle up to Glacier Bay, Alaska, set a non-stop record in an open version of the same boat across 728 miles (1171km) of the Atlantic from Virginia to Bermuda in 36$\frac{1}{2}$ hours and, taken on the Pacific in a similar manner, crossed the 1,328 miles (2137km) from Oahu, Hawaii to Midway Island in eight days. More recently, Graff took the first 36-ft Glacier Bay Ocean Runner sports fisher on a 55-day 8,000-mile (12874-km) round America promotional tour, down the west coast from Seattle to San Carlos before overlanding to Galveston, Texas and running up the east coast as far as

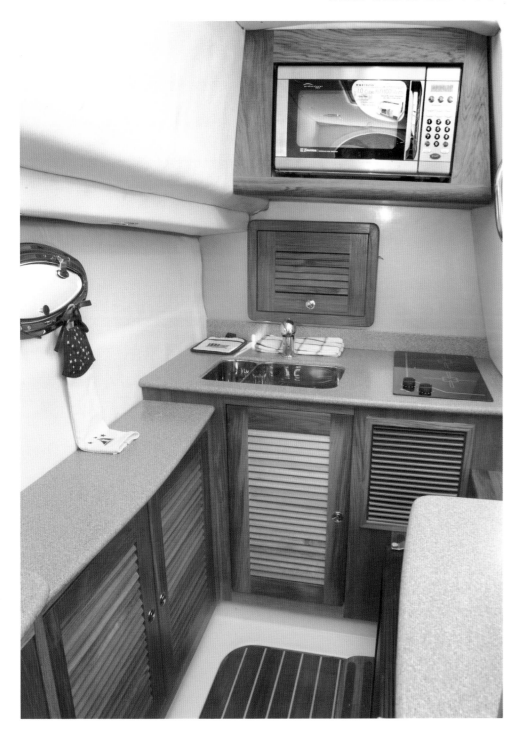

Portland, Maine. Making 22 stops en route to meet dealers and potential owners, and never running more than 20 minutes late, Graff returned to Seattle with 19 orders for similar boats.

Catamarans offer several advantages over deep-V monohulls of similar length. Not only do they give a much smoother ride in heavy seas, where they are much more stable, but also consume 25 per cent less fuel – more when trolling at low speeds. Being rectangular in shape they also have 40 per cent more deck space and have better separation of living quarters, which can be divided between a central saloon and separate cabins in each hull. The downside is that they are more expensive than an equivalent-sized monohull, since they are more expensive to tool up and require 50 per cent more materials and resin. Neither can they match the top speed of most monohull sport fishers. That said, the deck and interior volume offered by a cat can only be matched by a monohull that is at least 20 per cent longer, when price comparisons become more equal and the fuel economy advantage of a catamaran increases dramatically.

OPPOSITE
Glacier Bay Ocean Runner 3470 catamaran.

ABOVE
Helm of a Glacier Bay 3470.

LEFT
The galley.

cuddy has a double bed and a toilet fitting into the port hull. This leaves a wide aft deck for fishing, fitted with large lockers for fish and storing gear.

GLACIER BAY 2240SX RENEGADE/2260 CANYON RUNNER/2270 ISLE RUNNER SPORTS FISHING BOAT

DIMENSIONS

Length overall:	22ft 00in/6.70m
Beam:	8ft 05in/2.56m
Draft:	16in/41cm
Displacement:	3,400lb/1542kg
	3,200/3,500lb
	(1451/1588kg)
Tow Weight:	6,000lb/2722kg
Engine Options:	Twin 115-hp
	outboards
	40mph/64km/h
Design:	Larry Graff

GLACIER BAY 26

Like the 22, Glacier Bay produces several versions of its 26-ft model. These include the 260 Canyon Runner centre console model with a built-in head, the 2640 Renegade bowrider sports boat, the 2670 cuddy Isle Runner and 2680 and 2690 versions of the Coastal Runner with an enclosed bridge deck and steering position.

GLACIER BAY 22

Glacier Bay produces three versions of the 22-ft trailable sports catamaran. Powered by twin outboards up to 115hp each, the 2240 Renegade is a bowrider with a walk-through wraparound screen and enclosed head, and is fitted with a 30-gal (136-litre) live well, two large fish lockers and an ice box. Optional equipment includes a bimini hood and sunbeds. The 2260 Canyon Runner is a centre console sports fishing boat with an enclosed head and enormous stowage boxes for fish bait and tackle. The 2270 Isle Runner is a cuddy sports boat tailored for extended fishing trips. The

LEFT and OPPOSITE
Glacier Bay Ocean Runner 3470 catamaran.

GLACIER BAY 260 CANYON RUNNER/2640 RENEGADE/2670 ISLE RUNNER/2680/2690 COASTAL RUNNER SPORTS FISHING BOAT

DIMENSIONS

Length overall:	26ft 00in/7.92m
Beam:	8ft 06in/2.59m
Draft:	16in/41cm
Displacement:	4,600/4,800/ 5,250/5,200lb (2086/2177/2381/ 2359kg)
Tow Weight:	8,200/8,800lb (3719/3992kg)
Engine Options:	Twin 150-hp outboards 41mph/66km/h
Design:	Larry Graff

The latest 36-ft Glacier Bay catamaran is a true ocean-goer with enormous potential for game fishing and diving. Owners have the option of outboard or inboard/outdrive power that gives the boat a cruising speed of 23mph and a top speed of 30mph. The accommodation is enormous, with a large bridge deck saloon and sleeping cabins in each hull. The cockpit is just as impressive, with plenty of room for a large fishing party and good stowage space for bait, fish and gear.

GLACIER BAY 3470 OCEAN RUNNER SPORTS FISHING BOAT

DIMENSIONS

Length overall:	36ft 06in/11.12m
Beam:	13ft 03in/4.04m
Draft:	2ft 06in/0.76m
Displacement:	15,400lb/6985kg
Engine Options:	Twin 300-hp outboards 30mph/48km/h Twin 370-hp inboard/outdrives
	30mph/48km/h
Design:	Larry Graff
www.glacierbaycats.com	

ABOVE
Edgewater 140.

OPPOSITE
Edgewater 175.

The Edgewater range of outboard utility tenders starts with the 145CC models, which offer 19-in deep walkaround cockpits, have seating for four people and a carrying capacity of 1,000lb. The 155 and 175CC centre console models measure 15 and 17ft 6in, and double as good sports fishing boats in sheltered waters, while the 185, which is available as a centre console or deck boat, can carry up to six people, has the same 25-in freeboard, and is fitted with all the storage one would want for bait, fish and tackle.

EDGEWATER 145CC CONSOLE TENDER

DIMENSIONS

Length overall:	14ft 00in/4.27m
Beam:	6ft 04in/1.93m
Draft:	10in/25cm
Displacement:	650lb/295kg
Engine Options:	50-hp outboard

EDGEWATER 155CC CONSOLE TENDER

DIMENSIONS

Length overall:	15ft 01in/4.60m
Beam:	6ft 07in/2.00m
Draft:	10in/25cm
Displacement:	1,200lb/544kg
Engine Options:	90-hp outboard

EDGEWATER 175CC CONSOLE TENDER

DIMENSIONS

Length overall:	17ft 06in/5.33m
Beam:	7ft 03in/2.20m
Draft:	11in/28cm

EDGEWATER

The Edgewater range of boats is the brain child of Bob Dougherty, who spent 30 years with Boston Whaler before starting his own business, where he developed strong ideas as to how to produce better boats. Thus his Edgewater range, which starts with a 14-ft centre console and runs through to a 26-ft Express sports cruiser, carries the same 'unsinkable' tag as Boston Whaler. But that, according to Bob, is only part of the story.

He firmly believes that a boat should keep you out of harm's way, which starts with engineering its construction.

'You can enjoy a day on the water with your family, fish offshore, or cross a harbor bar, but its when a sunny afternoon turns black and threatening, and you have to traverse an open body of water, where it counts. A boat not worthy of such things should never ever pass the breakwater, unsinkable or not. And it should never be left alone with your children.' Wise words when it comes to choosing a boat.

Based at Edgewater, Florida, all the boats produced by Dougherty Marine, which is part of the North Marine Group, are moulded with an internal sub-frame. Hull and decks are tooled to very close tolerances and are sandwiched between a pre-formed foam core to create a much stronger union than simply filling the empty cavity with expanding foam.

Displacement:	1,800lb/816kg
Engine Options:	130-hp outboard

EDGEWATER 185CC CONSOLE/185DC DECK TENDER
DIMENSIONS

Length overall:	18ft 06in/5.64m
Beam:	7ft 04in/2.23m
Draft:	1ft 01in/0.33m
Displacement:	1,950lb/884kg
Engine Options:	150-hp outboard

The 205CC sports fishing and Express cuddy models mark the divide between utility tender and the dedicated offshore fishing boat. The 205CC carries a deep-V deadrise of 20° to provide a better offshore ride and has the option of a portable toilet fitted within the console or forward cuddy on the EX sports boat model.

EDGEWATER 205CC SPORTS FISHING/205EX EXPRESS CUDDY BOAT
DIMENSIONS

Length overall:	20ft 06in/6.25m
Beam:	8ft 06in/2.59
Draft:	1ft 08in/0.51m
Deadrise:	20°
Displacement:	2,200/2,800lb
	(998/1270kg)
Engine Options:	200-hp outboard

The 225 and 245 models are based on the same hull shape. The 225 is available either with a centre console or cuddy cabin for those wanting a more general purpose boat than one dedicated to the sport of

OPPOSITE
205EX Express cuddy boat.

ABOVE
Edgewater 205CC sports fishing boat.

FAR RIGHT
Edgewater 205CC with outboard.

RIGHT
Helm.

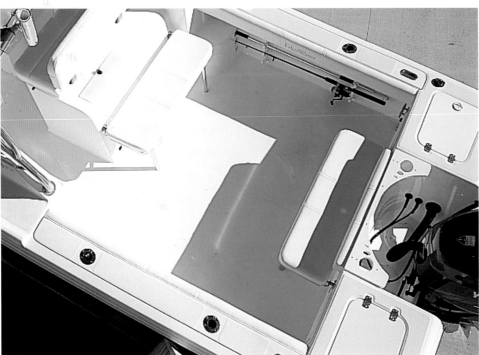

fishing. The 247CC is only an inch longer than the newer 245, but has a shallower V-hull similar in form to that of the 200CC, making her the better option for fishing inshore. Both have a maximum trailable beam of 8ft 6in.

The 245 and larger 26ft 6-in 265 are true blue-water boats, more than capable of running the gauntlet across the Gulf Stream as far as the Bahamas. Indeed, Edgewater organizes a Bahamas rendezvous each year and encourages other Edgewater owners with 21-ft boats and above to join them for the 180-mile (290-km) crossing from West Palm Beach in a series of flotilla fleets controlled by these bigger boats.

The 265, which is available with a centre console or with a four-berth cabin, is

moulded with a carbon sub-frame for additional strength.

ABOVE LEFT
Edgewater 225 Express cuddy tender.

ABOVE
The Edgewater 225 has a large V-berth with accommodation for two.

LEFT
Aft seating and outboard on an Edgewater 225.

OPPOSITE
225 Express.

EDGEWATER 225CC CONSOLE/225 EXP CUDDY TENDER

DIMENSIONS

Length overall:	22ft 06in/6.86m
Beam:	8ft 06in/2.59m
Draft:	1ft 05in/0.43m
Deadrise:	20°
Displacement:	3,000/3,400lb
	(1361/1542kg)
Engine Options:	250-hp outboard

EDGEWATER 245CC SPORTS FISHING BOAT

DIMENSIONS

Length overall:	24ft 06in/7.47m
Beam:	8ft 06in/2.59m
Draft:	1ft 07in/0.48m

OPPOSITE
Edgewater 245 used by the U.S. Harbor Patrol.

LEFT
Helm of the Edgewater 245CC.

BELOW LEFT
Edgewater 245CC.

BELOW
Edgewater 265 centre console.

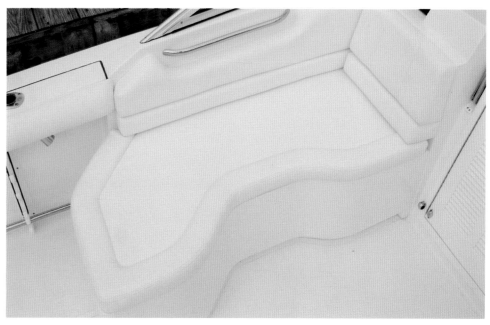

OPPOSITE
Edgewater 265CC sports fishing boat.

THIS PAGE
An Edgewater 265EX, showing cabin and cockpit seating.

Deadrise:	20°
Displacement:	3,400lb/1542kg
Engine Options:	300-hp outboard

EDGEWATER 247CC SPORTS FISHING BOAT

DIMENSIONS

Length overall:	24ft 07in/7.49m
Beam:	8ft 06in/2.59m
Draft:	1ft 05in/0.43m
Displacement:	3,400lb/1542kg
Engine Options:	Twin 200-hp outboards

EDGEWATER 265CC SPORTS FISHING BOAT/265 EXPRESS

DIMENSIONS

Length overall:	26ft 06in/8.08 m
Beam:	9ft 06in/2.89
Draft:	1ft 10in/0.56m
Displacement:	5,000/5,400lb
	(2268/2449kg)
Engine Options:	Twin 250-hp
	outboards

www.ewboats.com

OYSTER BAY BOATS

Oyster Bay, based at Foley, Alabama, builds this round-bilged centre console sports fishing boat for those of us with an eye for the traditional, a love of wood and a desire for something a little special. Her 21-ft fibreglass hull and curved deck combing are reminiscent of motor launches of the 1920s, but a large outboard, teak swim platform, large fish box and live bait well, with storage for rods under the gunwales, makes it an ideal boat for fishing in sheltered waters.

OYSTER BAY 21 CENTRE CONSOLE FISHING BOAT

DIMENSIONS

Length overall:	21ft 06in/6.55
Beam:	7ft 00in/2.13m
Draft:	1ft 02in/0.35m
Displacement:	2,450lb/1111kg
Engine Options:	Max outboard
	175hp 45mph/72km/h
Design:	Oyster Bay Boats

ABOVE
The helm of the Oyster Bay 21.

ABOVE LEFT
Oyster Bay 21, showing layout.

LEFT
Oyster Bay 21.

OPPOSITE
Running shot of an Oyster Bay 21.

PRO-LINE BOATS

Pro-Line, based at Crystal River, Florida, has been building fishing boats since 1968. Its range now extends across 24 models, from 19-ft inshore bay boats, centre- and dual-console fishing boats and overnight sports cruisers, right up to the tuna-towered 33-ft Express.

These fishing boats are all moulded using the Fibreglass Integrated Structural Technology process (FIST), which ensures a strong, wood-free, rot-free structural stringer system that is integral within the construction. Their build meets NMMA, U.S. Coastguard and European CE requirements and each boat carries a ten-year transferable hull warranty

Though designed principally for fishing, Pro-Line builds a host of non-fishing amenities into these models so that they can be used not only to catch the big fish, but also for a variety of other family and water-related sports. The company was one of the first to incorporate an enclosed toilet in its centre console models and this

facility is now present in its 19-footer – the smallest boat in the line-up.

PRO-LINE BAY BOAT SERIES

Launched in 2003, the three-line Bay Boat Series comprises the same basic hull form,

ABOVE
Pro-Line 33 Express.

ABOVE RIGHT
Helm of the Pro-Line 27 Express.

RIGHT
Pro-Line 30 Express.

LEFT
Forward cabin of the Pro-Line 30.

LEFT
Proline 18 sports utility, with outboard
and rod-holders.

FAR LEFT
Proline 18 flats.

BELOW LEFT
Proline 20 dual console.

BELOW
Proline 20 rod-holder and cockpit seat.

Deadrise:	13°
Displacement:	2,059lb/934kg
Tow weight:	2,437lb/1105kg
Max outboard:	200hp
Design:	Pro-Line

simply moulded in 20-, 22- and 24-ft lengths. These boats have an 8ft 6-in beam, 11-in draft and 13° deadrise to enable them to navigate more remote waters and be beached, while their moderate V-hulls retain good stability and have the ability to cope with 2–3-ft blue-water chop when used in exposed conditions.

Outboard-powered, these open boats come complete with ample storage and angling space, including a casting deck, purpose-built holders for rods and tackle, and a large bait well with a raw-water wash-down facility.

PRO-LINE 20 BAY BOAT
DIMENSIONS

Length overall:	20ft 05in/6.22m
Beam:	8ft 06in/2.59m
Draft:	11in/28cm

PRO-LINE 22 BAY BOAT
Dimensions

Length overall:	21ft 11in/6.68m
Beam:	8ft 06in/2.59m
Draft:	11in/28cm
Deadrise:	13°
Displacement:	2,284lb/1036kg
Tow weight:	3,248lb/1473kg
Max outboard:	225hp
Design:	Pro-Line

PRO-LINE 24 BAY BOAT
DIMENSIONS

Length overall:	23ft 11in/7.29m
Beam:	8ft 06in/2.59m
Draft:	11in/28cm
Deadrise::	13°
Displacement:	2,515lb/1141kg
Tow weight:	3,887lb/1763kg
Max outboard:	225hp
Design:	Pro-Line

PRO-LINE SPORT & DUAL CONSOLE SERIES

These deep-V boats are designed and built specifically with fishing in mind. Starting with the stern cockpit, plenty of thought has gone into giving ample space for fighting the big ones. Insulated bait boxes are close to hand, there are rod-holders everywhere, and the large fish boxes are foam-insulated and drain overboard. There is also plenty of storage space and the generous beam allows for easy access to the bow casting area, giving anglers plenty of room to spread out. The two dual console boats within the range, which share the same hulls as their sport

namesakes, have central access through an opening screen to the bow area.

The 19° deadrise (22° with the 23 models) gives them the deep V-shaped hull configuration that will cut through rough water, and their reverse chines are designed to throw the water and spray aside to provide a reasonably dry ride.

PRO-LINE 19 SPORTS FISHING BOAT

This is one of the most compact console sports fishing boats on the market and one of the few in this size range with an enclosed head. The boat also boasts rod racks and holders, a console tackle box and transom bait well. And for the non-

fishermen in the family, there is an integrated swim platform with fold-down ladder for diving, snorkelling and just plain swimming.

PRO-LINE 19 SPORTS FISHING BOAT
DIMENSIONS

Length overall:	19ft 02in/5.84m
Beam:	7ft 09in/2.36m
Draft:	1ft 00in/0.30m
Deadrise:	19°
Displacement:	2,000lb/907kg
Tow weight:	3,150lb/1429kg
Max outboard:	150hp
Design:	Pro-Line

PRO-LINE 20 & 22 SPORTS, DUAL CONSOLE AND WALK FISHING BOATS

These six boats share the same 8ft 3-in wide deep-V hull design, truncated at their appropriate length. The DC models have the versatility of runabouts and fishing boats with their opening windshields providing a walk-through to the forward casting deck. The port and starboard consoles contain large storage areas, and behind the captain's chair are insulated fish boxes and under-gunwale rod racks.

The centre console models carry enclosed heads and dedicated fishing amenities, including a raised casting platform forward, roomy aft cockpit and 25-gallon (114-litre) bait wells. The walk versions have a day cabin with fitted bunks, raised foredeck and deep freeboard.

PRO-LINE 20 SPORT/DUAL CONSOLE/WALK FISHING BOATS
DIMENSIONS

Length overall:	20ft 06in/6.25m
Beam:	8ft 02in/2.49m
Draft:	1ft 03in/0.38m
Deadrise:	19°
Displacement:	2,059/2,200/2,100lb (934/998/953kg)
Tow weight:	3,700/4,000/4,500lb (1678/1814/2041kg)
Max outboard:	200hp
Design:	Pro-Line

	(1225/1383/1361kg)
Tow weight:	4,500/4,179/4,900lb
	(2041/1896/2223kg)
Max outboard:	200hp
Design:	Pro-Line

PRO-LINE 22 SPORT/DUAL CONSOLE/ WALK FISHING BOATS

DIMENSIONS

Length overall:	22ft 05in/6.83m
Beam:	8ft 02in/2.49m
Draft:	1ft 03in/0.38m
Deadrise:	19°
Displacement:	2,700/3,050/3,000lb

PRO-LINE 23 SPORT AND WALK FISHING-BOAT SERIES

The hull has a deeper V than her Pro-Line sister vessels, making the 23 sport and walk models all the more suited to running in rough water conditions. With a dry tow weight of 6,500lb, these are one of the largest with the facility to be launched and recovered using a standard family car, without the need to upgrade to a four-wheel-drive or UT. The 23 Sport is dedicated to fishing, with ample stowage

OPPOSITE
Pro-Line 34 super sports.

ABOVE
Pro-Line 26 walk.

RIGHT
Pro-Line 26 walk casting deck seating.

ABOVE RIGHT
Pro-Line 30 walk central console.

FAR RIGHT
Pro-Line 30 walk – forward cabin.

for rods and tackle, a large bait well, a console cooler and insulated fish boxes. The 23 walk has the added benefit of an overnight cabin and a galley in which to cook the catch!

PRO-LINE 23 SPORT/WALK FISHING BOATS

DIMENSIONS

Length overall:	24ft 05in/7.44m
Beam:	8ft 06in/2.59m
Draft:	1ft 06in/0.46m
Deadrise:	22°
Displacement:	3,700lb/1678kg
Tow weight:	5,850/6,500lb
	(2654/2948kg)
Max outboard:	300hp
Design:	Pro-Line

PRO-LINE 25 SPORT/WALK FISHING BOATS

DIMENSIONS

Length overall:	25ft 08in/7.82m
Beam:	8ft 06in/2.59m
Draft:	1ft 02in/0.36m
Deadrise:	19°
Displacement:	3,600/4,100lb
	(1633/1860kg)
Tow weight:	5,750/7,000lb
	(2608/3175kg)
Max outboard:	300hp
Design:	Pro-Line

The 26 sport and walk models are the entry level to deep blue-water fishing in the Gulf Stream and beyond. Their twin outboards provide that extra confidence of always getting home on time, and with good-sized cockpits with a transom door to help land the fish, two 50-gal (227-litre) fish boxes and plenty of stowage space, they have all the amenities to sustain a full day's fishing. The walk model has the addition of an overnight cabin with galley and stand-up shower. The difference between their names and the actual sizes of the boats relates to the short walk-on bowsprit – a Pro-Line trademark – which holds the anchor away from the hull and allows you to see exactly where you are dropping the pick.

PRO-LINE 26 SPORT/WALK FISHING BOATS

DIMENSIONS

Length overall:	27ft 00in/8.23m
Beam:	8ft 06in/2.59m
Draft:	1ft 04in/1ft 05in
	(0.41/0.43m)
Deadrise:	19°
Displacement:	4,500/4,250lb
	(2041/1928kg)
Tow weight:	7,500/7,250lb
	(3402/3289kg)
Max outboard:	400hp
Design:	Pro-Line

The 27 sport, walk and top-level Express models boast 80-sq ft (7.4m²) of fighting cockpits, bowsprit and extended transom to carry the outboards that add 2ft (0.60m) to the hull length and full facilities for week-end fishing,

PRO-LINE 27 SPORT/WALK/EXPRESS FISHING BOATS

DIMENSIONS

Length overall:	29ft 01in/8.86m
Beam:	9ft 10in/3.00m
Draft:	1ft 06in/1ft 09in
	0.46/0.53m)
Deadrise:	19°
Displacement:	5,200/5,900lb
	(2359/2676kg)
Tow weight:	8,550/9,500lb
	(3878/4309kg)
Max outboard:	500hp
Design:	Pro-Line

The 30-ft sport, the top-level central-console boat in the Pro-Line range, shares the same hull as the 30 walk and Express to give a choice of day or overnight fishing with various levels of equipment. The 33 walk is Pro-Line's top-level, single-deck outboard-powered sports fishing boat. The 33 Express is a different boat altogether, with a further 1ft 6in of beam, deeper draft and greater displacement to carry a tuna tower. It can carry an inboard up to 840hp.

PRO-LINE 30 SPORT/WALK/EXPRESS FISHING BOATS

DIMENSIONS

Length overall:	32ft 06in/9.91m
Beam:	10ft 10in/3.30m
Draft:	1ft 10in/0.56m
Deadrise:	19°
Displacement:	6,300/7,550lb
	(2858/3425kg)
Tow weight:	11,000/11,700/
	14,000lb (4990/

	5307/6350kg)
Max outboard:	500hp
Design:	Pro-Line

PRO-LINE 33 WALK FISHING BOAT

DIMENSIONS

Length overall:	33ft 08in/10.26m
Beam:	11ft 00in/3.35m
Draft:	2ft 01in/0.63m
Deadrise:	19°
Displacement:	10,350lb/4695kg
Tow weight:	14,350lb/6509kg
Max outboard:	500hp
Design:	Pro-Line

PRO-LINE 33 EXPRESS TOWER FISHING BOAT

DIMENSIONS

Length overall:	33ft 00in/10.06m
Beam:	12ft 06in/3.81m
Draft:	3ft 05in/1.04m
Deadrise:	19°
Displacement:	14,500lb/6577kg
Tow weight:	18,000lb/8165kg
Max inboard:	840hp
Design:	Pro-Line

www.prolineboats.com

PURSUIT SPORTS FISHING BOATS

The heritage of S2 Yachts, builders of the Pursuit, Slickcraft and Tiara range, goes back to the mid-1940s when Leon Slikkers was cutting his teeth as a joiner, making cabin tops at Chris*Craft. He had a dream to become a boat-builder in his own right and during the 1950s began to build a line of 14-ft runabouts in his garage after work. He registered the name Slickcraft in 1954

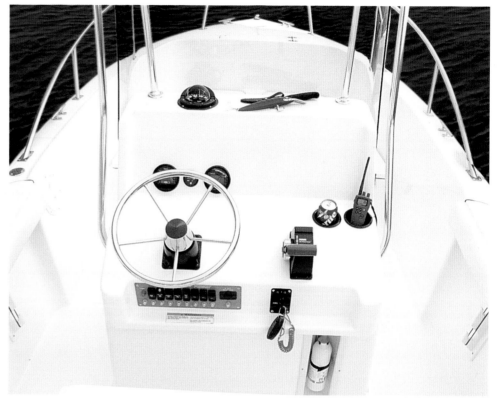

and a year later left Chris*Craft and sold his home to start building boats full-time in a small factory unit in Holland, Michigan. A year later he was experimenting with fibreglass and by 1961 his wooden models were replaced with moulded versions.

1964 saw the launch of the SS235, a forerunner to the deep-V trailable cabin sports fishing boats which became Slickcraft's most successful line. This success attracted the interest of the AMF Corporation, which bought out the company while leaving Leon Slikkers as president. He stayed in charge until 1973, when the urge to have his own business once more proved too great. A year later, he formed S2

Yachts in Holland, Michigan, and in 1977 the Pursuit line was launched. The first of the Tiara range followed two years later.

AMF produced the last Slickcraft in 1980 and Leon Slikkers bought back the brand name three years later and set up a second plant in Ft. Pierce, Florida. He also

ABOVE
Console of the Pursuit 2270 centre console sports fishing boat.

LEFT and PAGES 152 and 153
Pursuit 2270 centre console.

brought in his son, David, as president. The company has remained a family concern ever since, with younger sons Tom and Bob taking the corporate reins up later on.

The 19-strong Pursuit model range of sports fishing boats starts with the 22-ft go-anywhere centre console craft and ends with a 40-ft luxury tuna-towered fast offshore boat. All carry a five-year structural guarantee.

The Pursuit centre console models come in 22-, 26-, 28-, 30-, 33- and 34ft 6-in overall lengths. These deep-V hulls have a deadrise of between 20° and 24.4° and are finished to a high level with built-in fish boxes, rod racks and tackle storage. The 2270 is fitted with a single outboard, but the larger models can accommodate twin units. The 2470 and larger models also have a head and washing facilities built into the console. The 2670 has a forward cuddy with a V-berth to provide a rest area and secure waterproof storage for tackle and other marine gear. The 2670, 2870 and 3070 models also have a short bowsprit, which doubles as an anchor holder. The 30-ft 2870, 33-ft 3070 and the latest 34ft 6-in 3270 are all designed for serious offshore fishing or island-hopping and provide huge fore and aft cockpits. The two largest models are also big enough to carry tuna towers, which are available as optional extras.

The Pursuit walkaround and Denali models share some of the console hull designs but offer the addition of accommodation in their forward compartments for weekend fishing and family use. The 2460, 2665, and 2865

Denali boats are all powered by inboard/outdrives.

The outboard-powered 3070 and 35-ft 3370, and the inboard-powered 31-ft 3000, 34ft 6-in 3100, 36-ft 3400, 38ft 6-in 3500 and 41-ft 3800 offshore range all offer a high level of finish and equipment, together with luxury accommodation with V and pilot berths, galley, heads and dinette.

PURSUIT 2270 CENTRE CONSOLE SPORTS FISHING BOAT
DIMENSIONS

Length overall:	21ft 08in/6.60m
Beam:	8ft 00in/2.44m
Draft:	1ft 02in/0.36m
Deadrise:	20°
Displacement:	3,000lb/1361kg
Max Outboard:	225hp 47mph/76km/h
Design:	Pursuit

PURSUIT 2460 DENALI SPORTS UTILITY BOAT
DIMENSIONS

Length overall:	24ft 09in/7.54m
Beam:	8ft 06in/2.59m
Draft:	1ft 06in/0.46m
Deadrise:	21°
Displacement:	4,800lb/2177kg
Engine Options:	Mercury 5.7l EFI
	45mph/72km/h
	Mercury 350 Mag
	50mph/80km/h
	Volvo 5.7 GSI
	48mph/77km/h
Design:	Pursuit

PURSUIT 2470 CENTRE CONSOLE/ WALKAROUND SPORTS FISHING BOAT
DIMENSIONS

Length overall:	24ft 07in/7.49m
Beam:	8ft 06in/2.59m
Draft:	1ft 06in/0.46m
Deadrise:	21°
Displacement:	3,675/3,800lb
	(1667/1724kg)
Max Outboard:	300hp 46mph/74km/h
Design:	Pursuit

PURSUIT 2670 CUDDY CONSOLE/ DENALI LS SPORTS FISHING BOAT
DIMENSIONS

Length overall:	26ft 05in/8.05m
Beam:	9ft 03in/2.82m
Draft:	1ft 08in/0.51m
Deadrise:	21°
Displacement:	5,400lb/2449kg
Max Outboard:	400h 49mph/79km/h
Design:	Pursuit

LEFT and PAGE 156
Pursuit 2460 Denali sports utility boat.

OPPOSITE LEFT
Helm of Pursuit 2460.

OPPOSITE RIGHT
Forward berth of the Pursuit 2460.

PURSUIT 2665 DENALI LS FISHING BOAT

DIMENSIONS

Length overall:	26ft 05in/8.05m
Beam:	9ft 03in/2.82m
Draft:	3ft 00in/0.91m
Deadrise:	21°
Displacement:	5,400lb/2449kg
Engine Options:	inboard/outdrives
	Mercury 496 Mag 1
	45mph/72km/h
	Volvo 8.1L Gi
	45mph/72km/h
Design:	Pursuit

PURSUIT 2865 DENALI FISHING BOAT

DIMENSIONS

Length overall:	32ft 10in/10.00m
Beam:	9ft 06in/2.90m
Draft:	1ft 01in/0.33m
Deadrise:	21°
Displacement:	7,600lb/3447kg
Engine Options:	inboard/outdrives
	Mercury 496 Mag 1
	45mph/72km/h
	Volvo 8.1L Gi
	44mph/71km/h
	Volvo KAD300
	37mph/59.5km/h
Design:	Pursuit

Deadrise:	21°
Displacement:	7,500lb/3402kg
Max Outboards:	500hp 48mph/77km/h
Design:	Pursuit

PURSUIT 3270 CENTRE CONSOLE SPORTS FISHING BOAT

DIMENSIONS

Length overall:	34ft 06in/10.52m
Beam:	9ft 06in/2.90m
Deadrise:	24.4°
Max Outboards:	500hp
Design:	Pursuit

PURSUIT 2870 CENTRE CONSOLE/ WALKAROUND FISHING BOAT

DIMENSIONS

Length overall:	30ft 00in/9.14m
Beam:	9ft 06in/2.90m
Draft:	1ft 08in/0.51m
Deadrise:	22°
Displacement:	5,250/5,975lb (2381/2710kg)
Max Outboards:	450h 46mph/74km/h
Design:	Pursuit

PURSUIT 3070 CENTRE CONSOLE/ OFFSHORE FISHING BOAT

DIMENSIONS

Length overall:	32ft 08in/9.96m
Beam:	10ft 06in/3.20m
Draft:	1ft 06in/0.46m

ABOVE
Pursuit 2470 walkaround sports fishing boat.

ABOVE LEFT
Pursuit 2470 centre console sports fishing boat.

PURSUIT 3000 OFFSHORE SPORTS FISHING BOAT

DIMENSIONS

Length overall:	31ft 02in/9.50m
Beam:	12ft 01in/3.68m
Draft:	3ft 00in/0.91m
Deadrise:	19°
Displacement:	11,500lb/5216kg
Engine Options:	Twin inboards
	Cummins 6B3151
	Mercury 7.4 MPI L21
	34.7mph/56km/h
	Volvo KAMD 300 1B

LEFT and OPPOSITE
Pursuit 2665 Denali LS fishing boat.

ABOVE
Helm of a Pursuit 2665 Denali LS.

OPPOSITE
Pursuit 2670 cuddy console sports fishing boat.

LEFT
Pursuit 2670 Denali LS sports fishing boat.

ABOVE
Helm of a Pursuit 2670 Denali LS.

OPPOSITE
Pursuit 2865 Denali fishing boat.

ABOVE
Berth in a Pursuit 2865 Denali.

ABOVE LEFT
Helm of a Pursuit 2865 Denali.

LEFT
Pursuit 2870 centre console fishing boat.

35mph/56km/h,
Volvo KAMD
42 33.6mph/54km/h
Volvo KAMD 44
34mph/55km/h,
Crusader 8.1L Mplo
40.5mph/65km/h

PURSUIT 3370 OUTBOARD/3100 INBOARD OFFSHORE SPORTS FISHING BOAT

DIMENSIONS

Length overall:	35ft 01in/34ft 06in (10.69/10.52m)
Beam:	10ft 06in/3.20m
Draft:	2ft 04in/3ft 03in (0.71/0.99m)
Deadrise:	21°
Displacement:	9,520/10,500lb (4318/4763kg)
Engine Options:	Outboards 600hp 49mph/79km/h Twin Inboards Crusader 5.7l 31mph/50km/h Yanmar 6LPA-STP 37mph/59.5km/h
Design:	Pursuit

PURSUIT 3400 OFFSHORE SPORTS FISHING BOAT

DIMENSIONS

Length overall:	36ft 04in/11.07m
Beam:	12ft 09in/3.89m
Draft:	3ft 09in/1.14m
Deadrise:	18°
Displacement:	14,000lb/6350kg

OPPOSITE and THIS PAGE
Pursuit 3000 offshore sports fishing boat, with interior and exterior details.

PAGE 166 LEFT
Helm of a Pursuit 3070 centre console
fishing boat.

PAGE 166 RIGHT
Tackle station and rod-holders in a
Pursuit 3070.

PAGE 167
Pursuit 3070.

RIGHT
Pursuit 3070 centre console/offshore
fishing boat.

Engine Options: Twin Inboard
Design: Pursuit

PURSUIT 3800 OFFSHORE SPORTS
FISHING BOAT
DIMENSIONS

Length overall: 40ft 11in/12.47m
Beam: 14ft 02in/4.32m
Draft: 3ft 11in/1.19m
Deadrise: 18°
Displacement: 21,800lb/9888kg
Engine Options: Twin Inboard
                    Caterpillar 3126B
                    36mph/58km/h
                    Cummins 420C/450C
                    34mph/55km/h
                    Volvo 74P
                    36mph/58km/h
Design: Pursuit
www.pursuitboats.com

TOP and RIGHT
Pursuit 3070 centre console/offshore
fishing boat.

ABOVE
3070 helm.

OPPOSITE and FAR LEFT
Pursuit 3800 offshore sports fishing
boat.

LEFT
Pursuit 3800 rod store.

BELOW LEFT
Engine.

BELOW
Cabin.

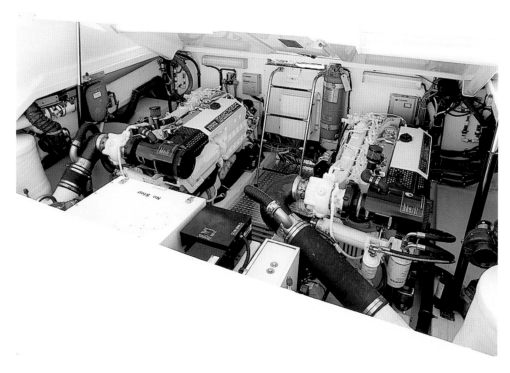

REGULATOR

Regulator Marine has been building specialist centre-console sports fishing boats at Edenton, North Carolina, since 1993. Its extreme deep-V fibreglass hulls are designed to cope with the rough and tumble of the Gulf Stream, and their web site tells tales of owners chasing grouper, kingfish, sunfish, tuna and wahoo as far across as the Bahamas.

This range of rugged outboard-driven fishing boats range between 21 and 32ft overall, carry a five-year hull warranty, and come professionally-equipped with fish, bait and storage boxes, centre console, leaning post and footrests, ready to wrestle with the big ones.

The Regulator 21FS would be as much at home as a fly-fishing platform in the shallow Carolina marshlands as it is

chasing shoals offshore. She can carry a single outboard up to 225hp and has the option of a portable toilet sited within a forward seating area in the bow, rather than within the centre console, which has a large cool box that doubles as a forward-facing seat.

REGULATOR 21FS SPORTS FISHING BOAT

DIMENSIONS

Length overall:	20ft 06in/6.25m
Beam:	8ft 02in/2.49m
Draft:	1ft 04in/0.41m
Deadrise:	20°
Displacement:	2,800lb/1270kg
Engine Options:	225-hp outboard

OPPOSITE and THIS PAGE
Regulator 21FS offshore sports fishing boat.

OPPOSITE
Regulator 23 offshore sports fishing boat.

RIGHT
Regulator 24.

BELOW
Regulator 24FS.

BELOW RIGHT
Regulator 26FS.

The Regulator 23 carries a deeper deadrise of 24°, making her more of a blue-water boat, and her transom will take either a single 300-hp outboard or twin installations up to 200hp each. Rods and tackle can be locked away from prying eyes in a storage compartment alongside two large fish boxes within the floor forward. There is also a 35-gallon (159-litre) live well built into the floor aft, and bait boxes are close to hand at each corner of the transom. There is further stowage within the console, which also incorporates a cool box in the base of the forward facing seat.

REGULATOR 23 SPORTS FISHING BOAT

DIMENSIONS

Length overall:	23ft 04in/7.11m
Beam:	8ft 04in/2.54m
Draft:	2ft 00in/0.61m
Deadrise:	24°

Displacement:	3,800lb/1724kg
Engine Options:	Twin 200-hp outboards
	Single 300-hp outboard

The 24 and 24FS (the latter denotes forward seating) is the first in the range with a toilet compartment built into the centre console. As sisters within the Regulator range, in addition to the in-floor storage areas this is the first with a walk-through door in the transom, which also incorporates a 28-gallon (125-litre) live well and beer cooler. The boat can be fitted with single or twin outboard configurations up to 400hp. These are serious fishing boats, sharing the same hull as the 26 and 26FS, with a 48° bow entry narrowing down to 24° at the

fully-upholstered seating and a canvas cuddy is available to provide protection from the wind and spray.

The transom has a walk-through door, there are acres of storage locker space all around, and the boat, which can carry twin outboards of up to 300hp, has a 310-gallon (1409-litre) fuel tank to keep you on the move all day, if necessary.

REGULATOR 32/32FS SPORTS FISHING BOAT

DIMENSIONS

Length overall:	32ft 00in/9.75m
Beam:	10ft 05in/3.17m
Draft:	2ft 00in/0.61m
Deadrise:	24°
Displacement:	7,400/7,500lb
	(3357/3402kg)
Engine Options:	Twin 300-hp
	outboards

www.regulatormarine.com

transom to slice through the worst that the weather can offer. The 26 models dispense with the transom door but carry a 2-ft wide engine step on the stern to extend the overall length.

REGULATOR 24/24FS SPORTS FISHING BOAT

DIMENSIONS

Length overall:	24ft 08in/7.52m
Beam:	8ft 06in/2.59m
Draft:	2ft 00in/0.61m
Deadrise:	24°

Displacement:	4,300/4,400lb
	(1950/1996kg)
Engine Options:	Twin 200-hp
	outboards

REGULATOR 26/26FS SPORTS FISHING BOAT

DIMENSIONS

Length overall:	25ft 10in/7.87m
Beam:	8ft 06in/2.59m
Draft:	2ft 00in/0.61m
Deadrise:	24°
Displacement:	5,000/5,100lb

	(2268/2313kg)
Engine Options:	Twin 250-hp
	outboards

The 32 models are the flagships within the Regulator range and, as such, are fitted out to satisfy the needs of the serious fisherman while offering some of the home comforts that the rest of the family will appreciate. The head, for instance, sited in the centre console, not only offers standing headroom, but is fully lined and fitted with a fresh-water shower. The boat also has

OPPOSITE
Regulator 32FS offshore sports fishing boat.

ABOVE
Regulator 32.

SEA FOX/MARIAH

The Renken family began building sports fishing and runabouts in Charleston, South Carolina, back in 1957. The company, which produces the Sea Fox and Mariah brands of trailable sports boats, is still family owned and run by the third generation of Renkens, Ed and Fred. Both ranges carry a ten-year hull warranty and have closed cell foam injected between hull and floor mouldings to provide a high level of built-in buoyancy in the event of an accident. The Sea Fox range is outboard-powered and all are predominantly sports fishing boats, while the Mariah brand concentrates on family runabouts and sports cruisers, mostly powered by inboard/outdrives.

The Sea Foxes include three low-profile specialist flats fishing boats measuring 16ft, 18ft 8in and 20ft in length. All have a draft of less than 1ft and have shallow V-hulls to provide maximum stability. They have flat casting decks fore and aft of the central steering console, with 33-gallon (147-litre) aerated live wells; tubular alloy poling platforms are available as optional extras.

SEA FOX 160 FLATS FOX

DIMENSIONS

Length overall:	16ft 02in/4.93m
Beam:	7ft 04in/2.23m
Draft:	10in/25cm
Deadrise:	10°
Displacement:	1,050lb/476kg
Engine Options:	60hp

SEA FOX 180 FLATS FOX

DIMENSIONS

Length overall:	18ft 08in/5.69m
Beam:	8ft 02in/2.49m
Draft:	10in/25cm
Deadrise:	11°
Displacement:	1,250lb/567kg
Engine Options:	115hp

SEA FOX 200 FLATS FOX

DIMENSIONS

Length overall:	20ft 01in/6.12m
Beam:	8ft 02in/2.49m
Draft:	11in/28cm
Deadrise:	11°
Displacement:	1,400lb/635kg
Engine Options:	150hp

ABOVE and OPPOSITE
Sea Fox 160 centre console sports
fishing boat.

The centre console and bay fisher models within the Sea Fox line-up range from 16 to 28ft, with V-hulls from 15–21°. These boats are built principally for fishing and carry aerated live fish wells, storage lockers, self-bailing cockpits and forward casting decks. The centre consoles on the 19ft 8-in 197 and 225 bay fisher models and upwards all have an enclosed toilet compartment, and the 21-ft 217 model and above are equipped with a bimini as standard.

The two dual console models at 18ft 5in and 22ft overall, are more dual-purpose family sports bowrider boats with walk-through screens and aerated live fish wells. Sea Fox and Mariah share the same hull moulds for the 21-ft deck boat, the 211 being totally open, while the 212 has a walk-through screen. The Sea Fox versions utilize the foredeck to take two casting chairs as part of a fish & ski option that includes an aerated live well, ski pole, rod-holders and tackle box. The Mariah range of family-orientated deck boats then continue with a 25-ft inboard/outdrive-powered model.

The Sea Fox range also includes three

ABOVE
Sea Fox 172 centre console sports fishing boat.

RIGHT
Sea Fox 185 bay fisher.

OPPOSITE
Sea Fox 197 centre console.

sports cabin boats, from the sporty-looking 20-ft cuddy fish to the 21- and 23-ft walkaround models. The latter have the option of a bimini and, with more space in the cabins, carry portable toilets.

SEA FOX 160 CENTRE CONSOLE

DIMENSIONS

Length overall:	16ft 01in/4.90m
Beam:	6ft 02in/1.88m
Draft:	09in/23cm
Deadrise:	16°
Displacement:	1,085lb/492kg
Engine Options:	50hp

SEA FOX 195 BAY FISHER
DIMENSIONS

Length overall:	19ft 06in/5.94m
Beam:	7ft 10in/2.39m
Draft:	0ft 09.05-in/24-cm V-hull
	0ft 08-in (20-cm) tunnel hull
Deadrise:	16°
Displacement:	1,700lb/771kg
Engine Options:	150hp

SEA FOX 197 CENTRE CONSOLE
DIMENSIONS

Length overall:	19ft 08in/5.99m
Beam:	8ft 06in/2.59m
Draft:	1ft 00in/0.30m
Deadrise:	19°
Displacement:	1,900lb/862k
Engine Options:	115hp

SEA FOX 204 CUDDY FISH BOAT
DIMENSIONS

Length overall:	20ft 04in/6.20m
Beam:	9ft 06in/2.90m
Draft:	0ft 14in/36cm
Deadrise:	18°
Displacement:	2,250lb/1021kg
Engine Options:	230hp

SEA FOX 205 BAY FISHER
DIMENSIONS

Length overall:	20ft 06in/6.25m
Beam:	8ft 06in/2.59m
Draft:	0ft 10in/25cm
Deadrise:	16°
Displacement:	2,050lb/930kg
Engine Options:	200hp

SEA FOX 172 CENTRE CONSOLE
DIMENSIONS

Length overall:	17ft 01in/5.21m
Beam:	6ft 10in/2.08m
Draft:	0ft 10in/25cm
Deadrise:	15°
Displacement:	1,390lb/630kg
Engine Options:	90hp

SEA FOX 185 BAY FISHER
DIMENSIONS

Length overall:	17ft 10in/5.43m
Beam:	7ft 10in/2.39m
Draft:	0ft 08in/20cm
Deadrise:	16°
Displacement:	1,275lb/578kg
Engine Options:	150hp

SEA FOX 186 DUAL CONSOLE
DIMENSIONS

Length overall:	18ft 05in/5.61m
Beam:	7ft 03in/2.21m
Draft:	0ft 11.05in/29cm
Deadrise:	19°
Displacement:	1,600lb/726kg
Engine Options:	135hp

OPPOSITE
Sea Fox 200.

LEFT
Sea Fox 204 cuddy fish boat.

BELOW LEFT
Sea Fox 205 bay fisher.

SEA FOX 206 DUAL CONSOLE
Dimensions

Length overall:	20ft 02in/6.15m
Beam:	8ft 06in/2.59m
Draft:	1ft 1.5in/0.34m
Deadrise:	21°
Displacement:	2,050lb/930kg
Engine Options:	200hp

SEA FOX 210 CENTRE CONSOLE
DIMENSIONS

Length overall:	21ft 00in/6.40m
Beam:	8ft 06in/2.59m
Draft:	1ft 02in/0.36m
Deadrise:	18°
Displacement:	2,200lb/998kg
Engine Options:	200hp

SEA FOX 210 WALKAROUND
DIMENSIONS

Length overall:	21ft 00in/6.40m
Beam:	8ft 06in/2.59m
Draft:	1ft 03in/0.38m
Deadrise:	18°
Displacement:	2,500lb/1134kg
Engine Options:	150hp

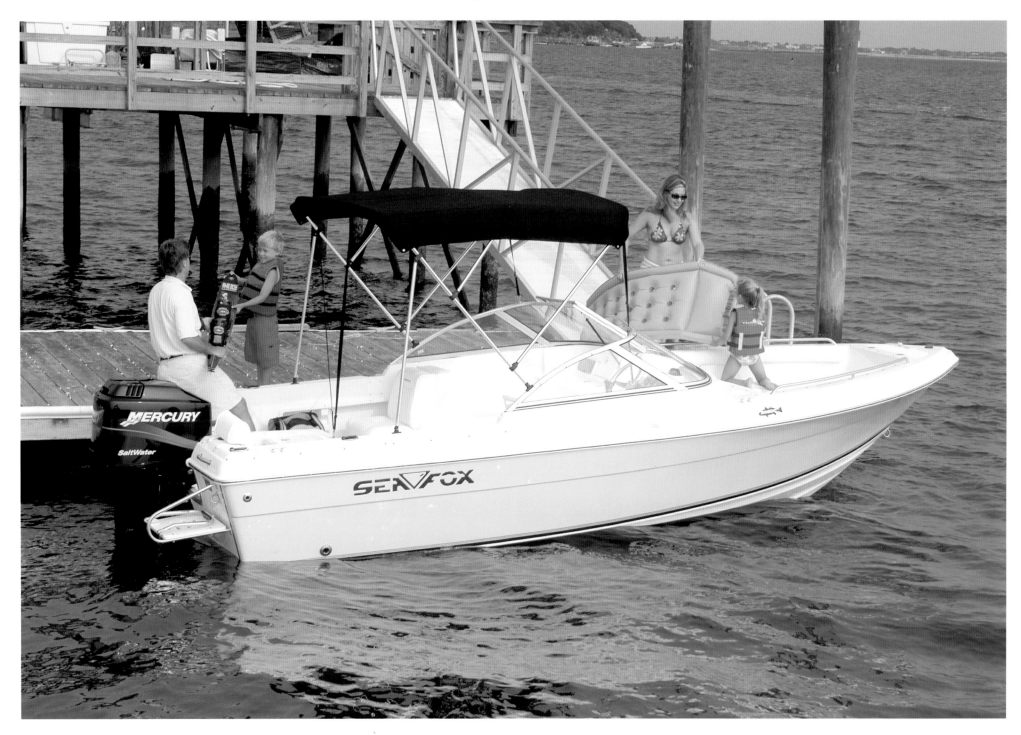

SEA FOX 215 BAY FISHER

DIMENSIONS

Length overall:	21ft 07in/6.58m
Beam:	7ft 10in/2.39m
Draft:	0ft 10-in/25-cm V-hull
	0ft 08.5-in/22-cm tunnel hull
Deadrise:	16°
Displacement:	2,050lb/930kg
Engine Options:	150hp

SEA FOX 217 CENTRE CONSOLE

DIMENSIONS

Length overall:	21ft 03in/6.48m
Beam:	8ft 05in/2.56m
Draft:	1ft 03in/0.38m
Deadrise:	21°
Displacement:	2,300lb/1043kg
Engine Options:	200hp

SEA FOX 225 BAY FISHER

DIMENSIONS

Length overall:	22ft 06in/6.86m
Beam:	8ft 06in/2.59m
Draft:	0ft 10in/25cm
Deadrise:	16°
Displacement:	2,350lb/1066kg
Engine Options:	225hp

OPPOSITE
Sea Fox 200 flats Fox.

BELOW
Sea Fox 206 dual console.

SEA FOX 230 CENTRE CONSOLE

DIMENSIONS

Length overall:	23ft 00in/7.01m
Beam:	8ft 06in/2.59m
Draft:	1ft 02in/0.36m
Deadrise:	18°
Displacement:	2,400lb/1089kg
Engine Options:	250hp

SEA FOX 230 WALKAROUND

DIMENSIONS

Length overall:	23ft 00in/7.01m
Beam:	8ft 06in/2.59m
Draft:	1ft 03in/0.38m
Deadrise:	18°
Displacement:	2,700lb/1225kg
Engine Options:	150hp

SEA FOX 245 BAY FISHER

DIMENSIONS

Length overall:	24ft 00in/7.31m
Beam:	8ft 06in/2.59m
Draft:	10in/25cm
Deadrise:	16°
Displacement:	2,700lb/1225kg
Engine Options:	250hp

SEA FOX 257 DUAL CONSOLE

DIMENSIONS

Length overall:	25ft 07in/7.80m
Beam:	8ft 06in/2.59m
Draft:	1ft 04in/0.41m
Deadrise:	20°
Displacement:	4,000lb/1814kg
Engine Options:	400hp

SEA FOX 257 WALKAROUND

DIMENSIONS

Length overall:	25ft 07in/7.80
Beam:	8ft 06in/2.59m
Draft:	1ft 05in/0.43m
Deadrise:	20°
Displacement:	4,300lb/1950kg
Engine Options:	250hp

SEA FOX 287 CENTRE CONSOLE

DIMENSIONS

Length overall:	28ft 00in/8.53m
Beam:	9ft 08in/2.95m
Draft:	1ft 08in/0.50m
Deadrise:	20°
Displacement:	4,800lb/2177kg
Engine Options:	Twin 200-hp outboards

www.seafoxboats.com

OPPOSITE
Sea Fox 217 centre console.

ABOVE
Mariah DX213 bowrider.

The Mariah range of bowriders and cuddy cabin boats carry the same ten-year hull warranty as their Sea Fox cousins. These runabouts are powered by a choice of Mercruiser inboard/outdrives to give each model within the 18–25-ft range an impressive speed of between 50 and 60mph. The 19- and 21-ft bowriders and cuddy models share the same-sized hull moulds and all are aimed at the family fun and ski market.

SEA FOX/MARIAH 211/ 212/MARIAH DX213 DECK BOATS

DIMENSIONS

Length overall:	21ft 00in/6.40m
Beam:	8ft 06in/2.59m
Draft:	1ft 03in/0.38m
Deadrise:	16°
Displacement:	2,200lb/2,700lb (DX) (998/1225kg)
Engine Options:	225-hp outboard
	DX model:
	4.3l Mercruiser inboard/outdrive
	47mph/76km/h
	5.0L Mercruiser inboard/outdrive
	53mph/85km/h

MARIAH DX251 DECK BOAT

DIMENSIONS

Length overall:	25ft 00in/7.62m
Beam:	8ft 06in/2.59m
Draft:	1ft 04in/0.41m
Deadrise:	16°
Displacement:	3,200lb/1451kg
Engine Options:	350 MAC MPI Mercruiser inboard/outdrive
	48mph/77km/h

MARIAH SX18 BOWRIDER

DIMENSIONS

Length overall:	18ft 00in/5.49m
Beam:	7ft 08in/2.34m

Draft:	1ft 00in/0.30m
Deadrise:	18°
Displacement:	2,310lb/1048kg
Engine Options:	3L Mercury Mercruiser inboard/outdrive
	46mph/74km/h
	4.3L Mercury Mercruiser inboard/outdrive
	50mph/80km/h

MARIAH SC19 CUDDY/SX19 BOWRIDER

DIMENSIONS

Length overall:	19ft 03in/5.87m
Beam:	8ft 02in/2.49m
Draft:	1ft 01in/0.33m

Deadrise:	19°
Displacement:	2,980/2,780lb 1352/1261kg
Engine Options:	3.0L Mercury Mercruiser inboard/outdrive
	45mph/72km/h
	4.3L Mercury Mercruiser inboard/outdrive
	49mph/79km/h
	5.0L Mercury Mercruiser inboard/outdrive
	52mph/84km/h

BELOW
Mariah SC19 bowrider.

OPPOSITE
Mariah SC21 bowrider.

MARIAH SX20 BOWRIDER

DIMENSIONS

Length overall:	20ft 00in/6.10m
Beam:	8ft 02in/2.49m
Draft:	1ft 02in/0.36m
Deadrise:	19°
Displacement:	2,800lb/1270kg
Engine Options:	4.3L Mercury Mercruiser inboard/outdrive
	44mph/71km/h

OPPOSITE
Mariah SX25 bowrider.

BELOW
Mariah SX18 bowrider.

5.7L Mercury
Mercruiser inboard/
outdrive
49mph/79km/h

MARIAH SX21 BOWRIDER/SC 21 CUDDY
DIMENSIONS
Length overall:	20ft 09in/6.32m
Beam:	8ft 06in/2.59m
Draft:	1ft 03in/0.38m
Deadrise:	20°
Displacement:	3,100/3,300lb (1406/1497kg)

Engine Options:	4.3L Mercury Mercruiser inboard/ outdrive 44mph/71km/h
	5.0L Mercury Mercruiser inboard/ outdrive 49mph/79km/h
	5.7L Mercury Mercruiser inboard/ outdrive 55mph/88.5km/h

MARIAH SX22 BOWRIDER
DIMENSIONS
Length overall:	22ft 02in/6.76m
Beam:	8ft 06in/2.59m
Draft:	1ft 03in/0.38m
Deadrise:	20°
Displacement:	3,000lb/1361kg
Engine Options:	5.7L Mercury Mercruiser inboard/ outdrive 55mph/88.5km/h
	350MPI Mercury Mercruiser outdrive/ outdrive 59mph/95km/h

MARIAH SX25 BOWRIDER
DIMENSIONS
Length overall:	25ft 02in/7.67m
Beam:	8ft 06in/2.59m
Draft:	1ft 04in/0.41m
Deadrise:	20°
Displacement:	3,600lb/1633kg
Engine Options:	5.7L Mercury Mercruiser inboard/ outdrive 44mph/71km/h
	MX 6.2 350MPI Mercury Mercruiser outdrive/outdrive 58mph/93km/h

www.mariah-boats.com

TRIUMPH BOATS

Triumph Boats is one of the world's largest producers of sports fishing boats. Based at Durham, North Carolina, Triumph is a member of the Genmar Group, which also owns Glastron, Four Winds and Wellcraft, and specializes in high technology solutions to mass-produced boats. The Triumph line-up, which ranges from a 12-ft tender to a 21-ft centre console sports fishing model, is all 'hot moulded' in the naturally buoyant marine-grade plastic, polyethylene. This material, which Genmar dubs 'Roplene', has five times the impact resistance of straight fibreglass and, tooling aside, is significantly less expensive. It is also fully recyclable. This would seem to suggest that the boats have a limited life, but that is before you see Triumph salesmen knocking seven bells out of a boat with a baseball bat – guaranteed to attract attention at boat shows!

The polyethylene moulding process has been used successfully since the 1970s and there are many boats still around to testify to the soundness of their construction. The problem has always been to decide on a design that will sell in such quantity to offset the high cost of tooling. Triumph has solved that by marketing several versions of the same hull moulding,

ABOVE and OPPOSITE
Triumph 120SDCC open tender.

such as its 18ft 6-in 191 model, which is available in walk-thu (WT), dual console (DC), Fish & Ski (FS) and single console (SC).

All these boats pop out of a mould like peas from a pod in a fully automated process. It starts with a specially-formulated polyethylene compound powder, which is poured into a high-temperature mould. The mould is mounted in a large convection oven and rotated both vertically and horizontally. The oven's heat melts the powder, which forms the boat shape, and the mould continues to rotate during the cooling stage to ensure an even, consistent thickness.

High load areas, such as cleats and tow eyes, are strengthened with stainless steel attachment points at the outset of the moulding process and the hull and deck comes out as a one-piece unit without seams and joins. All cavities are filled with closed foam to provide additional panel stiffness and flotation.

One disadvantage is that polypropylene is less hard-wearing than a glassfibre gel coat, so the surface can be damaged more easily when running the boat up a beach or coming alongside a pier or other rough surface. However, the material is easily repaired, even when the hull has been torn open. Most dealers will use a welding gun to heat the surrounding

plastic, but repairs can also be undertaken at home using a heat gun, a Teflon skillet and a putty knife. This is effected by first heating the damaged area with the heat gun, then filling it with Triumph's colour-matched welding material, overfilling the hole or gouge so that the additional plastic is higher than the surrounding area. Once cooled, it is then a simple case of sanding the area down to a smooth surface and buffing it up until it matches the surrounding area.

TRIUMPH 120SDCC OPEN TENDER

This tender, which is available as an open boat or fitted with a central steering console (120SDCC) has the looks and attributes of a RIB, but without the problem of deflating tubes. They have a carrying capacity of 650lb (295kg), built-in storage compartments and, in the case of the centre console version, are sold with an icebox, navigation lights, a padded bench seat and a galvanized trailer.

TRIUMPH 120SDCC OPEN TENDER
DIMENSIONS

Length overall:	12ft 00in/3.66m
Beam:	5ft 07in/1.70m
Draft:	04in/10cm

Deadrise:	10°
Displacement:	450lb/204kg
Engine Options:	25-hp outboard
Design:	Triumph/Genmar

The 14ft 6-in 150 and 16ft 10-in 170 models are available in a variety of colours and guises, including a camouflaged sports version built specifically for duck hunting. All come equipped with a rear casting deck with an aerated bait well, built-in fish boxes, storage lockers for rods and guns, a

ABOVE
Triumph 150DC deck boat.

LEFT
Triumph 150CC fishing boat.

OPPOSITE
Triumph 150COOL sports boat.

cooler and a fuel tank. Navigation lights, automatic bilge pump and a galvanized trailer are also included, while the console models come complete with speedo, tachometer and fuel gauge.

The hull shape of the 150 and 170 is identical, with 6ft 5-in beam, a draft of just 6in, and a shallow deadrise of 13°, which makes them ideal for boating and fishing on sheltered waters. The 170 has a carrying capacity of 1,300lb (590kg) and the 150 can cope with over 1,000lb (454kg).

TRIUMPH150CC/COOL/SPORT/ BT/FISH/BASS/DC CONSOLE SPORTS FISHING BOAT
DIMENSIONS

Length overall:	14ft 10in/4.52m
Beam:	6ft 05in/1.95m
Draft:	0ft 06in/15cm
Deadrise:	13°
Displacement:	950lb/431kg
Engine Options:	60-hp outboard
Design:	Triumph/Genmar

TRIUMPH 170CC/COOL/SPORT/ BT/FISH/BASS/DC CONSOLE SPORTS FISHING BOAT
DIMENSIONS

Length overall:	16ft 10in/5.13m
Beam:	6ft 03in/1.90m
Draft:	0ft 06in/15cm
Deadrise:	13°
Displacement:	1,030lb/467kg
Engine Options:	75-hp outboard

The 18ft 6-in 190 Triumph is also available as a general-purpose fish & ski boat or as centre console boats dedicated to fishing. They have a forward casting deck, aerated bait well, storage lockers for rods and nets, and all the accessories for a bow trolling motor built in, including storage space in the floor for two batteries. There are lockable stowage areas in the aft cockpit, a live well with removable bait bucket, and flush-mounted pedestal bases to take removable casting seats. These boats also come complete with navigation lights, speedo, tacho and fuel indicator, and a trailer with brakes.

The 191 model carries the same overall length, but has a steeper V-hull and 5in (13cm) more freeboard for use at sea and in less sheltered inland waters.

OPPOSITE
Triumph 150 fish boat.

ABOVE LEFT
Triumph 150 sport boat.

ABOVE
Triumph 170 fish boat.

TRIUMPH 190SC/BAY/DC/CONSOLE SPORTS FISHING BOAT

DIMENSIONS

Length overall:	18ft 06in/5.64m
Beam:	8ft 01in/2.46m
Draft:	0ft 11in/28cm
Deadrise:	14°
Displacement:	1,535lb/696kg
Engine Options:	150-hp outboard
Design:	Triumph/Genmar

TRIUMPH 191WT/DC/FS/SC CONSOLE SPORTS FISHING BOAT

Dimensions

Length overall:	18ft 06in/5.64m
Beam:	8ft 02in/2.49m
Draft:	0ft 10in/25cm
Deadrise:	16°
Displacement:	1,875lb/850kg
Engine Options:	175h-p outboard
Design:	Triumph/Genmar

TRIUMPH 210

The 20ft 6-in 210 Triumph models carry 19° of deadrise to cope with choppy offshore conditions and come as a complete package that includes trailer, navigation lights and bimini. The cockpit is self-draining, there is plenty of stowage for rods and tackle, and there are a live bait well and fish lockers, full instrumentation, leaning post, and stereo system.

TRIUMPH 210GLE/210CC CENTRE CONSOLE SPORTS FISHING BOAT

DIMENSIONS

Length overall:	20ft 06in/6.25m
Beam:	8ft 06in/2.59m
Draft:	1ft 02in/0.36m
Deadrise:	19°
Displacement:	2,300lb/1043kg
Engine Options:	200-hp outboard
Design:	Triumph/Genmar

www.triumphboats.com

ABOVE
Triumph 170BT sports fishing boat.

OPPOSITE
Triumph 170 bass.

SPORTS & FISHING BOATS

CROWNLINE

Crownline Boats, based at West Frankfort, Illinois, is one of America's largest producers of inboard/outdrive-powered sports bowriders, deck boats and cruisers. They range in size from 18 to 31ft, with some models, like the 23-ft BR (bowrider) sharing the same hull as the CR (cabin cruiser). They compete in the same competitive family market sector as Chaparral, Glastron and Mariah, providing healthy competition that has improved levels of quality and value all round. The entire range carries a five-year unlimited warranty and a lifetime guarantee on the plywood stringer construction as well as the cockpit gauges.

A lot of thought has gone into maximizing space and storage for everything from clothing to skis, coolers, food and drink. Upholstery is cut from a

BELOW
Crownline 206 LS bowrider.

OPPOSITE
Crownline 210 LX bowrider.

stain-, grease- and salt water-resistant vinyl and bucket seats are all fitted with a shock-absorbing system to cushion slamming. The boats are also available in a wide range of co-ordinated colours and trims.

The Crownline bowriders range in size from 18 to 28ft 8in and have walk-through screens, a bimini that Crownline calls a 'Sunbrella', cooler, Sony stereo system, automatic bilge pump and fire extinguisher. There is also an optional fish package for the 18- and 19-ft models, which adds bow and stern casting chairs and aerated live well and connections for a trolling motor on the bows. The 23-ft bowriders and above also have an enclosed head opposite the helm position.

The three deck boats within the Crownline range measure 21 and 23ft 7in overall, and are also fitted with enclosed toilets, and with flatter hulls than their bowrider cousins offer a stable platform on which to walk and picnic. Other features include a wet bar with fresh-water facilities, an enclosed trash bin and settee-style seating fore and aft.

OPPOSITE
Crownline 210 LX bowrider.

BELOW
Crownline 210 razor bowrider.

CROWNLINE 180 BR SPORTS BOWRIDER

DIMENSIONS

Length overall:	18ft 00in/5.49m
Beam:	7ft 08in/2.34m
Draft:	1ft 03in/0.38m
Deadrise:	18°
Displacement:	2,600lb/1179kg
Engine Options:	220-hp Mercruiser inboard/outdrive
Design:	Crownline

CROWNLINE 192 BR SPORTS BOWRIDER

DIMENSIONS

Length overall:	19ft 01in/5.82m
Beam:	8ft 00in/2.44m
Draft:	1ft 01in/0.33m
Deadrise:	16°
Displacement:	3,000lb/1361kg
Engine Options:	280-hp Mercruiser inboard/outdrive
Design:	Crownline

CROWNLINE 202 BR/210 BR/202 LPX SPORTS BOWRIDER

DIMENSIONS

Length overall:	20ft 02in/20ft 04in (6.15/6.20m)
Beam:	8ft 06in/2.59m
Draft:	1ft 04in/0.41m
Deadrise:	16°
Displacement:	3,300/3,500lb (1497/1588kg)
Engine Options:	320-hp Mercruiser inboard/outdrive
Design:	Crownline

OPPOSITE
Crownline 210 razor bowrider.

ABOVE
Crownline 216 LS bowrider.

PAGE 206
Crownline 240 EX deck boat.

PAGE 207
Crownline 240 EX and 260 EX deck boats.

SPORTS & FISHING BOATS

CROWNLINE 212 DB SPORTS DECK BOAT

DIMENSIONS

Length overall:	21ft 02in/6.45m
Beam:	8ft 06in/2.59m
Draft:	1ft 06in/0.46m
Deadrise:	14°
Displacement:	4,000lb/1814kg
Engine Options:	320-hp Mercruiser inboard/outdrive
Design:	Crownline

CROWNLINE 225 BR/225 LPX SPORTS BOWRIDER

DIMENSIONS

Length overall:	22ft 05in/6.83m
Beam:	8ft 06in/2.59m
Draft:	1ft 06in/0.46m
Deadrise:	18°
Displacement:	3,800lb/1724kg
Engine Options:	425-hp Mercruiser inboard/outdrive
Design:	Crownline

CROWNLINE 230 BR SPORTS BOWRIDER

DIMENSIONS

Length overall:	23ft 00in/7.01m
Beam:	8ft 06in/2.59m
Draft:	1ft 06in/0.46m
Deadrise:	18°
Displacement:	4,200lb/1905kg
Engine Options:	425-hp Mercruiser inboard/outdrive
Design:	Crownline

CROWNLINE 238 DB/239 DB SPORTS DECK BOAT

DIMENSIONS

Length overall:	23ft 07in/7.19m
Beam:	8ft 06in/2.59m
Draft:	1ft 07in/0.48m
Deadrise:	15°
Displacement:	4,400/4,700lb (1996/2132kg)
Engine Options:	320-hp Mercruiser inboard/outdrive
Design:	Crownline

CROWNLINE 288 BR SPORTS BOWRIDER

DIMENSIONS

Length overall:	28ft 08in/8.74m
Beam:	9ft 08in/2.95m
Draft:	1ft 09in/0.53m
Deadrise:	24°
Displacement:	8,000lb/3629kg
Engine Options:	425-hp Mercruiser inboard/outdrive
Design:	Crownline

The cuddy and full sports cabin cruisers within the Crownline range start with the 21-ft CCR and grow to 29ft. These have V-berths with a dinette in the saloon, a galley with a microwave oven, and a separate full-sized head and shower compartment. The 262 model and above also have a second double berth compartment fitted under the cockpit floor, which becomes an ideal bolt-hole for kids; on the top-of-the-range 290 model, this provides sufficient room for an adult to sit up. The cockpits have two settee areas, a

wet bar and transom access to the swim platform over the outdrive unit.

CROWNLINE 215 CCR SPORTS CRUISER

DIMENSIONS

Length overall:	21ft 01in/6.43m
Beam:	8ft 06in/2.59m
Draft:	1ft 06in/0.46m
Deadrise:	18°
Displacement:	4,200lb/1905kg
Engine Options:	320-hp Mercruiser inboard/outdrive
Design:	Crownline

CROWNLINE 230 CCR SPORTS CRUISER

DIMENSIONS

Length overall:	23ft 00in/7.01m
Beam:	8ft 06in/2.59m
Draft:	1ft 06in/0.46m
Deadrise:	18°
Displacement:	4,500lb/2041kg
Engine Options:	425-hp Mercruiser inboard/outdrive
Design:	Crownline

CROWNLINE 262 CR SPORTS CRUISER

DIMENSIONS

Length overall:	25ft 10in/7.87m
Beam:	8ft 06in/2.59m
Draft:	1ft 06in/0.46m
Deadrise:	18°
Displacement:	6,800lb/3084kg
Engine Options:	Single 375-hp Mercruiser inboard/outdrive Twin 270-hp

	Mercruiser inboard/outdrives
Design:	Crownline

CROWNLINE 290 CR SPORTS CRUISER

DIMENSIONS

Length overall:	31ft 02in/9.50m
Beam:	11ft 02in/3.40m
Draft:	1ft 05in/0.43m
Deadrise:	16°
Displacement:	10,500lb/4763kg
Engine Options:	Single 425hp Mercruiser inboard/outdrive Twin 320-hp Mercruiser inboard/outdrives
Design:	Crownline

www.crownline.com

OPPOSITE
Crownline 260 EX deck boat.

BELOW
Crownline 270 CR sports cruiser.

CHRIS*CRAFT

The year 2004 was the 130th anniversary of Chris*Craft, one of America's oldest boat-builders. Christopher Columbus Smith began by building the best duck-hunting punts in 1874 and went on to produce a succession of record-breaking powerboats. The company may have navigated through some pretty rough waters during the interim period, but the brand name and image remain as strong as ever.

Between 1922 and 1972, Chris*Craft built more than 100,000 of its distinctive boats and it is a credit to their design and construction that many of these mahogany masterpieces continue to win Concours d'Elégance trophies at classic events around the world.

Throughout its history, the company

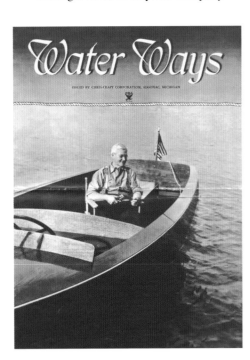

has managed to blend traditional craftsmanship with innovation, and the advent of fibreglass enabled it to achieve new standards in deep-V hull design and manufacture. It may no longer build boats with wooden hulls, but wood is still a significant feature in every boat that leaves the yard at Sarasota, Florida.

Today, the company is owned by Stephen M. Julius and Stephen F. Heese

ABOVE
A Chris*Craft advertisement from the 1950s.

ABOVE LEFT
A classic Chris*Craft, circa 1930s.

FAR LEFT
An old Chris*Craft publication.

LEFT
A Chris*Craft of the 1920s.

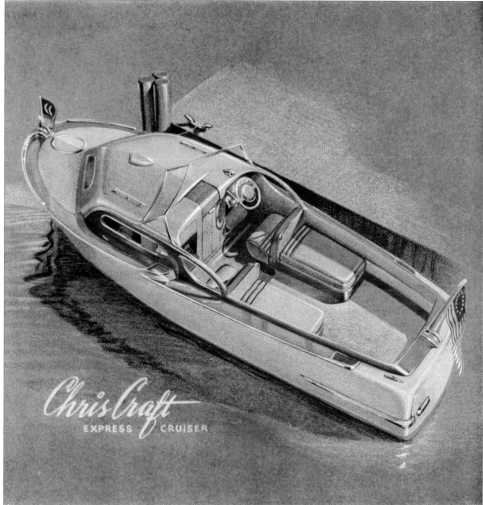

Keep your spirits high—speed Victory

Buy U. S. War Bonds Today—
Tomorrow command your own
CHRIS-CRAFT

CHRIS-CRAFT CORPORATION, ALGONAC, MICH. ★ WORLD'S LARGEST BUILDERS OF MOTOR BOATS

An advertisement reprinted from FORTUNE, Dec., 1943

LEFT
Chris*Craft.

FAR LEFT
A Chris*Craft advertisement from
Fortune magazine, 1943.

BELOW
Chris*Craft 21-ft utility boats from
1937.

who acquired the brand because of their
passion for this all-American icon and have
ensured that the new range of boats
continues to combine classic design with
contemporary technology.

1937 21-ft. Utility Boats are
available with or without
cabin as shown.   Prices
begin at $1395. The built-
in cabin is $250 additional.
There's nothing better afloat
in the Utility boat class.

THIS PAGE
Chris*Craft Corsair 25.

OPPOSITE
Chris*Craft Corsair 28.

The Chris*Craft Launch models range in size from 22 to 28ft. These luxury deep-V speedboats utilize the bow area to provide settee seating in their forward cockpits, which is accessed through walk-through windshields. The Corsair models utilize the same powerful 25- and 28-ft hulls but have a two-berth mini cabin

beneath their foredecks. Powered by Volvo inboard/outdrives, all are capable of providing an exhilarating 50mph plus.

CHRIS*CRAFT LAUNCH 22
DIMENSIONS

Length overall:	22ft 00in/6.70m
Beam:	8ft 06in/2.59m
Draft:	1ft 05in/0.43m
Deadrise:	20°
Displacement:	3,500lb/1588kg
Engine Options:	Volvo Penta 5.7 1 Gi
	53mph/85km/h
Design:	Michael Peters

CHRIS*CRAFT LAUNCH/CORSAIR 25

DIMENSIONS

Length overall:	25ft 00in/7.62m
Beam:	8ft 06in/2.59m
Draft:	1ft 05in/0.43m
Deadrise:	20°
Displacement:	4,600lb/2087kg
Engine Options:	Volvo Penta 8.1 1 GXi 60mph/196.5km/h
Design:	Michael Peters

CHRIS*CRAFT LAUNCH/CORSAIR 28

DIMENSIONS

Length overall:	28ft 00in/8.53m
Beam:	10ft 00in/3.05m
Draft:	1ft 08in/0.51m
Deadrise:	20°
Displacement:	7,500lb/3402kg
Engine Options:	Twin Volvo Penta 5.7 1 Gi 56mph/90km/h
Design:	Michael Peters

CHRIS*CRAFT CORSAIR 25

DIMENSIONS

Length overall:	22ft 00in/6.71m
Beam:	8ft 06in/2.59m
Draft:	1ft 05in/0.43m
Deadrise:	20°
Displacement:	3,500lb/1588kg
Engine Options:	Volvo Penta 5.7 1 Gi 53mph/85km/h
Design:	Michael Peters

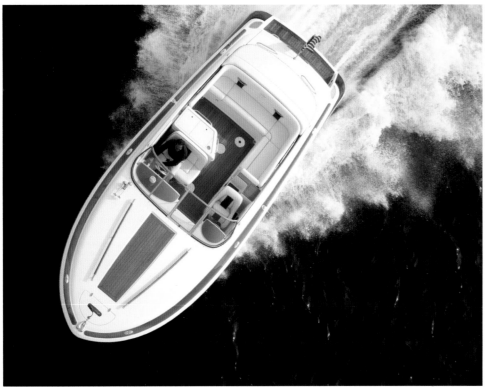

The Chris*Craft fast motor cruisers share the same style and luxury finish as their sports boat counterparts. The 34-ft Express cruiser is the most enduring model, offering a speed of almost 50mph coupled with two double berth cabins, dinette saloon, full galley and head.

The Roamer 36 has a shallower V-hull but equally eye-catching lines. With a choice of cockpit layouts, this boat offers similar accommodation to the Express but spread out over a larger area. Powered by twin Volvo 480-hp engines, she has a top speed of 34mph.

The Roamer 43 has similar speed potential and equally attractive lines. Her greater size allows for a separate owner's stateroom forward and a twin-bedded cabin

OPPOSITE LEFT,
ABOVE and BELOW
Chris*Craft Corsair 28s.

OPPOSITE RIGHT
Chris*Craft at the Fort Lauderdale Boat Show, 2003.

ABOVE and ABOVE LEFT
Chris*Craft Express cruiser 33.

LEFT
Helm of a Chris*Craft Express cruiser 33.

PAGES 216 and 217
Chris*Craft Roamer 36 and interior.

running the full width amidships, each with en suite facilities. The saloon is just as luxurious.

CHRIS*CRAFT EXPRESS CRUISER 33

DIMENSIONS

Length overall:	34ft 10in/10.62m
Beam:	11ft 10in/3.61m
Draft:	2ft 02in/0.66m
Deadrise:	20°
Displacement:	12,000lb/5443kg
Engine Options:	Twin Volvo Penta 5.7 1 Gi 47mph/76km/h
Design:	Michael Peters

CHRIS*CRAFT ROAMER 36

DIMENSIONS

Length overall:	36ft 03in/11.05m
Beam:	12ft 06in/3.81m
Draft:	2ft 11in/0.89m
Deadrise:	17°
Displacement:	18,200lb/8255kg

Engine Options:	Twin Yanmar 370hp 34mph/55km/h
Design:	Michael Peters

CHRIS*CRAFT ROAMER 43

DIMENSIONS

Length overall:	43ft 06in/13.26m
Beam:	14ft 00in/4.27m
Draft:	3ft 02in/0.96m
Deadrise:	20°
Displacement:	27,000lb/12247kg
Engine Options:	Twin Volvo Penta 480hp 35mph/56km/h
Design:	Michael Peters

CHRIS*CRAFT LAUNCH 22

DIMENSIONS

Length overall:	22ft 00in/6.70m
Beam:	8ft 06in/2.59m
Draft:	1ft 05in/0.43m
Deadrise:	20°
Displacement:	3,500lb/1588kg
Engine Options:	Volvo Penta 5.7 1 Gi 53mph/85km/h
Design:	Michael Peters

www.chriscraft.com

OPPOSITE
Chris*Craft Roamer 36.

THIS PAGE
Chris*Craft Roamer 43.

BERTRAM YACHTS

Bertram Yachts is synonymous with offshore fishing. Once Dick Bertram had proved Ray Hunt's deep-V hull concept in the 1960 Miami/Nassau race, moulds were made of *Moppie*'s hull and the Bertram 31 flybridge cruiser launched the company in 1961. A year later, the Bertram 25, a scaled-down version of the 31, was unveiled, and became one of the most popular models ever. This was followed first by the Bertram 38, then the 20-ft baby of the fleet, and the Bertram 35 in 1967.

In 1968, the company was bought out by the Whittaker Corporation, which led to considerable expansion of the production facilities in Miami. The thousandth Bertram was launched in 1971 and the Bertram 46 convertible and the Bertram 42 were introduced a year later. The demand now was for ever bigger sports fishing boats and in 1977 the Bertram 58 was unveiled – the first production model fitted with an aluminium superstructure. The next major milestone was the innovative 54 convertible, which made its debut in 1981 after two years of extensive research and tank testing at the Hovercraft laboratories in England and six months of proving trials running the prototype off Bimini and Miami.

Bertram underwent a major restructuring in 1985 following the leveraged buyout by Investcorp and merger with Trojan Yachts. This was marked by the introduction of the 37 convertible with sleek new styling that made other models in the range look decidedly dated. The

ABOVE LEFT
Moppie, in the 1960 Miami-Nassau race.

ABOVE
Bertram deep-V hull.

LEFT
Richard Bertram and family, circa 1947.

OPPOSITE
The Bertram range.

following year, the 50 convertible made its debut and was dubbed 'the slickest Bertram yet' by *Boating* magazine. This model was a turning point for Bertram and proved so popular that two production lines were built to keep pace with demand. This was followed by Bertram's biggest boat to-date, the 72, then the 43 convertible in 1987.

The 1990s witnessed a greater concentration on styling and interior design to compete with the high standards set by European imports. The Bertram 60, for instance, introduced in 1990, was relaunched in '93 with four staterooms. In 1994, the Bertram 50, one of the most popular models in the range, also underwent a major facelift. In 1993, however, the business filed for bankruptcy after the introduction of a 10 per cent luxury tax led to a decrease in orders.

OPPOSITE
Bertram 390.

ABOVE
Flybridge of the Bertram 390.

LEFT
Bertram 390 with tuna tower.

The name lived on, however, and in 1998 the company was acquired by the Ferretti group, headquartered in Italy, a takeover that was to herald major changes in the way the boats were designed and manufactured. The introduction of advanced composite technologies has led to much tighter manufacturing tolerances, stronger, lighter hulls and improved performance figures. Design, styling and interiors are now managed by Zuccon International, Italian stylists that are also responsible for the Ferretti range built in Italy. Their rich wood finishes now give this range of sports fishing boats a luxurious European appearance, as well as making better use of space within the interiors and cockpits.

THIS PAGE
The interior of a Bertram 390, showing its luxurious appointments.

OPPOSITE
Bertram 390.

The Bertram range now encompasses seven models: the 390, 450, 510, 570, 60, 630 and 670 – the latter two available with the option of an open or closed flybridge. These tough, all-weather boats are marked by the lack of forward windows in their coach roofs to avoid problems of glass breaking under the weight of green water that can be thrown up when crossing the Gulf Stream. However, those not expecting

such heavy conditions or who enjoy boating in cooler climates do have the option of forward windshields in the 390, 450 and 510 models, together with an inside pilot position.

While the aft decks and tuna towers on all these Bertrams are dedicated to professional fishing, the fighting chairs, rod-holders, trawl arms, live bait and fish boxes, cutting table, sink and fresh-water washdowm facilities are what we have come to expect. But for those who have not been aboard a Bertram recently, it is the level of luxury and finish inside that comes

as the surprise. The 390, for example, has beautifully polished wooden furnishings throughout, matched with exquisite but practical fabrics. The saloon is fitted out with a dinette table to starboard, a large L-shaped settee to port and the galley is but a step down the companionway leading to the forward sleeping quarters. This is divided between an owner's suite forward and twin-bedded cabin amidships. Noise levels on all the Bertrams are minimized by positioning the fuel tank athwartships between engine room and accommodation, which also minimizes any change of trim as fuel loads

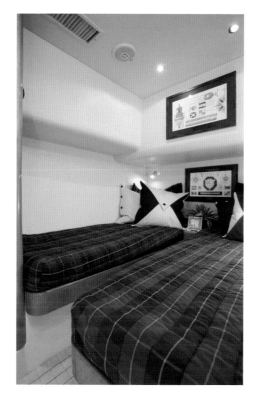

drop. The flybridge carries the steering console aft and a large bench seat forward, which is protected by a wraparound windshield. Fitted with an option of twin Volvo 480-hp or Yanmar 500-hp diesels, she can cruise all day at 31mph and has a top speed of more than 36mph.

BERTRAM 390 SPORTS FISHING CRUISER

DIMENSIONS

Length overall:	41ft 08in/12.70m
Beam:	13ft 04in/4.06m
Draft:	4ft 00in/1.22m
Deadrise:	20°
Displacement:	34,398lb/15603kg
Engine Options:	Twin Volvo 74 EDC
	6l diesels
	36.2mph/58km/h
	Twin Yanmar 500-hp
	diesels
	37.9mph/61km/h
Design:	Bertram/
	Ferretti/Zuccon

OPPOSITE
Bertram 390.

TOP LEFT
Stateroom of a Bertram 390.

FAR LEFT
Saloon of the Bertram 390.

LEFT
The wake with fishing rods.

The 450 Bertram has a similar layout to the 390, though has more space to include a separate shower and heads in the guest cabin, a larger galley and full bar in the saloon. There is more space on the flybridge too, which doubles the guest seating area and wet bar. On top, the position of the tuna tower is the same as on the 390 model, with a bimini for shade. Fitted with optional MAN diesels, she has a top speed of 39mph.

OPPOSITE
Bertram 450 at sunset.

ABOVE
Bertram 450 flybridge and tuna tower

RIGHT
Fighting seat at rear.

BERTRAM 450 SPORTS FISHING CRUISER

DIMENSIONS

Length overall:	48ft 03in/14.71m
Beam:	14ft 11in/4.55m
Draft:	4ft 04in/1.32m
Deadrise:	20°
Displacement:	46,305lb/21004kg
Engine Options:	Twin CAT 6L 3196
	DITA diesels
	35.6mph/57km/h
	Twin MAN V8
	D2848LE diesels
	39.1mph/63km/h
Design:	Bertram/
	Ferretti/Zuccon

THIS PAGE
Interior of the Bertram 450.

OPPOSITE
Bertram 450 flybridge and tuna tower.

RIGHT
Bertram 510.

OPPOSITE
Bertram 510, with views of cockpit,
flybridge and tuna tower.

The Bertram 510, introduced in 2004,
has a choice of interiors that surpasses
almost any five-star hotel. The saloon is
divided between a large U-shaped galley
with dinette table opposite, and a
lounge/entertaining area with an L-shaped
settee facing a flat-screen TV in the
opposite corner. The sleeping quarters
include the owner's stateroom forward, a
second double cabin with en suite shower,
heads on the port side and a smaller twin-
bedded crew cabin opposite. The twin pilot
console on the flybridge carries a variety of
navigational and fish-finding monitor
screens, which retract when not in use, and
has a large U-shaped settee forward and
wraparound windshield to protect the
guests. Fitted with twin MAN 1,300-hp
diesels, this is one of Bertram's fastest
models, with a top speed of 45mph.

BERTRAM 510 SPORTS FISHING CRUISER

DIMENSIONS

Length overall:	54ft 10in/16.71m
Beam:	16ft 02in/4.93m
Draft:	5ft 00in/1.52m
Deadrise:	20°
Displacement:	65,489lb/29706kg
Engine Options:	Twin CAT 3406E DITA diesels 35.6mph/57km/h Twin MAN V10 D2840 LE diesels 39.7mph/64km/h Twin MAN V12 D2842 LE diesels 45.6mph/73km/h
Design:	Bertram/ Ferretti/Zuccon

OPPOSITE
Helm of the Bertram 510.

THIS PAGE
Stateroom, heads, crew quarters and saloon of the Bertram 510.

OPPOSITE
Two views of the Bertram 510.

ABOVE
Bertram 570.

RIGHT
Bertram 570 cockpit with fighting chair.

The 570 has a three- or four-cabin layout below and a choice of designs within the saloon. Unlike her smaller sisters, the master suite is positioned amidships with a queen-sized bed and adjoining heads. There is room for a second double bed in the forward cabin, but owners have the option of having split over/under single berths built here if preferred. A third cabin on the starboard side has twin beds. All have private en suite head and shower facilities.

The choice of layouts in the saloon centre around the galley. Plan A offers a full-sized upright refrigerator, four-burner range, double sink and ample preparation areas married to an attractive U-shaped

settee arrangement aft, which protrudes out at 45°. Plan B carries all the appliances under the counter, matched to a more traditional L-shaped sofa facing the wide-screen TV opposite. Both options share the same five-seater dinette on the starboard side.

The cockpit measures 147sq ft (137m²), with plenty of space for two anglers and their mates to work simultaneously. It is fitted with a large transom door and gate ready to land the bigger fish. The bait and tackle centre, with fitted sink, salt and fresh-water faucets, cutting board, top-loading freezer and circulating bait well are positioned in the shelter of the flybridge, which, in addition to the fully-fitted pilot and co-pilot station with its retractable screens, has a wet bar and seating for six around a dinette table. Fitted with the option of MAN, CAT or MTU diesels, this Bertram has a cruising speed of 38mph and a top speed of 43mph.

LEFT
Bow of the Bertram 570.

OPPOSITE
Helm, stateroom and two-bedded berth of Bertram 570.

BERTRAM 570 SPORTS FISHING CRUISER

Dimensions

Length overall:	60ft 06in/18.44m
Beam:	16ft 09in/5.10m
Draft:	5ft 03in/1.60m
Deadrise:	20°
Displacement:	76,073lb/34507kg
Engine Options:	Twin MTU 12V 2000 M91 diesels

37.3mph/60km/h
Twin CAT C30 12V diesel
41.9mph/67km/h
Twin MAN V12 D2842 LE diesels
43.9mph/71km/h

Design: Bertram/Ferretti/Zuccon

ABOVE LEFT
Bertram 570.

ABOVE
Bertram 570 galley.

LEFT
Fishing reels at the ready.

TOP
Bertram 570 aft cockpit tackle station with sink.

ABOVE
Flybridge deck.

LEFT
Master stateroom.

The Bertram 60 shares the same expansive fighting cockpit features as the 570. Below decks, there is a choice of three of four cabin layouts, with a large master suite situated amidships, with the choice of a queen-sized bed or upper and lower bunks forward and two pilot bunk beds on the starboard side. All have their own entertainment centres with TV, VCR and stereo sound, together with adjoining stall shower and heads.

There is a large U-shaped galley on the forward port side of the saloon, opposite a five-seater dining table, leaving the aft section devoted to a lounge area with L-shaped settee, bar and entertainment centre. The flybridge is fitted with a swivel fighting chair that doubles as the helm seat and there is an L-shaped settee forward for guests. Fitted with twin CAT diesels, this Bertram has a cruising speed of 37mph and a top speed of 42mph.

OPPOSITE
Bertram 60.

TOP
Bertram 60 dining area.

ABOVE LEFT
Cockpit with fighting chair and transom door.

LEFT
The well-proportioned galley.

BERTRAM 60 SPORTS FISHING CRUISER

DIMENSIONS

Length overall:	62ft 02in/18.95m
Beam:	16ft 11in/5.16m
Draft:	5ft 06in/1.68m
Deadrise:	17°
Displacement:	93,492lb/42408kg
Engine Options:	Twin CAT 3412 E DITA diesels 42.55mph/68km/h
Design:	Bertram/ Ferretti/Zuccon

ABOVE
Bertram 60 forward berth.

FAR LEFT
Double berth.

LEFT
Head.

OPPOSITE
Master stateroom.

The Bertram 630 is available with a variety of six- or eight-berth cabin layouts, centred around a master suite amidships, and with either an open or enclosed flybridge. There is also a choice of engine packages with twin MTU 2000-hp engines making this the fastest Bertram, with a top speed of 46mph.

Below decks, there is a choice of a VIP guest suite forward or a split V-berth arrangement with a small double bed to port and overhead single to starboard. There is a further twin-bedded cabin on the starboard side amidships ahead of an optional twin-bunk cabin, which takes the place of head and shower in the four-cabin model.

The layout options for the saloon are the same as in the Bertram 60, with the exception of an internal spiral staircase to the flybridge.

BERTRAM 630/630E SPORTS
FISHING CRUISER
DIMENSIONS

Length overall:	66ft 09in/20.34m
Beam:	18ft 01in/5.51m
Draft:	5ft 03in/1.60m
Deadrise:	20°
Displacement:	90,672/91,672lb
	(41129/41582kg)
Engine Options:	Twin CAT C-30 12v
diesels	41.4mph/67km/h
	Twin MTU 16v 2000
	M91 diesels
	46mph/74km/h
Design:	Bertram/
	Ferretti/Zuccon

The 670, Bertram's flagship, is also available with an open or enclosed flybridge. In the open version this is large enough to provide an open entertainment and dining area, with galley, grill and fridge ahead of the pilot station with its power-activated electronics pod that adjusts to any position out of the console. The fighting cockpit has 168sq ft (15.6m²) of space and boasts all the amenities, including chair, stand-up rod storage, live bait well and freshwater washdown.

The interior living area offers a mix of intimacy and space in four distinct areas, divided by a medley of angles and curves. Aft portside is a living room with a couch flanked by armchairs to provide seating for eight to ten people with a bar area opposite. A raised open galley with under-counter refrigerators overlooks the living area and connects directly to the eight-seater dinette. A forward companionway then leads down to a lavish 18-ft (5.5-m) wide master suite. There is another VIP stateroom in the bows, a twin-berth cabin to starboard and upper and lower crew quarters opposite – all finished in the same high-gloss cherry with polished Italian granite and marble on the surfaces.

The 670 cruises at 37mph and has a top speed of 43mph.

OPPOSITE and RIGHT
Bertram 670.

BERTRAM 670/670E SPORTS FISHING CRUISER

DIMENSIONS

Length overall:	71ft 06in/21.79m
Beam:	18ft 08in/5.69m
Draft:	5ft 07in/1.70m
Deadrise:	20°
Displacement:	108,045lb/49009kg
Engine Options:	Twin MTU 12V 2000 M91 diesels 37.4mph/60km/h Twin CAT C-30 12v diesels 37mph Twin MTU 16v 2000 M91 diesels 43.7mph/70km/h
Design:	Bertram/Ferretti/Zuccon

ABOVE
Engine room of the Bertram 670.

LEFT
Aft cockpit stairs.

FAR LEFT
Helm.

OPPOSITE
LEFT
Bertram 670 at night.

ABOVE RIGHT
The galley.

BELOW CENTRE
Berth with bunk beds.

BELOW RIGHT
Heads.

OPPOSITE
LEFT
Bertram 670.

RIGHT ABOVE
Upper deck of the Bertram 670.

RIGHT BELOW
Stateroom.

LEFT
Saloon with dining area.

OPPOSITE
Bertram 670E.

FAR LEFT
Aft cockpit and pilot house.

LEFT
Aft deck showing stairs.

BELOW
Pilot house.

PAGE 254
LEFT
Bertram 670E.

RIGHT
Spiral staircase to pilot house.

PAGE 255
Pilot house and helm.

COBALT 343

If anyone has their doubts about stepped hulls, then they should take a look at the Cobalt 343. Cobalt certainly has, and in three decades of building classic performance powerboats has never strayed into this territory. Stepped hulls may be faster in a straight line, but what about the skidding, stability and handling problems associated with this race-boat technology whenever the wheel is turned? The truth is, of course, that the cut-and-thrust of racing has led to enormous improvements since efforts during the Second World War to build fast gunboats led to some very sick navy crews whenever the weather cut up rough.

But there was still some convincing to do within the Cobalt hierarchy. So much so that the design team from Neodesha spent eight months examining every stepped hull on the market and documenting its design characteristics and safety features. Then a further ten months was spent simulating potential designs on computer before building a trial hull for its new 343. This stripped-out hull was fitted with twin 500-hp engines and was pushed to the limits at 80mph off Palm Beach. Surprisingly, to some diehards, she refused to skip outside

her track, however hard and fast the turn.

The resulting boat was finally unveiled at the 2003 Fort Lauderdale Boat Show. A 34-footer, with an additional 3-ft swim platform, is arguably Cobalt's best-looking sports boat to date – in the same class as Riva's famed Aquarama. The difference is that, along with a generous cockpit with all the amenities of plush seating, sunbeds, cockpit bar and a clever bimini cover that slides out from the radar arch, there is a cabin with an occasional V-berth that doubles as a dining table, also an enclosed head.

THIS PAGE and OPPOSITE
Cobalt 343.

But it is the boat's performance that has Cobalt's designers in raptures. Sean Callan says that the 343 has an almost eerie ability to correct itself after passing through a large wake or in response to a half-second flip of the trim switch. Niles Schurle is just as amazed at the 343's handling under extreme conditions offshore. 'On occasions when the boat was airborne, the landings were soft and controlled. We certainly don't advocate wave jumping, but it's good to know that she will perform even under the most difficult conditions.'

COBALT 343 SPORTS CRUISER

DIMENSIONS

Length overall:	37ft 02in/11.33m
Beam:	9ft 08in/2.95
Draft:	2ft 04in/0.71m
Deadrise:	24.5°
Displacement:	10,200lb/4627kg
Engine Options:	Twin 496 Mag MPI Bravo 1 375hp Mercruiser inboard/outdrives
	Twin 496 Mag HO Bravo 1XR 425hp Mercruiser inboard/outdrives
	Twin 525HP EFI B1 XR 500hp 1Mercruiser inboard/outdrives
Design:	Cobalt

www.cobaltboats.com

DONZI

A company that has led the way in stepped hull design and technology is Donzi, a name launched by the famous American powerboat racer, Don Aronow, some four decades ago, and which remains at the forefront of American racing today. The company, based at Tallevast, Florida, not only builds a series of race-bred powerboats from 16 to 45ft, all with stepped hulls, but also produces a range of high-performance sports fishing boats which use the same technology.

Ranging in size from 24ft 5in to 38ft 6in, these outboard-powered twin-step centre-console sports fishers are designed and built to be first out to the shoals and the last to leave. The 23ZF is powered by a single 250-hp outboard and has a large clear area forward of the console as well as a built-in fighting seat directly behind. And to ensure that the fish are landed, there is a transom door that opens out onto the engine well to get you closer to the water.

The 29ZF model is available with or without a forward cuddy and shares the same basic hull shape and facilities as the 32ZF, 35ZF and cuddy versions, which can be fitted with twin or triple engine rigs. The top boat in Donzi's sports fishing range is the 38ZF walkaround with a fully-fitted

RIGHT
Donzi 32ZF.

OPPOSITE
Donzi 23ZF.

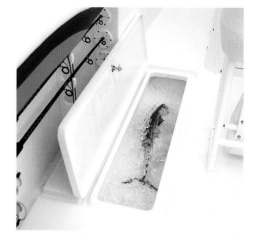

saloon, galley and head/shower for weekend fishing trips across the Gulf Stream to the Bahamas. Like the 35 models, she is powered by triple 250-hp outboards.

DONZI 23ZF CENTRE CONSOLE SPORTS FISHING BOAT
Dimensions

Length overall:	24ft 05in/7.44m
Beam:	8ft 06in/2.59m
Draft:	1ft 06in/0.46m
Deadrise:	22°
Displacement:	3,300lb/1497m
Engine Options:	250-hp outboard
Design:	Donzi

DONZI 29ZF/29ZFC CENTRE CONSOLE SPORTS FISHING BOAT
Dimensions

Length overall:	28ft 07in/8.71m
Beam:	9ft 00in/2.74m
Draft:	1ft 09in/0.53m
Deadrise:	22°
Displacement:	6,000lb/2722m
Engine Options:	250-hp outboard
Design:	Donzi

DONZI 32ZF CENTRE CONSOLE SPORTS FISHING BOAT
Dimensions

Length overall:	28ft 07in/8.71m
Beam:	9ft 00in/2.74m
Draft:	1ft 09in/0.53m
Deadrise:	22°
Displacement:	6,000lb/2722m

OPPOSITE
Donzi 26ZF offshore sports fishing boat.

ABOVE LEFT
Donzi 29ZF Daytona.

TOP
Fishbox.

ABOVE
Cockpit and console.

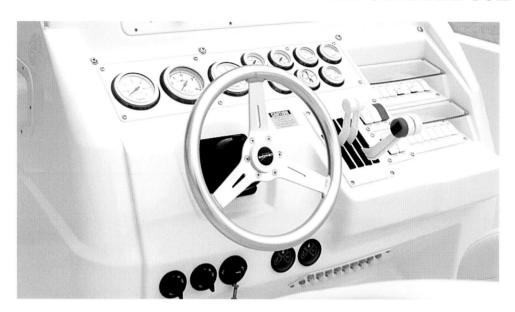

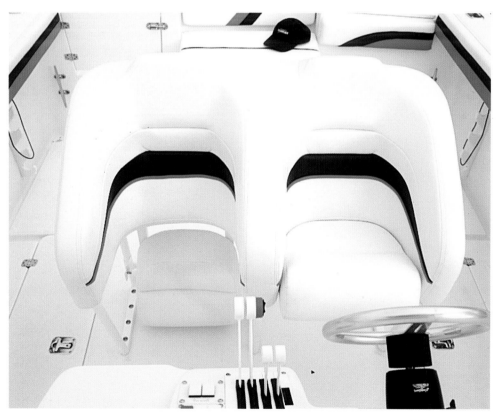

| Engine Options: | Twin 250-hp outboards |
| Design: | Donzi |

DONZI 35ZF/35ZF CUDDY CENTRE CONSOLE SPORTS FISHING BOAT

DIMENSIONS

Length overall:	33ft 04in/10.16m
Beam:	9ft 02in/2.79m
Draft:	2ft 08in/0.81m
Deadrise:	22°
Displacement:	8,000lb/3629kg
Engine Options:	Triple 250-hp outboards
Design:	Donzi

OPPOSITE
Donzi 29ZF.

ABOVE
Cabin in the Donzi 29ZF.

ABOVE LEFT
Helm.

LEFT
Helm seating.

DONZI 38ZF SPORTS FISHING CRUISER

DIMENSIONS

Length overall:	38ft 06in/11.73m
Beam:	10ft 06in/3.20m
Draft:	2ft 00in/0.61m
Deadrise:	22°
Displacement:	12,750lb/5783kg
Engine Options:	Triple 250-hp outboards
Design:	Donzi

In this age of retro design, the Donzi Classic series of runabouts combine the simple appeal of the first Aronow-inspired boats built four decades ago, with today's lightweight composite engineering and latest inboard/outdrives. Available in 16-, 18- and 24ft 6-in sizes, these deep-V hulls have a common deadrise of 24°, a beam of 7ft and give probably the most exhilarating experience on the market.

LEFT
Donzi 32ZF.

OPPOSITE
Donzi 32ZF ProSeries offshore sports fishing boat.

OPPOSITE
Donzi 39ZSC offshore sports cruiser.

ABOVE
The helm of the Donzi 39ZSC.

ABOVE LEFT
Cabin.

FAR LEFT
Aft deck seating.

LEFT
Head.

OPPOSITE
Donzi Z22 offshore sports cruiser.

ABOVE LEFT
Donzi Z32 offshore sports cruiser.

ABOVE
Donzi Z32, with forward cabin, galley and dinette.

LEFT
Donzi Z32 Express fish offshore sports fishing boat.

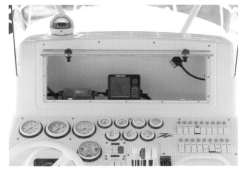

LEFT
Donzi 35ZF offshore sports fishing boat.

TOP
Helm.

ABOVE
Cuddy cabin.

OPPOSITE
ABOVE LEFT
Donzi 16C Classic speedboat.

ABOVE RIGHT
Donzi 18C Classic speedboat.

BELOW
Donzi 22C Classic speedboat.

DONZI 16C CLASSIC RUNABOUT
DIMENSIONS

Length overall:	16ft 05in/5.00m
Beam:	6ft 11in/2.11m
Draft:	1ft 00in/0.30m
Deadrise:	24°
Displacement:	2,500lb/1134kg
Engine Options:	260-hp inboard/ outdrive
Design:	Donzi

DONZI 18C CLASSIC RUNABOUT
DIMENSIONS

Length overall:	18ft 05in/5.61m
Beam:	7ft 00in/2.13m
Draft:	1ft 02in/0.35m
Deadrise:	24°
Displacement:	2,700lb/1225kg
Engine Options:	260-hp inboard/ outdrive
Design:	Donzi

DONZI 22C CLASSIC RUNABOUT

DIMENSIONS

Length overall:	22ft 06in/6.86m
Beam:	7ft 00in/2.13m
Draft:	1ft 04in/0.41m
Deadrise:	24°
Displacement:	3,400lb/1542kg
Engine Options:	425hp inboard/outdrive
Design:	Donzi

The Donzi range of extreme performance speedboats continues with the ZX, ranging from 22 to 45ft. The boats are offered with a wide range of engine options, including a staggered engine-mount arrangement in the larger models to pack even more horsepower into the stern compartment. These boats, which are all race-bred, will rocket up to 80mph plus. For greater enjoyment at more sedate speeds, each carries a large sunbed over the engine hatches and the 28 model is available with a bowrider deck option.

Donzi also produces one sports cruiser model – the 39ZSC. She carries all the attributes of a sun chaser, with a large, open cockpit laid out with a U-shaped settee that doubles as a sunbed, a wet bar and secondary sunbathing areas on the stern and foredeck. Below, owners are rewarded with full standing headroom in

RIGHT
Donzi 22ZX offshore speedboat.

OPPOSITE
Donzi 26ZX offshore speedboat.

the saloon, a V-berth forward and a galley and shower/head facility.

The 38ZR series has enjoyed considerable success on the race circuits, winning the F2 APBA national championship in 2002 and 2003; but for those looking at a speed of 100mph plus, and less of the racing, Donzi produces an adrenalin-charging Poker Run version of the 38 which was voted 'Offshore V-bottom Boat of the Year' in 2003.

DONZI 22ZX PERFORMANCE POWERBOAT

Dimensions

Length overall:	22ft 03in/6.78m
Beam:	7ft 09in/2.36m
Draft:	1ft 05in/0.43m
Deadrise:	22°
Displacement:	3,800lb/1724kg
Engine Options:	350-hp Mercruiser inboard/outdrive
Design:	Donzi

DONZI 26ZX PERFORMANCE POWERBOAT

DIMENSIONS

Length overall:	26ft 05in/8.05m
Beam:	8ft 06in/2.59m
Draft:	2ft 00in/0.61m
Deadrise:	22°
Displacement:	5,800lb/2631kg
Engine Options:	Twin 235-hp Mercruiser inboard/outdrives
Design:	Donzi

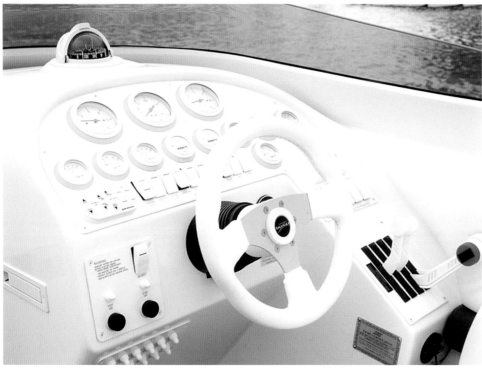

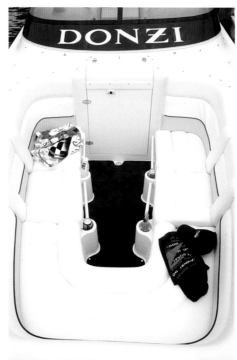

ABOVE LEFT
Forward cabin of the Donzi 26ZX.

ABOVE
Cabin of the Donzi 28ZX offshore speedboat.

FAR LEFT
Donzi 28ZX helm.

LEFT
Bow seating in a Donzi 28ZX.

OPPOSITE
Donzi 28ZX.

DONZI 28ZX PERFORMANCE POWERBOAT

DIMENSIONS

Length overall:	27ft 07in/8.41m
Beam:	8ft 06in/2.59m
Draft:	2ft 00in/0.61m
Deadrise:	22°
Displacement:	6,500lb/2948kg
Engine Options:	Twin 235-hp

Mercruiser inboard/outdrives

Design:	Donzi

DONZI 26ZX/ZXO PERFORMANCE POWERBOAT

DIMENSIONS

Length overall:	26ft 05in/8.05m
Beam:	8ft 06in/2.59m
Draft:	2ft 00in/0.61m
Deadrise:	22°
Displacement:	5,800lb/2631kg
Engine Options:	470-hp Mercruiser inboard/outdrive
Design:	Donzi

DONZI 33ZX PERFORMANCE POWERBOAT

DIMENSIONS

Length overall:	32ft 06in/9.91m
Beam:	9ft 03in/2.82m
Draft:	2ft 03in/0.68m
Deadrise:	22°
Displacement:	9,800lb/4445kg
Engine Options:	Twin

OPPOSITE
Donzi 28ZX Scorpion offshore
speedboat.

LEFT
Forward cabin of the Donzi 28ZX.

FAR LEFT
Cockpit seating in the Donzi 33ZX.

LEFT
Engine cover of the Donzi 33ZX.

BELOW
Cabin in the Donzi 33ZX.

OPPOSITE
Donzi 33 Daytona offshore speedboat.

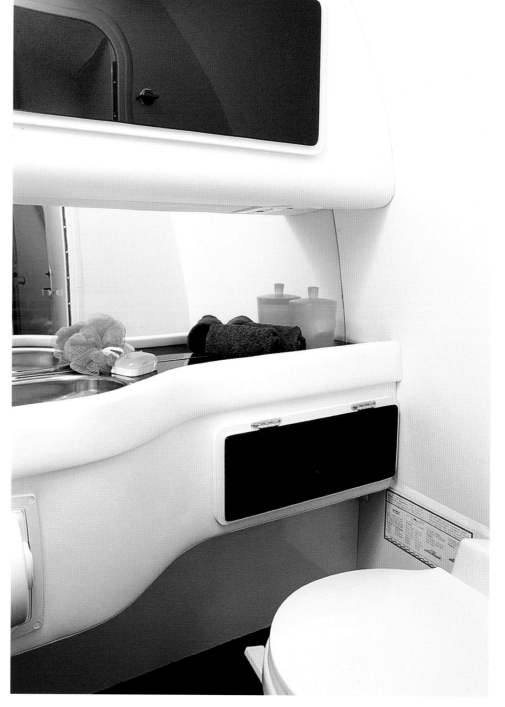

550-hp Mercruiser
inboard/outdrives
80mph/129km/h

Design: Donzi

OPPOSITE
Donzi 38ZX offshore speedboat.

ABOVE
Cabin with V-Berth, galley and head on a Donzi 38ZX.

RIGHT
Donzi 38ZX head.

DONZI 38ZX PERFORMANCE POWERBOAT
DIMENSIONS

Length overall:	37ft 09in/11.51m
Beam:	9ft 03in/2.82m
Draft:	2ft 04in/0.71m
Deadrise:	22°
Displacement:	11,500lb/5216kg
Engine Options:	Twin 550-hp Mercruiser inboard/ outdrives 88mph/149km/h
Design:	Caldwell/Donzi

OPPOSITE
Donzi 38 Daytona offshore speedboat.

ABOVE
Donzi 38ZX head.

ABOVE RIGHT
V-berth and head.

DONZI 39ZFC SPORTS CRUISER

DIMENSIONS

Length overall:	39ft 10in/12.14m
Beam:	12ft 02in/3.71m
Draft:	2ft 05in/0.74m
Deadrise:	22°
Displacement:	16,800lb/7620kg
Engine Options:	940-hp Mercruiser inboard/outdrive
Design:	Donzi

DONZI 45ZX PERFORMANCE POWERBOAT

DIMENSIONS

Length overall:	45ft 00in/13.72m
Beam:	9ft 03in/2.82m
Draft:	2ft 03in/o.68m
Deadrise:	24°
Displacement:	16,000lb/7258kg
Engine Options:	Twin 1,2750-hp Mercruiser inboard/ outdrives 100mph+ (161km/h+)
Design:	Donzi

DONZI 38ZR CUSTOM & RACING
SPORTS BOAT
Dimensions

Length overall:	38ft 01in/11.61m
Beam:	8ft 02in/2.49m
Draft:	1ft 10in/0.56m
Deadrise:	Variable
Displacement:	8,700lb/3946kg
Engine Options:	Twin 1,000-hp inboard/outdrives
Design:	Donzi

www.donzimarine.com

OPPOSITE
Donzi 45ZX offshore speedboat.

ABOVE LEFT
Cabin of the 45ZX.

ABOVE
Cockpit seating.

LEFT
Galley.

CHAPTER SIX
CRUISERS & POWERBOATS

FAIRLINE

Fairline is one of Britain's flagship boat-builders, producing a line of luxurious power cruisers ranging from 34 to 75ft. The company's 40th anniversary in 2003 was celebrated with the launching of the 10,000th Fairline, a special-edition Squadron 65.

The marque was born on the back of a marina developed by Jack Newington in England's Fen Country and a ready market from berth-holders for new boats. The first was a 19-ft fibreglass river cruiser, designed to explore the local Norfolk Broads, but it was not until Jack's son, Sam, took over the helm in 1971, after graduating from Columbia University with an MBA, that the business of building boats was given a clear commercial directive. Sam began by establishing an international network of agents and that

RIGHT and OPPOSITE
Fairline Targa 34.

year, Fairline posted its first profit. The following year saw the launch of the first Phantom, a 32-ft inboard/outdrive model, and the launch of the Fairline 40 in 1974, which continued in production for a record 11 years. By 1979, staff levels had grown from 14 to 140 and turnover was now a buoyant $7.5 million.

The first Targa sports cruiser was delivered in 1985 and its success in U.S. and Mediterranean markets led to a range of open-cockpit boats that range between 34 and 62ft. In 1991, the company launched its Squadron range of super-luxury flybridge cruisers with the Squadron 62, and the Squadron 74, introduced in 2003, now carries the Fairline marque into the league of superyachts.

FAIRLINE TARGA 34 SPORTS CRUISER

The most striking aspect of the five models within Fairline's Targa range of sports cruisers is their enormous accommodation. Richly furnished in American cherry and honey maple, even the 34, which has a top speed of almost

45mph, has separate sleeping cabins and 6ft 6in (1.98m) of headroom in the roomy central saloon. The forward master cabin has a big double bed angled across the boat to maximize space, there is a twin-bedded cabin aft and the settee in the saloon quickly converts into a second double bed when required. There are also the standard heads and washing facilities together with a fully-functional galley.

On deck, a wide helm seat allows for three guests to ride alongside the helmsman, and a second settee arrangement in the aft cockpit has a hide-away table that creates an al fresco dining area in seconds. This also converts into an enormous sunbed with a drinks bar, fridge and sink all within reach. Aft is a large teak-decked bathing platform, with hot and cold shower, which is roomy enough to house a dinghy.

FAIRLINE TARGA 34 SPORTS CRUISER
DIMENSIONS

Length overall:	36ft 03in/11.05m
Beam:	11ft 04in/3.45m
Draft:	3ft 00in/0.91m
Deadrise:	20°
Displacement:	13,440lb/6096kg
Engine Options:	Twin Volvo KAD43/DP 39mph/63km/h Twin Volvo KAD44/DP 43.7mph/70km/h Twin Volvo DAD300/DP 44.8mph/72km/h
Design:	Bernard Olesinski

OPPOSITE
Fairline Targa 34.

LEFT
Saloon and dining table.

The Targa 40 is Fairline's most popular model, with 6ft 4-in headroom below, two sleeping cabins, a luxurious saloon and an integral RIB garage built into the transom, which also acts as a platform for one of two double sunbed areas. This garage is one of the boat's most useful features. The launch and recovery system is child's play and allows for the tender to be stowed without removing the outboard motor.

The interior design is similar to the Targa 34 with the exception of a larger master cabin forward, with its own access to the boat's en suite facilities, which includes a shower. On deck, the extra 6ft of length is maximized with a large fixed dinette and bar and the two sunbed areas on the foredeck and above the garage.

FAIRLINE TARGA 40 SPORTS CRUISER

DIMENSIONS

Length overall:	41ft 06in/12.65m
Beam:	12ft 00in/3.66m
Draft:	3ft 02in/0.96m
Deadrise:	20°
Displacement:	16,800lb/7620kg
Engine Options:	Twin Volvo
	KAD44/DP
	41.4mph/67km/h
	Twin Volvo
	DAD300/DP
	42.5mph/68km/h
Design:	Bernard Olesinski

OPPOSITE
Fairline Targa 40.

ABOVE
Galley.

LEFT
Forward cabin.

FAIRLINE TARGA 43 SPORTS CRUISER

The most striking aspect of Fairline's Targa 43 is the boat's luxuriously appointed interior. This is a boat that successfully blends the accommodation of a fully-enclosed cruiser with the open space of a sports boat. With 6ft 2in (1.88m) of headroom in the saloon and 6ft 6in in the two sleeping cabins, one's first impression is one of space. The large forward master cabin has its own exclusive heads and shower facilities with the same toilet arrangement mirrored on the opposite side of the saloon for guests. The extra space in the saloon is taken up by a large semi-circular settee and table that converts into an occasional double bed. The galley extends the length of the saloon, with a serving area centred next to the companionway steps. The second sleeping cabin aft is fitted with twin beds, its own settee and ample storage space.

On deck, a large wet bar area is sited in the shelter of the screen, opposite the helmsman's seat, and the main cockpit is occupied by a large oval settee and wide folding table that seats eight. The garage aft is big enough to house an RIB or personal watercraft and the teak swim platform can be accessed from both sides. Like the Targa 40, the boat also carries bathing areas above the garage and on the foredeck.

OPPOSITE, BELOW and RIGHT
Fairline Targa 43.

FAIRLINE TARGA 43 SPORTS CRUISER

DIMENSIONS

Length overall:	45ft 01in/13.74m
Beam:	12ft 05in/3.78m
Draft:	3ft 03in/0.99m
Deadrise:	20°
Displacement:	20,720lb/9398kg
Engine Options:	Twin Volvo TAMD 63P 36.8mph/59km/h
	Twin Volvo TAMD 74L 38mph/61km/h
	Twin Caterpillar 3126 38mph/61km/h
	Twin Volvo TAMD 75P 40.2mph/65km/h
Design:	Bernard Olesinski

ABOVE
Galley of the Fairline Targa 43.

RIGHT
Saloon.

FAIRLINE TARGA 52 SPORTS CRUISER

The Targa 52 is big enough to provide owners with several layout options, including an office, children's den or utility room or to maximize the accommodation to cater for six. There is 6ft 6in (1.98m) of headroom in the bedroom areas and 6ft 9in (2.06m) in the saloon, all beautifully appointed with high-gloss American cherry furniture. The forward master stateroom has a king-size bed, en suite shower and toilet facilities and generous hanging locker space. A second shower/heads for other guests is sited on the port side of the boat, just ahead of a fully-fitted galley. The six-seat dinette, opposite, also coverts to a double bed. The central area ahead of the engine room can either be divided into two twin-bedded cabins or the port side can be fitted out to become a den or office with the flexibility of converting the sofa into a single bed. Alternatively, the area can be used as a utility/storage room.

On deck, there is a garage on the port quarter to house an RIB or personal watercraft and two sundeck areas aft, with another on the foredeck. The centre cockpit has an eight-seater settee with wet bar and the forward area has two helm seats and another settee for guests to share the exhilaration of speeding at 40mph plus.

FAIRLINE TARGA 52 SPORTS CRUISER

DIMENSIONS

Length overall:	53ft 03in/16.23m
Beam:	14ft 00in/4.27m
Draft:	3ft 07in/1.09m
Deadrise:	20°
Displacement:	38,976lb/17679kg
Engine Options:	Twin Volvo D12
	EVC615
	38mph/61km/h
	Twin Caterpillar 3196
	40.2mph/65km/h
	Twin Volvo D12
	EVC715
	41.4mph/67km/h
	Twin Caterpillar C12
	41.4mph/67km/h
Design:	Bernard Olesinski

ABOVE
Saloon of the Fairline Targa 52.

LEFT
Galley.

FAIRLINE TARGA 62 SPORTS CRUISER

To blur the differences between an open sports cruiser and a coupé, the Targa 62, due to be launched in late 2004, has a retractable hardtop that folds away at the press of a button. Utilizing a modified version of the well-proven Fairline 62 hull, the interior designers have given owners the option of ordering the boat with a fully-fitted all-enclosed deck saloon with stainless steel-framed doors opening out to the cockpit, or the standard arrangement of a sports cruiser-style cockpit that remains open at the aft end. Whatever the preference, the folding roof gives owners the option of open-air boating whenever the weather obliges.

Below deck, the accommodation includes two lavish full-width staterooms, each with king-size beds with private shower and toilet facilities. The master stateroom is amidships, where motion is less troublesome, and has three vertical portholes port and starboard, hanging wardrobe, dressing table, a sofa and LCD TV and stereo system. The forward guest stateroom, though smaller in size, is equally well appointed though without a settee. The main saloon has an enormous settee and table on the port side and a galley to starboard with a full-height fridge/freezer alongside a single-berth cabin, which can be made into a utility room if preferred. A second single berth, with en-suite facilities, is sited aft opposite the RIB garage to provide pilot or skipper's accommodation.

Top speed is an impressive 40mph plus.

FAIRLINE TARGA 62 SPORTS CRUISER

DIMENSIONS

Length overall:	61ft 11.5in/18.88m
Beam:	15ft 07in/4.75m
Draft:	4ft 06in/1.37m
Deadrise:	20°
Displacement:	51,968lb/23573kg
Engine Options:	Twin Volvo D12 EVC715 34.5mph/55.5km/h Twin Caterpillar 3406E 36.8mph/59km/h Twin MAN D2848 36.8mph/59km/h Twin Caterpillar C18 1015 40.2mph/65km/h Twin MAN D2840 41.4mph/67km/h
Design:	Bernard Olesinski

RIGHT & OPPOSITE
Fairline Targa 62.

OPPOSITE
Fairline Targa 62.

LEFT & FAR LEFT
En suite bathroom in the Fairline Targa 62.

BELOW LEFT
The cockpit, with fully-powered opening roof panel, central dining area and cockpit galley.

BELOW
The master stateroom amidships, with a king-size double bed.

OPPOSITE and FAR LEFT
Fairline Targa 62.

ABOVE
The saloon dining area.

LEFT
Galley.

FAIRLINE PHANTOM 40 FLYBRIDGE CRUISER

The Phantom marque distinguishes Fairline's mid-range of flybridge cruisers that combine the outdoor appeal of the sports cruiser with the interior space of a coupé. The design of the 40, the latest addition to the range, has been influenced by the success of the Phantom 50 and provides a remarkable amount of room for a boat of this size. Designed for extended cruising, this four-berth design with the option of a double settee bed in the saloon, has a master cabin forward, with en suite facilities, and a twin-bedded cabin beneath the saloon which also has its own shower and toilet. The low-level galley is fully equipped and is two steps down from the saloon. The internal pilot/navigator position to starboard carries an array of radar and position-plotting screens in the

OPPOSITE and BELOW
Fairline Phantom 40.

OPPOSITE and THIS PAGE
Views of Fairline Phantom 40, with shot of helm below.

dashboard; directly behind is an eight-seater dinette with a smaller sofa opposite to provide a spacious entertainment area. This opens via a sliding glass door to the aft cockpit, sheltered by the boat's extending flybridge, which has a central steering position, large seating area and optional wet bar.

Twin Caterpillar diesels give the boat a top speed of 35mph.

FAIRLINE PHANTOM 40 FLYBRIDGE CRUISER

DIMENSIONS

Length overall:	41ft 01in/12.52m
Beam:	13ft 00in/3.96m
Draft:	3ft 02in/0.96m
Deadrise:	20°
Displacement:	25,536lb/11583kg
Engine Options:	Twin Volvo TAMD 63P 33.4mph/54km/h
	Twin Caterpillar 3126 35.7mph/57km/h
Design:	Bernard Olesinski

OPPOSITE
Fairline Phantom 40 saloon.

ABOVE LEFT
Extendable dining table in the saloon.

ABOVE
Starboard guest cabin.

LEFT
Forward master cabin with king-size bed.

FAIRLINE PHANTOM 43 FLYBRIDGE CRUISER

The Phantom 43 has the most balanced lines in its class. Similar in concept to Fairline's 40, with the extra length providing additional area to the aft cockpit and flybridge, it boasts a large semi-circular settee, table and wet bar. The second twin-bedded cabin also has some welcome extra space and there is the addition of a utility locker large enough to take an optional washing machine.

This boat has four diesel-engine options, which provide a maximum speed range of between 32 and 38mph.

FAIRLINE PHANTOM 43 FLYBRIDGE CRUISER

DIMENSIONS

Length overall:	44ft 07in/13.59m
Beam:	13ft 06in/4.11m
Draft:	3ft 08in/1.12m
Deadrise:	20°
Displacement:	26,880lb/12193kg
Engine Options:	Twin Volvo TAMD 63P 32.2mph/52km/h
	Twin Caterpillar 3126 34.5mph/55.5km/h
	Twin Volvo TAMD 74L 35.6mph/57km/h
	Twin Volvo TAMD 75P 38mph/61km/h
Design:	Bernard Olesinski

OPPOSITE and RIGHT
Fairline Phantom 43.

FAIRLINE PHANTOM 46 FLYBRIDGE CRUISER

The Phantom 46 offers six berths split into three cabins and the option of an extra single bed for a crew member in self-contained accommodation accessed through the cockpit floor. The large saloon benefits from the huge expanse of tinted glass, including split side windows, and features a six-seater settee to starboard and a two-seater to port. The helm position has all the navigation equipment necessary and a traditional drop-down chart table for those of us still preferring paper to electronic charts.

The extensive galley has been built for entertaining and is positioned on the port side, one step away from the saloon. The main accommodation is sited on one level forward, with the master bedroom in the bows and a twin-bedded guest cabin to

BELOW and OPPOSITE
Fairline Phantom 46.

starboard, both of which have full en suite facilities; there is a third smaller cabin fitted out with two bunk beds opposite.

The flybridge has seating for four in line with the helmsman, a wet bar and a large semi-circular settee which converts easily into a sunbed.

FAIRLINE PHANTOM 46 FLYBRIDGE CRUISER

DIMENSIONS

Length overall:	47ft 10in/14.58m
Beam:	14ft 02in/4.32m
Draft:	3ft 08in/1.12m
Deadrise:	20°
Displacement:	32,032lb/14530kg
Engine Options:	Twin Volvo TAMD 74L 34.5mph/55.5km/h Twin Caterpillar 3126B 34.5mph/55.5km/h Twin Volvo TAMD 75P 35.7mph/57km/h
Design:	Bernard Olesinski

FAIRLINE PHANTOM 50 FLYBRIDGE CRUISER

The Phantom 50 has space in abundance for six to seven people, with a lower-level plush master stateroom forward, a double-bedded guest cabin, each with their own en suite facilities, and a third twin-bedded cabin on the port side. A separate single

RIGHT and OPPOSITE
Fairline Phantom 46.

berth with a washbasin is sited in the stern for a skipper or crew member.

The large saloon opens up via a sliding glass doorway to a spacious cockpit to provide an enormous entertaining area with a galley set forward, opposite the interior helm position, to service guests and the six-place dining table.

Fitted with twin Volvo Penta 12-cylinder diesels, the 50 has a top speed close to 40mph.

FAIRLINE PHANTOM 50 FLYBRIDGE CRUISER

DIMENSIONS

Length overall:	51ft 11in/15.82m
Beam:	14ft 10in/4.52m
Draft:	4ft 00in/1.22m
Deadrise:	20°
Displacement:	38,080lb/17273kg
Engine Options:	Twin Volvo D12 EVC 615 35.6mph/57km/h
	Twin Volvo D12 EVC 675 39.1mph/63km/h
Design:	Bernard Olesinski

FAIRLINE SQUADRON 55 FLYBRIDGE MOTOR YACHT

Fairline's Squadron range marks the company's entry to the superyacht class, where the term luxury verges on understatement and cost, if mentioned, is measured in terms of opulence. The 55, Fairline's entry-level motor yacht, has a proven track record with some 150 models now basking in the Florida and Mediterranean sun. These are boats as much for socializing as for cruising long

distances. The vast saloon is split into two distinct seating areas, serviced by a central galley/bar set at a lower level, which leads to a utility room fitted out with a washer/dryer, freezer and ironing board. There is also a stairway providing direct access to the forward flybridge area to complement the open stairs from the cockpit.

Amid all this exotic hand-matched lacquered wood and leather-bound furnishings is an opulent steering position and navigation station, while at a lower level forward, the accommodation is divided between a large owner's stateroom with private en suite facilities forward and two twin-bedded cabins, which share the second shower and

toilet suite. A further self-contained twin-bedded cabin with toilet and washing facilities is sited in the stern as quarters for crew.

The flybridge has a large settee which doubles as a sunbed, a bimini cover, wet bar and grill, and the foredeck provides another self-contained place to socialize with sunbeds and a central drinks stowage area.

Powered by twin Volvo 12-cylinder diesels, they can propel this 20 tons of luxury at speeds of up to 39mph.

OPPOSITE and ABOVE
Fairline Squadron 55.

FAIRLINE SQUADRON 55 FLYBRIDGE
MOTOR YACHT
DIMENSIONS

Length overall:	56ft 11in/17.35m
Beam:	15ft 03in/4.65m
Draft:	3ft 08in/1.12m
Deadrise:	20°
Displacement:	44,800lb/20321kg
Engine Options:	Twin Volvo D12 EVC 615 34.5mph/55.5km/h Twin Volvo D12 EVC 675 36.8mph/59km/h Twin Caterpillar C12 39mph/63km/h Twin Volvo D12 EVC 715 39.1mph/63km/h
Design:	Bernard Olesinski

OPPOSITE
Fairline Squadron 55.

ABOVE
Fairline Squadron 55 forward
stateroom.

RIGHT
Saloon with galley and main helm.

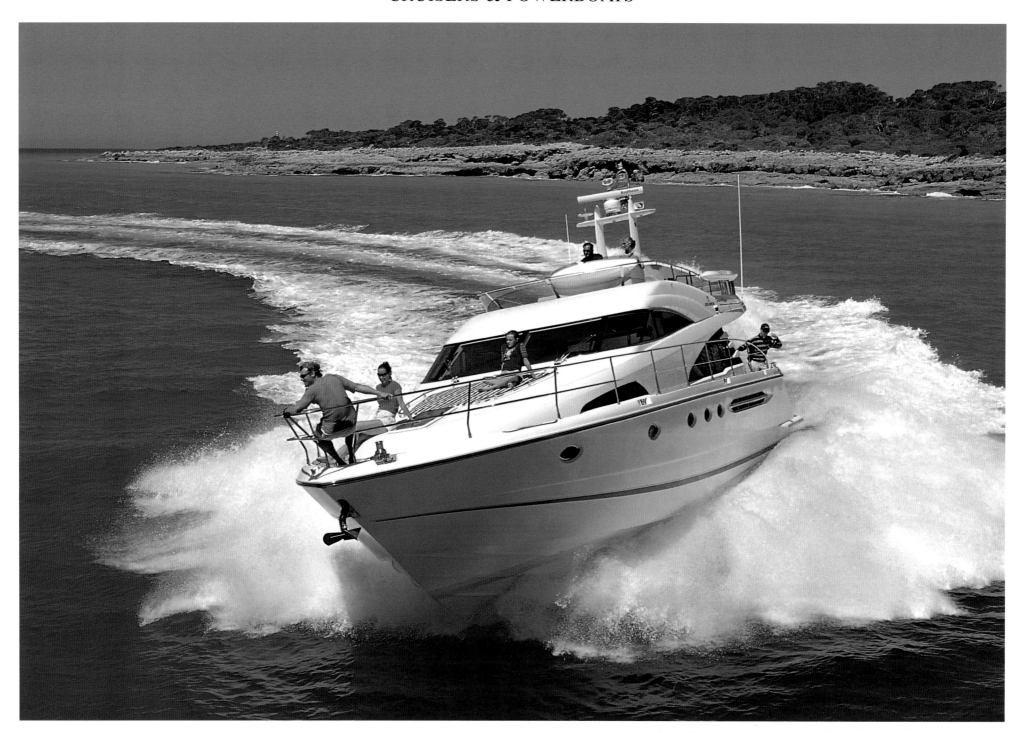

FAIRLINE SQUADRON 58 FLYBRIDGE MOTOR YACHT

The Squadron 58 shares the same opulence and split-level saloon arrangement and forward accommodation as her 55 sister. However, the extra 3ft of length provides an extra-large flybridge divided by a central mast into two distinct areas, a larger stern cockpit and the option of various mid-cabin configurations. These can be a twin-berth cabin for crew or guests, a single berth with en suite facilities or a single berth devoted to domestic appliances.

FAIRLINE SQUADRON 58 FLYBRIDGE MOTOR YACHT

DIMENSIONS

Length overall:	58ft 10in/17.93m
Beam:	16ft 00in/4.88m
Draft:	4ft 07in/1.40m
Deadrise:	20°
Displacement:	49,280lb/22353kg
Engine Options:	Twin Volvo D12 EVC 675 34.5mph/55.5km/h Twin Caterpillar C12 35.6mph/57km/h Twin Volvo D12 EVC 715 35.6mph/57km/h Twin Caterpillar 3406E 39.1mph/63km/h
Design:	Bernard Olesinski

OPPOSITE and RIGHT
Fairline Squadron 58.

ABOVE
Fairline Squadron 58 flybridge seating and bimini top.

LEFT
Galley.

FAR LEFT
Bow.

OPPOSITE
Master stateroom.

FAIRLINE SQUADRON 66 FLYBRIDGE MOTOR YACHT

This, the newest within Fairline's flagship range, is due to be launched in 2004 and draws heavily on the innovative features and design concepts pioneered by the Squadron 74. This 66 is in fact closer to 70ft and is available with several layout options. These centre around an owner's suite amidships, lit by striking portrait portholes with a large settee, en suite toilet, bidet and shower facilities, and a walk-in closet. The principal guest cabin is sited in the bow and also enjoys private en suite facilities. A third toilet and shower is shared between a twin-bedded cabin on the port side and one with twin bunks on the opposite side of the central companionway, which owners have the option of turning into an office or laundry room. There is a further twin-bedded cabin, again with full standing headroom, sited beneath the aft deck, which can be used for guests or as crew quarters and which is accessed via the transom.

The flybridge is divided into three sections, with two large settees providing seating and eating areas around the helm position, and an aft viewing deck to watch the sun set.

The large aft cockpit provides access to the garage housing a personal watercraft and to the teak-laid swimming platform.

FAIRLINE SQUADRON 66 FLYBRIDGE MOTOR YACHT

DIMENSIONS

Length overall:	69ft 06in/21.18m
Beam:	17ft 09in/5.41m
Draft:	4ft 08in/1.42m
Deadrise:	20°
Displacement:	77,056lb/34953kg
Engine Options:	Twin MAN D2840
	Twin Caterpillar 3412E
	Twin MAN D2842
	Twin Caterpillar C30
Design:	Bernard Olesinski

FAIRLINE SQUADRON 74 FLYBRIDGE MOTOR YACHT

There is no standard Squadron 74, and so far the interior of each of these $3-million boats reflects their owners' distinct taste and preference for layout and furnishings. With structural bulkheads the only constraint, these build projects are as exciting for the owner as they are challenging to the interior designer. At this price, it is obvious that nothing but the finest materials, from hand-

The flybridge is an entertainment area in its own right, divided into three distinct areas with a large dining table, mini galley and sunbathing area aft.

With twin MTU 2000-hp diesels, this pampered vessel has a displacement of more than 40 tons and a top speed of 37mph.

FAIRLINE SQUADRON 74 FLYBRIDGE MOTOR YACHT
DIMENSIONS

Length overall:	74ft 05in/22.68m
Beam:	18ft 08in/5.69m
Draft:	5ft 03in/1.60m
Deadrise:	20°
Displacement:	90,944lb/41252kg
Engine Options:	Twin Caterpillar 3412E 35.6mph/57km/h Twin MAN D2842 36.8mph/59km/h Twin MTU 12V 2000 36.8mph/59km/h
Design:	Bernard Olesinski

www. fairline.com

polished marble work surfaces, best Connelly hides and hand-matched and lacquered exotic woods, are incorporated into the design.

There is a choice of three or four cabin layouts, and multiple options for seating around the banqueting table. A relaxed breakfast bar and stools may be preferred to

a settee and then there is the question of how many crew, which has its own separate quarters aft, there is to be catered for. There is the same freedom of choice when it comes to toys. The concealed transom garage can accommodate an 11-ft (3-m) RIB or a flybridge crane to store personal watercraft on the top deck may be preferred.

Below, the master suite amidships has a private dressing room as well as a king-size double bed, an en suite bathroom with a whirlpool bath, and a security safe to keep jewels under lock and key. The forward guest cabin is no less opulent, with its own private en suite facilities which are replicated in a third twin-bedded cabin.

OPPOSITE and ABOVE
Fairline Squadron 74.

FORMULA/THUNDERBIRD

The Formula/Thunderbird story is one that centres around three of America's powerboat pioneers. Formula was the first of Don Aronow's boat companies, which he formed in 1962 in Miami, Florida. The original 233 deep-V hull design was built at his direction and later earned notable victories on the national offshore racing circuit. While many of today's Formulas have matured well beyond the speed-only image he generated, the prestige originating from past racing victories is still evident in the performance-orientated range today.

Thunderbird was founded by Woodie Woodson in 1956 in Miami, where he produced cathedral hull boats. To prove their stability and staying power, an 18-ft Thunderbird made the first successful stern-drive crossing from Miami to Nassau in 1959

In 1961 Thunderbird was acquired by Alliance Machine and Foundry, which followed this by purchasing Formula in 1964. Both Formula and Thunderbird models were then produced in north

BELOW
Formula 27PC sports cruiser.

OPPOSITE
ABOVE
Formula 260 bowrider.

BELOW
Formula 260 sun sport.

Miami. Fuqua Industries, an Atlanta-based conglomerate, acquired the company in 1969.

In 1958 Vic Porter, the third pioneer in this story, began building and selling small fibreglass runabouts, enjoying success largely in the mid-west and north-east. This boat line was one of the first to utilize fibreglass technology, and was marketed under the Duo brand name. Starcraft, a larger regional boat manufacturer, purchased Duo in 1966 and for a time Vic Porter stayed on as president.

In 1970 Porter, and five business associates, founded the Signa Corporation to build a new line of cathedral hull boats

manufactured in Decatur and marketed throughout the mid-west and east. Their success attracted the attention of Fuqua Industries, which bought the company in 1973 and installed Porter as president of its entire small-boat division.

Three years later, Porter purchased Thunderbird and Formula from Fuqua and a second generation of Porters joined the management team as they completed their college studies. The cathedral hull design was discontinued in 1979, when the company centred production on the offshore deep-V hull configuration of the Formula models then manufactured in California. In 1988, the Thunderbird

production line was moved from south Florida to join Formula in a state-of-the-art facility in Decatur, Indiana.

The company continues as a family-run business under the Thunderbird brand name with Porter's four sons and a daughter now managing the day-to-day operations.

The year 2006 will mark Thunderbird's 50th anniversary in the production of fibreglass powerboats. The company now concentrates on producing a series of performance-orientated powerboats, including the 70mph + FAS3TECH speedboats, the super and sun sport fast power cruisers, and their luxurious performance cruiser models. All carry a five-year limited warranty.

The PC range of luxury sports cruisers starts with a 28-ft model and continues up to a 43-footer. Their open cockpits are designed for entertaining and enjoying the sun, with dinette seating that folds down to form sunbeds; there are wet bars and swimming platforms with fresh-water shower facilities. All have walk-through wraparound windshields, which open up to the forward sun deck.

Below, these boats are fitted out to a high level. The 27PC sleeps four with a V-berth dinette in the bows and a second double bed under the cockpit. She is equipped with a fully-fitted galley with microwave oven, a spacious toilet and shower facility, and a DVD/CD TV suite to keep the children amused.

The 31PC sleeps six and utilizes the extra length to provide a queen-size bed in

the bow and a six-seater fold-down dinette opposite the galley. Like the 27, a third double bed is fitted under the cockpit. On the 34 and 37PC, there is sufficient headroom beneath the cockpit for it to become the dining area with a fold-down dinette, which opens up the central saloon for entertainment with a long settee set opposite the galley.

On the 40 and 41PC models, the bow area is devoted to a private master cabin and the galley and entertainment centre is positioned opposite a settee and table. This

is open to a second entertaining area beneath the cockpit, with a large U-shaped dinette that converts to make a second double berth.

The 50-ft top-of-the-range Formula 47 yacht model has a large fixed canopy above the forward cockpit area to provide protection from the sun and elements, and like the 37, 40 and 41 has sufficient space on the aft swim platform to carry a small tender or jet ski. Below decks, this boat has the space to provide a master suite forward, a central entertaining area

amidships and to move the galley to a less prominent position beneath the cockpit floor, along with a second head and separate L-shaped settee.

ABOVE
Formula 280 bowrider.

OPPOSITE
Formula 280 sun sport.

FORMULA 27PC SPORTS CRUISER

DIMENSIONS

Length overall:	28ft 03in/8.61m
Beam:	9ft 07in/2.92m
Draft:	3ft 05in/1.04m
Deadrise:	18°
Displacement:	9,500lb/4309kg
Engine Options:	Twin Mercruiser T-50 MPI Bravo III inboard/outdrives 48mph/77km/h Twin Volvo T 5.7 GXI DP inboard/outdrives 52mph/84km/h Twin Mercruiser T-350 Mag MPI Horizon Bravo III inboard/outdrives 53mph/85km/h
Design:	Thunderbird

Formula's bowrider, sun sport and super sport models range from 26 to 40ft and are more performance-orientated than the PC models, offering top speeds in the 50–60-mph range. They do share very similar cockpit arrangements, however, with U-shaped dinettes that fold down to make sunbeds, with a wet bar, easy access to the swim platform and fresh-water shower facilities.

Below decks, the space in these narrower hulls is limited in the smaller models, up to the 330, to a V-berth, galley and head, and it is only in the 37- and 40-ft super sport models that a second double berth under the cockpit and a spacious galley and head/shower room is provided.

FORMULA 260 BOWRIDER/260 SUN SPORT

DIMENSIONS

Length overall:	26ft 00in/7.92m
Beam:	8ft 06in/2.59m
Draft:	2ft 08in/0.81m
Deadrise:	22°
Displacement:	5,250/5,450lb (2381/2472kg)
Engine Options:	Twin Mercruiser T-350 Mag MPI Bravo III inboard/outdrives 46mph/74km/h Twin Volvo T 8.1 GXi DP inboard/outdrives 54mph/87km/h
Design:	Thunderbird

FORMULA 280 BOWRIDER/280 SUN SPORT

DIMENSIONS

Length overall:	28ft 00in/8.53m
Beam:	9ft 02in/2.79m
Draft:	3ft 00in/0.91m
Deadrise:	21°
Displacement:	6,100/6,300lb (2767/2858kg)
Engine Options:	Twin Mercruiser 496 Mag Bravo III inboard/outdrives 50mph/80km/h Twin Volvo T 5.7 GXi DP inboard/outdrives 58mph/93km/h
Design:	Thunderbird

Formula's latest FAS3TECH sports boats carry the range full circle back to its race-boat roots when Don Aronow was at the helm. Ranging in size from 27 to 38ft, these stepped hull designs offer exhilarating performances with speeds between 65 and 75mph, depending on engine choice. At these white-knuckle speeds, seat padding and the close proximity of grab rails take on far greater importance than sunbeds, wet bars and certainly cabin facilities, which are limited by the narrow hull and low headroom.

FORMULA 271 FAS3TECH SPORTS CRUISER

DIMENSIONS

Length overall:	29ft 02in/8.89m
Beam:	8ft 03in/2.51m
Draft:	2ft 10in/0.86m
Deadrise:	24°
Displacement:	5,685lb/2579kg
Engine Options:	Twin Mercruiser 496 Mag Bravo I inboard/outdrives 60mph/96.5km/h Twin Mercruiser 575 SCi Bravo I XR inboard/outdrives 74mph/119km/h
Design:	Thunderbird

FORMULA 292 FAS3TECH SPORTS CRUISER

DIMENSIONS

Length overall:	29ft 02in/8.89m
Beam:	8ft 03in/2.51
Draft:	2ft 09in/0.84m
Deadrise:	24°
Displacement:	7,000lb/3175kg
Engine Options:	Twin Mercruiser T-5.0 MPI Bravo III inboard/outdrives 62mph/100km/h Twin Mercruiser T-377 Scorpion Bravo I inboard/outdrives 74mph/119km/h
Design:	Thunderbird

FORMULA 330 SUN SPORT CRUISER

DIMENSIONS

Length overall:	33ft 00in/10.06m
Beam:	10ft 02in/3.10m
Draft:	2ft 09in/0.84m
Deadrise:	20°
Displacement:	9,700lb/4400kg
Engine Options:	Twin Mercruiser T-350 Mag MPI Bravo III 53mph/85km/h Twin Volvo T 8.1 Gi DP 58mph/98km/h
Design:	Thunderbird

OPPOSITE
Formula 271 FAS3Tech performance boat.

PAGE 330
Formula 292 FAS3Tech.

PAGE 331
Formula 330 sun sport.

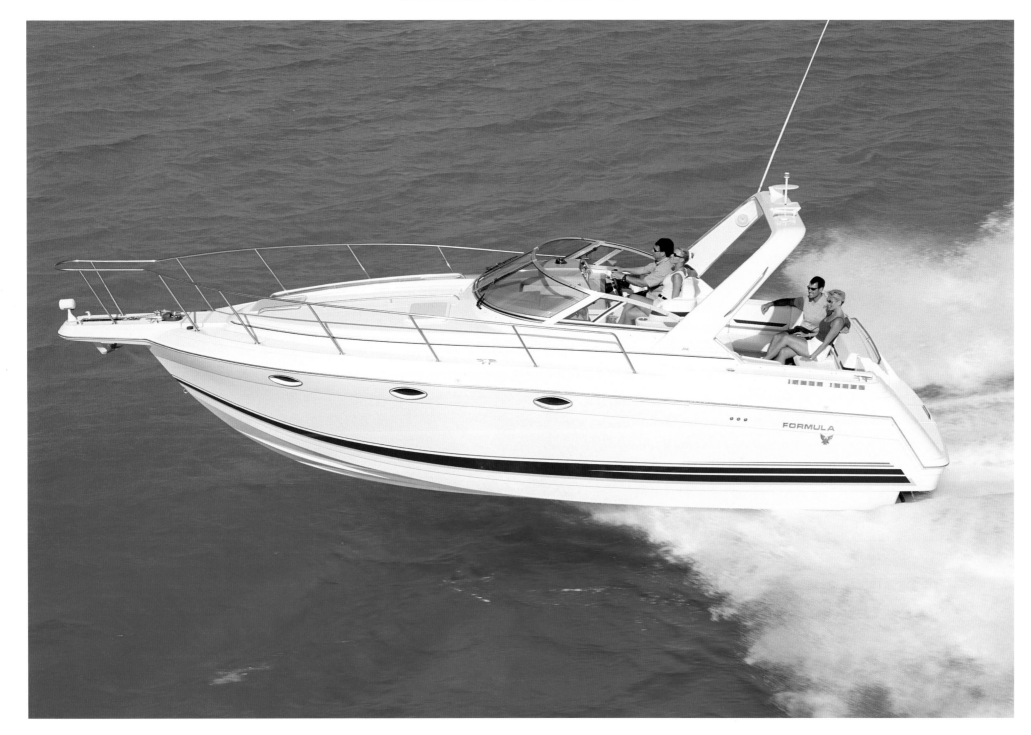

Engine Options: Twin Mercruiser T-496 Mag Bravo I inboard/outdrives 66mph/106km/h
Twin Mercruiser T-HP 525 ITS EFI Bravo IXR inboard/outdrives 78mph/125.5km/h

Design: Thunderbird

FORMULA 34PC SPORTS CRUISER
DIMENSIONS

Length overall:	35ft 07in/10.84m
Beam:	11ft 06in/3.50m
Draft:	3ft 00in/0.91m
Deadrise:	18°
Displacement:	13,916lb/6312kg
Engine Options:	Twin Mercruiser T-350 Mag MPI Horizon Bravo III 37mph/59km/h Twin Volvo T 8.1 Gi DP 48mph/77km/h
Design:	Thunderbird

FORMULA 31PC SPORTS CRUISER
DIMENSIONS

Length overall:	34ft 00in/10.36m
Beam:	11ft 00in/3.35m
Draft:	3ft 05in/1.04m
Deadrise:	19°
Displacement:	11,730lb/5321kg
Engine Options:	Twin Mercruiser T-350 Mag MPI Horizon Bravo III 42mph/67.5km/h Twin Volvo T 8.1 Gi DP 51mph/82km/h
Design:	Thunderbird

FORMULA 353 FAS3TECH SPORTS CRUISER
DIMENSIONS

Length overall:	35ft 03in/10.74m
Beam:	8ft 03in/2.51m
Draft:	3ft 00in/0.91m
Deadrise:	24°
Displacement:	8,575lb/3890kg

OPPOSITE
Formula 31PC sports cruiser.

ABOVE
Formula 353 FAS3Tech performance boat.

FORMULA 370 SUPER SPORT

CRUISER

DIMENSIONS

Length overall:	37ft 00in/11.28m
Beam:	10ft 06in/3.20m
Draft:	3ft 00in/0.91m
Deadrise:	21°
Displacement:	14,400lb/6532kg
Engine Options:	Twin Mercruiser T-496 Mag Bravo III Xi 51mph/82km/h Twin Volvo T 8.1

GXi DP
55mph/88.5km/h

Design: Thunderbird

FORMULA 382 FAS3TECH SPORTS

CRUISER

DIMENSIONS

Length overall:	38ft 02in/11.63m
Beam:	8ft 03in/2.51m
Draft:	2ft 09in/0.84m
Deadrise:	24°
Displacement:	10,450lb/4740kg

Engine Options:	Twin Mercruiser T-496 Mag HD Bravo IX inboard/outdrives 68mph/109km/h Twin Mercruiser T-HP 525 ITS SCI Bravo IXR inboard/outdrives 77mph/124km/h
Design:	Thunderbird

OPPOSITE
Formula 34PC sports cruiser.

ABOVE
Formula 370 super sport.

CRUISERS & POWERBOATS

FORMULA 37PC SPORTS CRUISER

DIMENSIONS

Length overall: 38ft 05in/11.71m
Beam: 12ft 00in/3.66m
Draft: 2ft 06in/0.76m
Deadrise: 18°
Displacement: 16,500lb/7484kg
Engine Options: Twin Mercruiser T-496 Mag Horizon Bravo III X 47mph/76km/h
Twin Volvo T 8.1 Gi DP 49mph/79km/h
Twin Yanmar T-6LY2A-STP diesels 40mph/64km/h
Design: Thunderbird

FORMULA 400 SUPER SPORTS CRUISER

DIMENSIONS

Length overall: 40ft 00in/12.19m
Beam: 11ft 00in/3.35m
Draft: 3ft 00in/0.91m
Deadrise: 22°
Displacement: 15,500lb/7031kg
Engine Options: Twin Mercruiser T-496 Mag Bravo III Xi 53mph/85km/h
Twin Mercruiser T-HP 500.EFI Bravo III Xi 58mph/93km/h
Design: Thunderbird

FORMULA 40PC SPORTS CRUISER

DIMENSIONS

Length overall: 42ft 07in/12.98m
Beam: 12ft 08in/3.86m
Draft: 2ft 11in/0.89m
Deadrise: 18°
Displacement: 18,510lb/8396kg
Engine Options: Twin Mercruiser T8.1S HO 33mph/53km/h
Twin Yanmar T-6LY2A-STP 36mph/58km/h
Design: Thunderbird

BELOW
Formula 382 FAS3Tech performance boat.

OPPOSITE
Formula 37PC sports cruiser.

336

FORMULA 41PC SPORTS CRUISER

DIMENSIONS

Length overall:	43ft 01in/13.13m
Beam:	13ft 06in/4.11m
Draft:	2ft 09in/0.84m
Deadrise:	18°
Displacement:	21,015lb/9532kg
Engine Options:	Twin Volvo T-TAMD 75P EDC T8.1S HO 38mph/61km/h Twin Cummins T-diesel 480 Diamond 38mph/61km/h
Design:	Thunderbird

OPPOSITE
Formula 400 super sports.

ABOVE LEFT and ABOVE
Formula 40PC sports cruiser.

LEFT
Formula 40PC main cabin.

FORMULA 47 YACHT SPORTS CRUISER

DIMENSIONS

Length overall:	50ft 00in/15.24m
Beam:	14ft 00in/4.27m
Draft:	3ft 01in/0.94m
Deadrise:	18°
Displacement:	32,650lb/14810kg
Engine Options:	Twin Volvo T-TAMD
	75P EDC T8.1S HO
	31mph/50km/h
	Twin Cummins 480
	31mph/50km/h
Design:	Thunderbird

FORMULA 47PC SPORTS CRUISER

DIMENSIONS

Length overall:	50ft 00in/15.24m
Beam:	14ft 00in/4.27m
Draft:	3ft 01in/0.94m
Deadrise:	18°
Displacement:	32,650lb/14810kg
Engine Options:	Twin Volvo T-TAMD
	75P EDC T8.1S HO
	31mph/50km/h
	Twin Cummins 480
	31mph/50km/h
Design:	Thunderbird

www.formulaboats.com

ABOVE
Formula 41PC sports cruiser.

OPPOSITE
Formula 47 yacht sports cruiser.

MAGNUM MARINE

Magnum has a special place in American powerboat history. Founded by the legendary Don Aronow, who used it as a vehicle to build offshore race boats, it was Filippo Theodoli who developed the market for fast luxury offshore boats based on racing hulls. After purchasing the company from Aronow in 1976, he launched the Magnum 53 a year later as the first open high-performance powerboat, combining the characteristics of a race boat with the comforts and accommodation of a yacht. She had a full 7ft (2.13m) of headroom across two double cabins, each with their own head, a saloon, galley and separate crew cabin. What made it so attractive, however, was the fact that here was a boat that an owner could command himself without the need of a professional crew. It was an immediate success, particularly in Europe, where owners appreciated the advantages of being able to reach the Balearic Islands, Sardinia or Corsica from the Côte d'Azur within a few hours – in perfect comfort.

This was followed by the Magnum 38, 40 and 45 models, all built with much the same philosophy.

Their impact was extraordinary. Within very few years, Magnum copies were everywhere, especially in Italy, where Carlo Riva built them under licence as the Riva Superamerica. Suddenly, the islands of Corsica and Sardinia, particularly the Agha Khan's exclusive

OPPOSITE & BELOW LEFT
Magnum 50 offshore powerboat.

Costa Smeralda development, became the places for the jet set to be seen – invariably in Theodoli- inspired Magnums or Rivas.

As the market developed, Magnum turned to the famous Italian car stylist, Pininfarina, to work its magic on the deck and interiors of its boats, work that is continued today by David Chipperfield, Andrew Winch, Hermes and Roberto Cavalli, customizers who continue to turn new Magnum owners' dreams into reality.

Today, the Magnum models range from 27 to 90ft, with the 50, 60 and 80 the most popular. The Magnum 50 is better known as 'The Beast', for its acceleration and brute power. Fitted with twin 1,400-hp diesels, this narrow deep-V hull has an impressive top speed of 72mph and capability to sustain a very high average, even in rough conditions.

Below decks, the bespoke interior is divided between a master stateroom with a queen-sized bed and private en suite facilities, a large saloon with galley, and a separate crew cabin.

MAGNUM 50 SPORTS CRUISER

DIMENSIONS

Length overall:	49ft 09in/15.16m
Beam:	13ft 08in/4.16m
Draft:	3ft 07in/1.09m
Deadrise:	20°
Displacement:	50,000lb/22680kg

Engine Options: Twin Caterpiller or MTU 1,400-hp diesels 72mph/116km/h

The Magnum 60 is another high-performance boat powered by twin 1,800-hp diesels to give a 70-mph top speed. The extra 10ft provides the interior space for a designer to include two en suite staterooms, if required, together with a large saloon and separate crew cabin.

MAGNUM 60 SPORTS CRUISER

DIMENSIONS

Length overall:	60ft 00in/18.29m
Beam:	15ft 09in/4.80m
Draft:	3ft 04in/1.02m
Deadrise:	20°
Engine Options:	Twin MTU 1,800hp diesels 70mph/113km/h
Design:	Pininfarina

RIGHT
Helm of the Magnum 60 offshore powerboat.

OPPOSITE
Magnum 60.

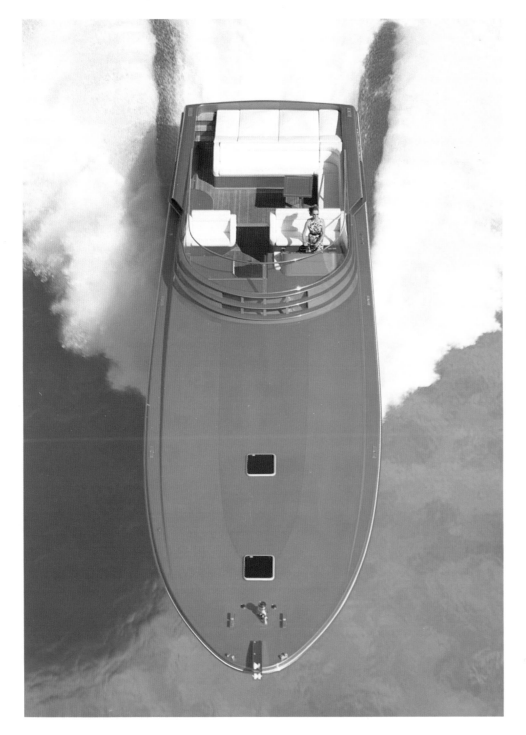

OPPOSITE
LEFT
Magnum 60 offshore powerboat.

OPPOSITE RIGHT, ABOVE and
BELOW
Saloon and forward stateroom.

THIS PAGE
Magnum 60 saloon, stateroom, galley
and second stateroom.

The 80-ft Pininfarina-designed Magnum is the latest in this line of high-performance power cruisers. Fitted with twin 1,800-hp diesels driving Arneson surface props, she has a top speed of 50mph, but has the capacity to accept much larger power units up to 3,650hp to increase this to 70mph plus. There is sufficient volume below decks for an interior designer to work their magic to include two VIP suites, two smaller double cabins, a large saloon and galley, and separate crew cabin.

MAGNUM 80 SPORTS CRUISER
DIMENSIONS

Length overall:	80ft 00in/24.38m
Beam:	20ft 00in/6.10m
Draft:	4ft 04in/1.32m
Deadrise:	20°
Displacement:	50,000lb/22680kg
Engine Options:	Twin MTU 3,650 diesels 60mph/96.5km/h
Design:	Pininfarina

www.magnummarine.com

OPPOSITE and RIGHT
Magnum 80 offshore powerboat.

SEALINE INTERNATIONAL
For three decades, the British builder, Sealine International, has been developing something quite unique – a range of luxury power cruisers between 23 and 60ft, where no two boats are exactly alike, for each one is designed to meet the individual needs of its buyer. What each model does have in common are advanced FRP hull and deck mouldings and a level of craftsmanship that is not possible with most mass-production techniques. Among the many innovations built into the range are electrically-operated sunroofs and bimini covers and an extending aft deck that, at the push of a button, slides backwards over the swim platform on the latest coupé and flybridge models. This clever option opens up 3ft of extra cockpit space for dining, relaxing and entertaining at anchor.

SEALINE S38 SPORTS CRUISER
This new offshore sports cruiser combines 35-knot open water performance with an incredible amount of space, thanks to some clever ergonomic design. The sunbed and cockpit table, for instance, both slide away into unobtrusive storage positions whenever a clear cockpit is required. There is also a wet bar and the option of a built-in fridge. The two-part canopy, with its two-stage bimini, also folds away with equal ease, and the full-width bathing platform provides easy access to the pontoon or the water. There is also a concealed swim ladder, a transom shower and provision for mounting a passerelle.

Below deck, the standard design offers

seven berths in two cabins plus the saloon.
There are also separate toilet and shower
compartments. Opposite the lavish dining
area is a fully-equipped galley and an
abundance of storage cupboards.

OPPOSITE
Helm of the Sealine S38.

ABOVE
Cockpit.

ABOVE RIGHT
Fore cabin.

RIGHT
Head.

FAR RIGHT
Saloon.

SEALINE S38 SPORTS CRUISER

DIMENSIONS

Length overall:	37ft 09in/11.51m
Beam:	12ft 03in/3.73m
Draft:	3ft 01in/0.94m
Displacement:	16,800lb/7620kg
Engine Options:	Twin Volvo KAD 300/EDC/DFG 34–36 knots Twin Volvo KAD 43P/EDC/DP 32–34 knots
Design:	Sealine

SEALINE S42 SPORTS CRUISER

With the option of a fixed V-drive or the greater flexibility of stern drives that allow you to explore shallow coral inlets, Sealine's S42 sports cruiser combines a remarkable amount of accommodation with great outdoor living space.

The boat's cockpit is designed on two levels. The lower section offers seating, a sunbed and wet bar, with the option of a built-in fridge and barbecue, a dedicated life-raft locker and access to the engine

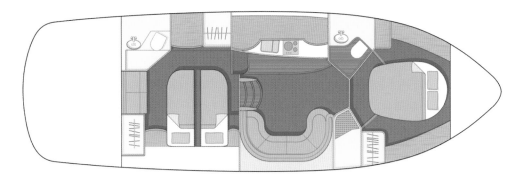

ABOVE RIGHT
Sealine S42 sports cruiser: diagram showing the general arrangement.

RIGHT
Cockpit.

OPPOSITE
Sealine S42 sports cruiser.

compartment. The teak-laid swim platform has provision for a passerelle, dinghy crane or davits. The upper al fresco deck seats seven in comfort, and with the co-pilot seat folded down offers additional seating around the table, which cleverly stows away in the bimini cover when not required. The helm seat module also doubles as a cool-box holder and has a sit/stand facility to suit individual driving positions.

Owners have the option of Sealine's patented Solar Protection System (SPS) – an integral bimini incorporating an electrically-operated sliding roof – a two-part canopy that completely encloses the cockpit rather than the standard two-stage bimini arrangement.

The luxurious saloon features a U-shaped settee and table that easily converts to provide an additional double berth. The large forward double cabin has en suite facilities, as does the master suite aft which has the option of being fitted out with a large double bed or two single berths.

SEALINE S42 SPORTS CRUISER

DIMENSIONS

Length overall:	42ft 03in/12.88m
Beam:	13ft 04in/4.06m
Draft:	3ft 04in/1.02m
Displacement:	20,700/23,500lb (9389/10660kg for V-Drive option
Engine Options:	Twin Volvo KAD 300/EDC/DFG 29–31 knots Twin Volvo KAD

RIGHT
Sealine S42 helm.

FAR RIGHT
Aft cabin.

BELOW
Galley.

BELOW RIGHT
Twin aft cabin.

OPPOSITE
Saloon.

75/EDC V-Drives
32–34 knots
Design: Sealine

SEALINE S48 SPORTS CRUISER

This is the premier boat within Sealine's range of sports cruisers and, as such, comes with a wide range of ingenious ideas and luxurious appointments. Take the cockpit, for instance. The design provides comfortable seating for up to ten around two cockpit tables, a walkaround bar, barbeque, fridge, cool box and the option of a built-in ice maker. From here it is but a step down to the water sports platform, with a dinghy lift that descends into the water, and which provides easy launching, recovery and stowage for a dinghy, PWW, or simply as a platform for swimming and snorkelling. There is also a 9-ft (2.74-m) hydraulic passerelle, which stows away unobtrusively when not in use. The option of Sealine's patented Solar Protection System houses a bimini extension to completely shade the aft cockpit and allows for the air conditioning unit to provide a curtain of cooling air.

Through a stainless steel sliding door, a curved stairway leads into a spacious saloon with dinette facility, feature bar and the

ABOVE RIGHT and OPPOSITE
Running shots of a Sealine S48 sports cruiser.

RIGHT
Plan showing the layout of the interior.

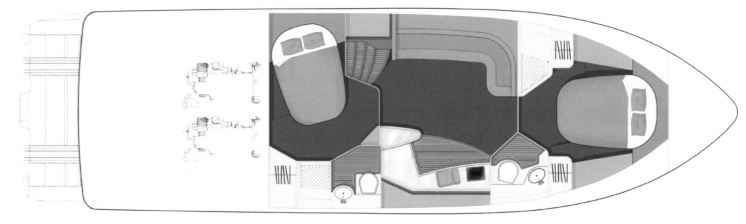

provision for flat-screen TV and surround-sound audio system within the maplewood and marble finish. Two large overhead hatches enhance the natural light from the oval portholes, and the phosphorescent strips and downlighting help to create a soft and attractive ambience. The eye-catching galley has state-of-the-art appliances and a dedicated drawer storage system. There is also the option of a dishwasher.

ABOVE
Port-side door of the Sealine S48 sports cruiser.

LEFT
Cockpit and helm.

ABOVE
Sealine S48 saloon.

ABOVE LEFT
Aft cabin.

LEFT
Forward cabin.

FAR LEFT
Galley.

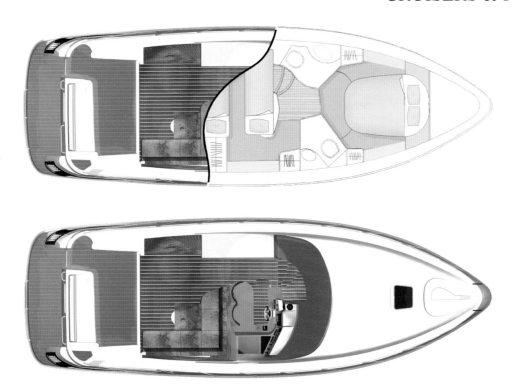

The two equally luxurious master cabins have their own en suite facilities and the aft cabin has the addition of a writing/laptop desk with a computer link to the boat's electronic information.

One final innovation is the option of Sealine's Docking System (SDS) which allows both engines and bow thruster to be controlled from a single point to simplify berthing – something that will be second nature to addicts of computer games!

SEALINE S49 SPORTS CRUISER

DIMENSIONS

Length overall:	48ft 07in/14.81m
Beam:	13ft 04in/4.06m
Draft:	3ft 08in/1.12m

Displacement:	35,000lb/15876kg
Engine Options:	Twin Cummins QSM11 34–36 knots
Design:	Sealine

SEALINE C39 COUPÉ CRUISER

This is the first in a new range of all-weather coupés from Sealine and shares the same basic hull as the C38 sports cruiser. She is equipped with Sealine's novel extending cockpit system, which provides 3ft (0.91m) of extra cockpit area at the touch of a button. The toughened glass sliding sunroof above the deck saloon, and the electronic bimini cover protecting the aft cockpit, means that the choice between wind-in-the-hair enjoyment and an air-conditioned environment can be made in seconds.

A three-section curved sliding door opens up the rear of the saloon and combined with the extended cockpit, provides a large entertaining area for a boat of this size. The large windows and modern styling provide an airy ambience and a clear all-round view from the helm/navigation position. The comfortable sofa converts easily into an occasional double berth, adding to the double cabins fore and aft which both have en suite toilet/shower facilities.

Top speed with twin Volvo Penta 300-hp diesels is 36 knots.

ABOVE
The extended cockpit of the Sealine C39 coupé cruiser.

ABOVE LEFT
Plans showing the general arrangement of the boat.

OPPOSITE
Sealine C39 coupé cruiser.

SEALINE **C39** COUPÉ CRUISER

DIMENSIONS

Length overall:	39ft 03in/11.96m
Beam:	12ft 03in/3.73m
Draft:	3ft 04in/1.02m
Displacement:	18,700lb/8482kg
Engine Options:	Twin Volvo KAD 300 EDC/DPG 34–36 knots
Design:	Sealine

SEALINE **F43** FLYBRIDGE CRUISER

The F43 is a popular import to American waters. Sealine offers a variety of layout options, which vary between three cabins or an open dinette in place of the mid-cabin. This converts easily to an occasional double berth to provide six-berth accommodation. The large saloon has

OPPOSITE
Sealine C39 coupé cruisers.

ABOVE
Helm of the Sealine C39.

ABOVE RIGHT
Galley.

RIGHT
Forward cabin.

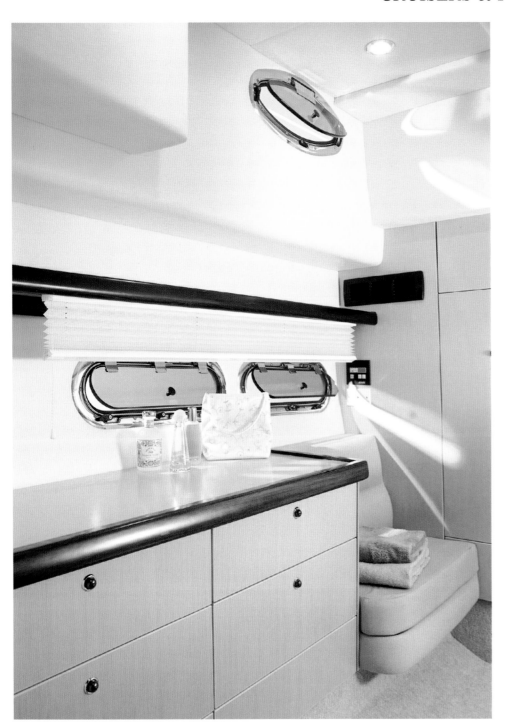

ample seating and a sturdy table, together with a sideboard unit that houses a fridge on the port side. There is also a pull-out double seat for added versatility.

The lower-level galley is fully-equipped with a hob, oven/grill, split sinks, large fridge and provision for a microwave and is well situated opposite a large dinette suite.

The deep aft cockpit has all-round seating, together with an occasional table and cockpit canopy that both stow away within the flybridge moulding. Moulded steps provide safe, easy access to the flybridge, where there is ample seating around the helm position and a large

LEFT and ABOVE
Sealine C39: views of mid-cabin.

OPPOSITE
Sealine F43 flybridge cruiser.

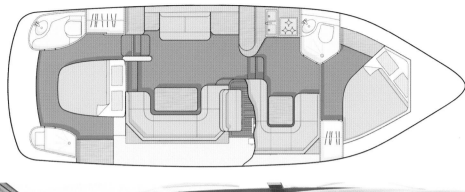

sunbed area protruding out over the cockpit.

The F43 is available with a choice of engines to give her a top speed of between 28 and 33 knots.

SEALINE F43 FLYBRIDGE CRUISER
DIMENSIONS

Length overall:	43ft 05in/13.23m
Beam:	13ft 08in/4.16m
Draft:	4ft 02in/1.27m

ABOVE
Galley of the Sealine F43 flybridge cruiser.

ABOVE LEFT
Plan of boat.

LEFT
Saloon.

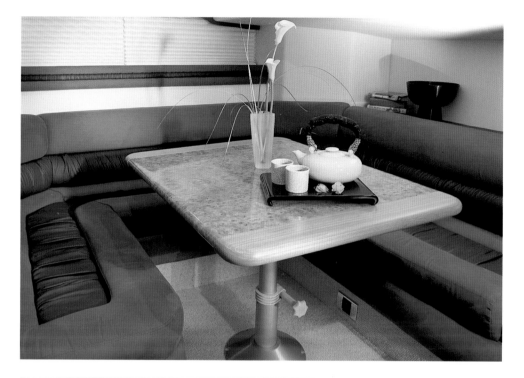

Displacement:	24,500lb/11113kg
Engine Options:	Twin Volvo TAMD
	75/EDC 31-33 knots
	Twin Volvo TAMD
	74/EDC 30–32 knots
	Twin Volvo TAMD
	63P 28–30 knots
Design:	Sealine

SEALINE F42/5 FLYBRIDGE CRUISER

As its name suggests, this is one of the Sealine models that extends itself from 42 to 45ft, thanks to the boat's novel electronically-extending cockpit and seating, which opens up a huge area for entertaining when berthed or at anchor. This is just one of a number of technical innovations that makes this flybridge cruiser remarkable. Another is the option of the Sealine Docking System (SDS), which links engines and thrusters to a single directional lever.

The boat's flybridge extends right over the cockpit to provide a great sunbathing

ABOVE
Forward cabin of the Sealine F43 flybridge cruiser.

ABOVE LEFT
Saloon.

LEFT
Head.

platform; with a little adaptation of the furniture, the area is quickly turned into a dining area for eight around a table that stows away in the helm seat.

Below deck, various layout options are available. The four- to six-berth plan offers 6ft 6-in (1.98-m) headroom throughout and comprises a master cabin forward, a spacious twin mid-cabin, which has the flexibility to convert into an office and single berth, and a saloon dinette that doubles as a fully sprung bed. Both cabins have en suite facilities. The galley is situated at the lower level in this configuration, but in another plan, this replaces two club chairs on the port side of the saloon to give the option of a further two-berth cabin amidships. Whichever is chosen, the galley comes fully equipped to cater for eight, with an oven/grill, fridge, twin sinks and provision for a microwave oven and ice-maker. There is also the option of a clever underfloor waste bin and storage system.

OPPOSITE
LEFT
Sealine F42/5 flybridge cruiser

RIGHT
Helm.

BELOW
Sealine F42/5.

FAR RIGHT
Galley.

The F42/5 is available with a choice of engines to give a top speed of between 27 and 33 knots.

SEALINE F42/5 FLYBRIDGE CRUISER

DIMENSIONS

Length overall:	42ft 04in extending to 44ft 10in (12.90 to 13.66m)
Beam:	13ft 10in/4.22m
Draft:	3ft 04in/1.02m
Displacement:	27,600lb/12519kg

Engine Options:	Twin Volvo TAMD 75/EDC 31-33 knots
	Twin Volvo TAMD 74/EDC 30-32 knots
	Twin Volvo TAMD 63P 27-29 knots
Design:	Sealine

Sealine's top-level T-line series of flybridge cruisers range from 47 to 60ft, with interiors that resemble a five-star hotel. These boats ooze quality, and with highly-polished maple and cherry furniture,

soft leather upholstery and enduring teak decks, offer uncompromising luxury.

The T47 has two large double staterooms furnished with highly-lacquered cherry and owners have the option of choosing double beds or wide singles. Each also has en suite facilities, individual shower rooms and natural marble surfaces. One of the many options available is a third cabin, in place of the low-level galley, to increase accommodation to cater for six to eight.

The saloon has a marble-topped island bar, large folding table and club chairs, sofa seating and a one-touch fold-out occasional third double berth. A fridge and ice-maker are built into the furniture and there is provision for a TV and surround-sound system.

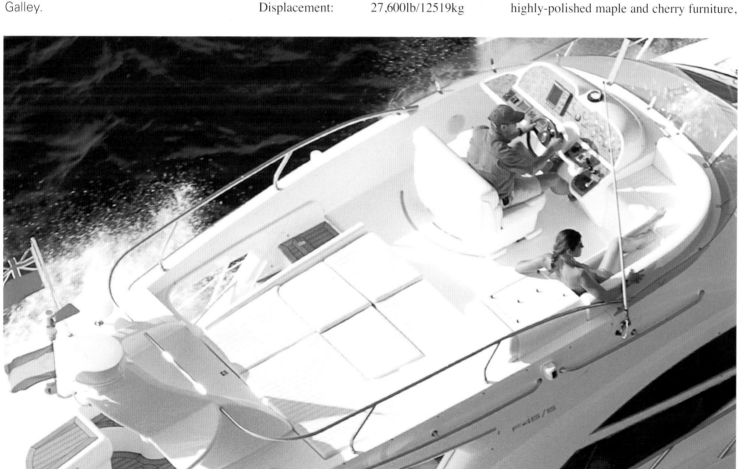

The galley is all-electric, with space for a freezer and dishwasher, while hidden away beneath the floor is a novel modular drawer storage system.

Outside, the spacious teak-laid cockpit and flybridge provide a wet bar, barbeque and fridge and there is easy access to the bathing platform which is big enough to accommodate a dinghy and passerelle.

Many owners happily employ a full-time skipper or mate to look after the boat and give them their own accommodation. This is accessed via a stairway hatch in the cockpit floor down to a single-berth cockpit cabin and the business end of the boat, where there is a laundry with

ABOVE
Saloon and helm of the Sealine F42/5 flybridge cruiser.

ABOVE LEFT
Forward cabin.

LEFT
Head.

FAR LEFT
Mid-cabin.

OPPOSITE
Sealine T47 flybridge cruiser.

washer/dryer, generator and walk-through access to the engine room, where fuel, water filters and sea cocks are clustered for checking and maintenance.

If fitted with twin Volvo diesel engines, the T47 has a top speed of between 30–32 knots.

SEALINE T47 FLYBRIDGE CRUISER
Dimensions

Length overall:	46ft 09in/14.25m
Beam:	14ft 02in/4.32m
Draft:	3ft 11in/1.19m
Displacement:	31,600lb/14334kg
Engine Options:	Twin Volvo TAMD 75/EDC 30–32 knots
Design:	Sealine

OPPOSITE
LEFT
Overhead view of the cockpit and helm of the T47.

RIGHT
Cockpit dining area.

ABOVE
T47 saloon.

ABOVE LEFT
Helm.

LEFT
Master cabin.

SEALINE T51 FLYBRIDGE CRUISER

The T51 carries the Sealine luxury to the top level; in fact, quality is the keyword from the moment you step aboard. There is an abundance of teak, from the integral bathing platform to the flybridge, which is equipped with a table, wet bar, fridge and barbeque. The cockpit, which is shaded by the extended sunbathing platform, has a passerelle, dinghy crane and large lazarette – space that can be used as a crew cabin if required.

Inside, the spacious split-level saloon has a large seating area, an entertainment centre and upper-level dinette, which is served by a fully-equipped all-electric galley. The steering position on the flybridge is protected by an all-weather helm station, which mirrors the navigation and engine instruments on the top deck.

The three-cabin accommodation plan provides for two doubles and a twin, while the forward master cabin has its own en suite toilet and circular shower. A second toilet and separate shower serves the two mid-cabins. There is also a secondary storage compartment which is large enough to accommodate a washer/dryer, dishwasher or fridge/freezer.

Highly-lacquered cherrywood joinery is in evidence throughout and complements

ABOVE RIGHT
Galley of the Sealine T51.

RIGHT and ABOVE FAR RIGHT
Saloon.

the wide choice of fabrics and hides that are available for the upholstery, which is cut and manufactured by specialist upholsterers employed at Sealine's English Midlands factory.

There is a choice between Swedish Volvo or American Cummins power units, which give the T51 a top speed of 32 knots.

SEALINE T51 FLYBRIDGE CRUISER
DIMENSIONS

Length overall:	51ft 05in/15.67m
Beam:	15ft 00in/4.57m
Draft:	4ft 07in/1.40m
Displacement:	41,000lb/18598kg
Engine Options:	Twin Volvo D12
	29–32 knots
	Twin Cummins QSMI
	29–32 knots
Design:	Sealine

SEALINE T60 FLYBRIDGE CRUISER

The T60 is the new flagship within the Sealine range, the first of which was due to

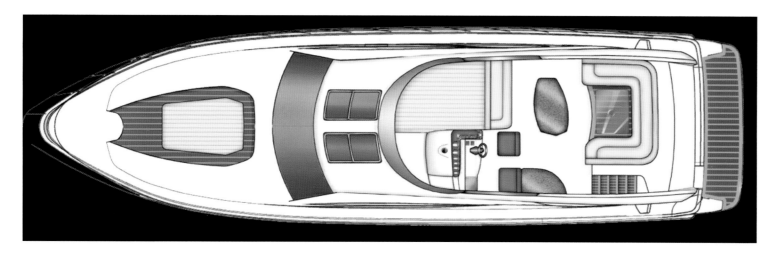

Sealine's extending deck system that adds 3ft (0.91m) to the area at the press of a button, while beneath is a single-berth crew cabin, laundry and engine room.

The spacious flybridge is fitted with a ten-seater dinette and table, a wet bar and a sunbathing area positioned in the lee of the windshield alongside the helm position. There is another bathing area built into the forward cabin top.

Fitted with a choice of engines which range in power from 715 to 1050hp and coupled to V-drives, the T60 has a top speed of around 30 knots.

SEALINE T60 FLYBRIDGE CRUISER
Dimensions

Length overall:	59ft 04in extending to 61ft 03in (18.08 to 18.67m)
Beam:	16ft 00in/4.88m
Draft:	4ft 08in/1.42m
Displacement:	52,000lb/23587kg
Engine Options:	Twin V-drives from 715–1050hp 30–32 knots
Design:	Sealine

www.sealine.com

be launched in the spring of 2004. Like the T51, this is a boat which can be designed and hand-built to reflect a discerning owner's personal tastes and preferences.

The three-deck layout in the first boat off the line offers two large staterooms, with the master bedroom amidships taking up the full width of the boat. There is also

a twin-bedded guest cabin forward of the spiral stairwell which leads up to the lounge. This has wide panoramic views and a high-level plasma television and audio system which retracts away when not in use. Behind is a wet bar, dining table and curved-glass sliding doors that open up the cockpit to provide a huge al fresco

entertainment deck. Here, on future boats, owners will have the choice of a fixed rectangular table with banquet seating.

The lower-level helm position has an electric sunroof and the area is accessed via the saloon or a door onto the side deck. The panelling and cabinetry throughout is pearwood. The cockpit is fitted with

ABOVE LEFT
Plan of the Sealine T60 flybridge cruiser.

BELOW LEFT
Side elevation.

STOREBRO BRUKS

Sweden has quite a name for innovative design, solid quality and superb craftsmanship in almost everything it produces, from cars and furniture right through to boats. Part of Storebro's reputation was built around the Solö – a 21-ft (6.4-m) mahogany-built weekender which became a classic in the same mould as the Chris*Craft and Riva Aquarama. Three thousand of these boats were built by Storebro Bruks between 1951 and 1977, and being such desirable craft, examples can still be found right across the globe, including the United States.

When it came to choose a worthy successor – a design that would pay homage to the distinctive deckline of the original Solö, which means 'sun' in Swedish, Storebro turned to the Argentine architect German Frers to produce a fresh design. It helped that Frers drives a Volvo, but it was the pleasing lines that his design studio provided for other Scandinavian boat-builders, such as Nautor Swan and Hallberg-Rassy, that made Storebro look across the Atlantic.

The result was the Storebro J34, a 33-ft deep-V weekender that cuts through waves like a knife through butter, has a top speed of 46mph and, thanks to its twin waterjet propulsion units, can turn on a dime. This very distinctive design has a large cockpit with settee seating around a central table and an integral swim platform that extends over the waterjet units. The deckline provides full standing headroom below, and the lavish woodwork within the

cabin gives the interior a distinctive Swedish look. This is divided between two V-berths forward, an enclosed toilet and shower facility, full galley and a dinette table arrangement that can seat four when the weather is bad.

STOREBRO J34 SPORTS CRUISER

DIMENSIONS

Length overall:	33ft 03in/10.13m
Beam:	14ft 06in/4.42m
Draft:	1ft 07in/0.48m
Deadrise:	aft 23°, midships 22°, fore 59°
Displacement:	11,200lb/5080kg
]Engine Options:	Twin 300-hp diesel engines 46mph/74km/h
Design:	German Frers

STOREBRO GRAND SERIES 62 FLYBRIDGE MOTOR YACHT

Storebro also commissioned Frers to design a modern successor to what had become a rather dated line of flybridge cruisers.

His answer is the distinctive Grand Series 62, which is best described as a scaled-down superyacht. The deep, safe bulwarks surrounding her deck certainly lead to the impression that it is a much larger boat, and the spacious layout, with a full-width master suite amidships, double guest cabin forward and twin-bedded cabin, all with en suite facilities, adds to the illusion.

A circular stairway leads up to an

ABOVE
Storebro Solö.

OPPOSITE, LEFT and RIGHT
Storebro J34, designed by German Frers.

OPPOSITE
Storebro Grand Series 62.

ABOVE
Grand Series 62, rear view.

RIGHT
Guest cabin.

FAR RIGHT
Saloon seating and dinette adjacent to
the helm.

equally spacious saloon, which has a semi-circular dinette sited opposite the pilot position for guests to watch what is happening through large panoramic tinted windows. The galley/bar is sited behind the helmsman in a central position to service the forward dinette, lounge area or the large flybridge, which is accessed via an internal stairway and another leading from the aft cockpit.

The most unique aspect of the Grand Series 62, however, is the lengths to which Storebro engineers have gone to dampen sound. Instead of being bonded to the hull, the interior sections are isolated from the mechanical installations with the aid of 'floating' dampers, similar to the way engines are mounted, which absorb much of the noise and vibration. The fibreglass hull and carbon composite superstructure make maximum use of modern materials to provide a strong, durable construction that is light enough to enhance the boat's stability and performance at sea.

OPPOSITE
Storebro Grand Series 62.

LEFT
Master stateroom of the Grand Series 62.

STOREBRO GRAND SERIES 62
FLYBRIDGE MOTOR YACHT
Dimensions

Length overall:	62ft 00in/18.90m
Beam:	17ft 08in/5.38m
Draft:	(waterjets) 2ft 10in (0.86m)
	(V-drives) 4ft 09in (1.45m)
Deadrise:	aft 22˚, midships 25˚, fore 62˚
Displacement:	53,760lb/24385kg
Engine Options:	Twin Scania DI 14/82M with V-drives. Twin MAN D 2840 LE 403EDC with waterjet system
Design:	German Frers

www.storebro.se

Grand Series 62: the saloon, dinette and steps leading up to the flybridge.

DERECKTOR 50/50

The Derecktor 50/50 was one of the stars at the 2003 Fort Lauderdale Boat Show. Built as a fast launch to be carried aboard a Feadship superyacht, her 50-knot performance means that she can make short work of island-hopping around the Caribbean during the winter and make the run between Monte Carlo and Cannes, during the busy Mediterranean summer months, far quicker than a car.

Designed by Doug Zurn, her 50-ft hull is moulded using high-tech composites to minimize weight and allow for an elegant teak superstructure and transom without compromising performance. She is equipped with two fighting chairs in the large cockpit, a well-appointed wheelhouse, large saloon, galley and heads amidships, and has the owner's double cabin forward with a single skipper's berth just behind.

The first in this line of semi-custom performance launches was fitted with twin 1,300-hp MAN diesel engines driving surface-piercing propellers, but future boats can be fitted with waterjet propulsion units if preferred.

The *Longevity*, at the Fort Lauderdale Boat Show in 2003, was built by Derecktor as a tender for a superyacht operating between Palm Springs and the Mediterranean. She can make the run between Portofino and Monaco within half an hour.

DERECKTOR 50/50

DIMENSIONS

Length overall:	50ft 00in/15.24m
Beam:	14ft 05in/4.39m
Draft:	2ft 11in/0.89m
Displacement:	38,000lb/17237kg
Engine Options:	Twin 1,300-hp MAN diesel 50 knots
Design:	Doug Zurn

www.derecktor.com

CARLO RIVA

The Riva name has been around since 1842 when Pietro Riva began building boats on the banks of Lake Como, Italy. A chance opportunity to repair a fleet of boats wrecked in a storm 70 miles (113km) away at Sarnico led him to move base and set up a wooden shed on the banks of the Oglio river, which is where the Riva dynasty remains.

Carlo Riva, born in 1922, took over the business in the perilously barren times immediately after the Second World War. As a 22-year-old, he was full of confidence and risked everything to expand the business. First, he had to find 2 million lire to pay off his father for materials – then 2 million more to cover new

investments. The banks refused to help so he turned to friends and leading boatmen around Sarnico to help. Gino Gervasoni, a schoolfriend, stepped in as a partner and for the next ten years they and the business lived a hand-to-mouth existence. Even in 1950, when they managed to obtain credit to exhibit the Riva speedboats on a stand at the Milan Trade Fair, they were sailing perilously close to the wind financially. By day, Carlo Riva wore a dapper suit, showing potential customers around his boats and setting up appointments in front of the best hotels, but by night he slept on the attic floor of a monastery.

The following year he went to the U.S.A. to import engines for his boats – which in Europe were still difficult to come by. With a little wheeling and

dealing, Carlo secured the mechanical lifeline the Riva business needed, with the result that the company went from strength to strength, building exotic powerboats for kings, emperors, sultans and the glitzy jet-set. Peter Sellers bought one of his boats for Princess Margaret and had it delivered to Windsor Castle as a wedding present, while David Niven, Princess Caroline of Monaco, Anita Ekberg, Brigitte Bardot, the Shah of Iran and even the grandson of Chief Sitting Bull were all proud owners.

The 29-ft (9-m) Riva Aquarama, first launched in 1971 and powered by twin 350-hp V8 American engines, which gave the boat a speed of 44 knots, epitomized the very best in boat-building. Constructed *from* a single log of mahogany to ensure

OPPOSITE
ABOVE and BELOW
Riva Aquariva Silver.

ABOVE and ABOVE LEFT
Riva 44 Rivarama.

LEFT
Cabin.

that all the planks matched, the brightly-varnished hulls, with their leather internal upholstery, took a month to construct and cost more than $200,000.

These were tough standards to maintain, and Carlo Riva saw the writing on the wall in the late 1960s when fibreglass began to rival wood as a building material and a series of strikes almost bled the company to death. In 1969, Riva sold the business to Whittaker, a ship-building conglomerate based in Los Angeles with considerable experience in fibreglass technology, which had bought Bertram Boats from Dick Bertram the previous year. Soon, Riva was building the Bertram 20 and 25 under licence, which helped the Italians to overcome the technology hurdle; but the strikes continued and it was only the return of Gino Gervasoni that saved the company from bankruptcy.

He re-structured the business and oversaw the launch of a new, very distinct line of performance power cruisers designed by Giorgio Barilani. Their racy good looks, fine Italian interior styling and exotic fabrics soon set the Riva marque ahead of its rivals and attracted the same Rolls Royce and Ferrari set that had so cherished the Aquarama.

When Gervasoni retired, the company lost its direction again and in 1985 the Whittaker Corporation sold a majority interest in Riva to the Arab financial group, Investcorp, that also owned the Tiffany jewellery marque. Three years later, the business was in the hands of the London

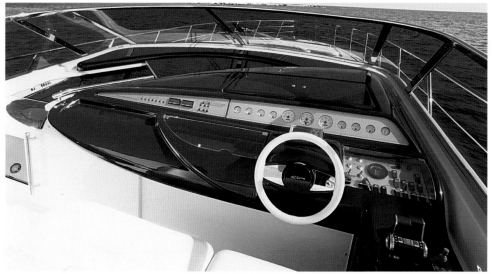

OPPOSITE and ABOVE
Riva 59 Mercurius.

LEFT
Helm.

banking group, Schroder Wagg, which sold it on to Rolls Royce Motors, then part of the Vickers Group. But these were turbulent times, particularly for prestige products, and when Vickers decided to auction off its Rolls Royce and Bentley names to BMW and VW, Riva also went under the hammer. It has since been acquired by the Ferretti Group, an Italian conglomerate that not only builds boats under its own name, but also owns Bertram Yachts in the U.S. Matters came to a full circle when Ferretti honoured Carlo Riva with a model of his famous Aquarama – the Rivarama 44 – to mark the company's return to Italian ownership.

LEFT
Riva 59 Mercurius, saloon.

BELOW LEFT
Head.

BELOW
Galley.

OPPOSITE
Master stateroom.

CIGARETTE POWERBOATS

Cigarette's reputation for building fast, brassy, throbbing powerboats has its roots deep in offshore racing's history. Back in the late 1960s, when speed was something of an obsession for an increasing number of high-income, high-energy customers, Don Aronow was the man to see. The first of his many victories was earned on the 176-mile (283-km) stretch from Long Beach, California to Ensenada, Mexico, when Don and his riding mechanic, 'Knocky' House, drove their 32-ft (9.75-m) deep-V-bottomed *Cigarette* across the line well ahead of the rest. The pair went on to capture 192 victories in this twin Mercruiser-powered prototype boat as far away as the Bahamas, Italy, France, England and right across the U.S., including the Hennessy Key West race, which marked their official debut on the national racing scene.

Aronow's *Cigarette*, named after a boat owned by a notorious rum-runner during the prohibition years, gained eight international victories and speed records in three countries. The Bahamas 500, a gruelling, rough-water duel, and one of America's most famous offshore contests, first saw *Cigarette* take the chequered flag in 1969. These Aronow-built boats then dominated the event from 1971 to '76. His Cigarettes also carried off World Championship titles from 1969 through to 1974 and again in 1976.

The name, Cigarette, quickly became an icon for powerboats, with a host of famous and infamous racers such as Dr. Bob Magoon, Tom Gentry and Vincenzo Balestrieri winning title after title in the U.S. and abroad. Even Carl Kiekhaeffer, the father of Mercury, created several new engine designs for the Cigarette boats he owned; in fact, Aronow and Keikhaeffer's shared quest for excellence evolved into part of the Mercury legend.

Over the years, the design of the 32-ft Cigarette was refined and led to a 36-ft (11-m) model that was to dominate the offshore racing world throughout the 1970s. This was replaced by the 35-ft (10.6-m) Cigarette and the range was then extended with a 40-ft (12-m) version, which was bought by kings, princes, presidents and even the U.S. Customs services, who joined the ranks of racing champions like Rocky Aoki and Roger Penske as Cigarette owners.

Aronow's untimely death in 1987 was a result of turbulent times and questionable customers on Thunder Boat Row in North Miami, where he built his powerboat fame and met his demise. He may have been gunned down by an assassin, but the business and legend that he developed lives on, immortalized by TV series such as *Miami Vice* to become one of America's strongest sporting brand names.

The company is now controlled by Cigarette devotees Skip Braver and Neill Hernandez, who have moved the business to a 100,000-sq ft factory at OpaLocka, Miami and oversee the continuing story. Indeed, Cigarettes continue to capture the top trophies, winning the 1998 SBI world title, the national title in 1999 and both world and national titles in 2000. In 2002, these distinctive boats won the Factory 2 world and national titles.

Today, the Cigarette range runs from 35 to 46ft (10.6 to 14m), packed with power and wearing the most remarkable paint jobs. Their supportive seating comes straight from the race circuits and the larger models have distinctive interior forward cabins, which seem superfluous until, after a hard day's racing at 100-mph plus, a bed seems all too inviting!

CIGARETTE 35 MISTRESS
POWERBOAT
DIMENSIONS

Length overall:	30ft 00in/9.14m
Beam:	8ft 00in/2.44m
Draft:	2ft 04in/0.71m
Deadrise:	20°

Displacement:	8,800lb/3992kg
Engine Options:	Twin Sterling 1,050-hp inboard/outdrives
Design:	Cigarette

The 36-ft Gladiator was introduced in 2001 as a no-frills, go-fast, lower-profile, no-cabin or rub-rail hull. Her race-rigged, staggered 800+ HP Zul engines, with 600-ci (9830cc) Tunnel RAM, give the boat quite a kick, with a top speed of 110mph. A new Herring six-blade propeller gives her a cruise speed of 75mph (121km/h) at 3,500rpm, with a redline of 6,000rpm.

CIGARETTE 36 GLADIATOR
POWERBOAT
DIMENSIONS

Length overall:	36ft 11in/11.25m
Beam:	8ft 00in/2.44m
Draft:	2ft 04in/0.71m
Deadrise:	20°
Displacement:	8,000lb/3629kg
Engine Options:	Twin 800-hp Zul inboard/outdrives 110mph/177km/h
Design:	Cigarette

OPPOSITE
Cigarette 36 Gladiator offshore racing powerboat.

THIS PAGE
Details of the 36 Gladiator.

CIGARETTE 38 TOP GUN

POWERBOAT

DIMENSIONS

Length overall: 37ft 06in/11.43m
Beam: 8ft 00in/2.44m
Draft: 2ft 03in/0.68m
Deadrise: 20°
Displacement: 9,300lb/4218kg
Engine Options: Twin Sterling
1,050-hp inboard/
outdrives
Design: Cigarette

THIS PAGE and OPPOSITE
Cigarette 38 Top Gun offshore racing
powerboat.

The 42-ft Tiger's triple-step hull and side-by-side engines has made it one of Cigarette's most popular models. In 2004, the company raised the performance of this model by staggering the engine positions to provide more power, with the option of two larger block units or a triple engine layout.

CIGARETTE 42 CONCEPT/XP/TIGER POWERBOAT

DIMENSIONS

Length overall:	41ft 07in/12.67m
Beam:	8ft 00in/2.44m
Draft:	3ft 00in/0.91m
Deadrise:	20°
Displacement:	9,800lb/4445kg
Engine Options:	Twin Mercury 1,050-hp inboard/ outdrives
Design:	Cigarette

CIGARETTE 46 CONCEPT/XP POWERBOAT

DIMENSIONS

Length overall:	45ft 07in/13.89m
Beam:	8ft 00in/2.44m
Draft:	4ft 00in/1.22m
Deadrise:	20°
Displacement:	12,200lb/5534kg
Engine Options:	Twin Sterling 1,050-hp inboard/ outdrives
Design:	Cigarette

www.cigaretteracing.com

OPPOSITE and FAR LEFT
Cigarette 42X offshore racing powerboat.

ABOVE and LEFT
Cigarette 46 American muscle powerboat and engine.

Don Joel Aronow (1927–1987), father of modern U.S. powerboating.

Don Aronow was one of the most

influential figures in American powerboat history. He not only formed some of the biggest names within the industry, such as Formula Marine, launched in 1963, but also Donzi Marine in 1964, Magnum Marine a year later and Cigarette in 1970. He was also a designer and racer and won most of the world's top events, including the Miami-Nassau and the Bahamas 500, partnering top owners from both sides of the Atlantic, such as Carl Keikhaefer, Don Shead, Jim Wynne, Walt Walters and Vincenzo Balastrieri, who all bought his boats.

His narrow deep-deadrise hull shapes took Ray Hunt's original deep-vee concept to another level, producing boats that could outrun any other type of craft. He won countless championships and titles as well as the custom of kings, presidents and Hollywood stars. Don Johnson, perhaps, did more to publicize the Cigarette name by featuring one of these extreme craft in the TV hit series, Miami Vice. But these boats were also used extensively by the darker elements of organized crime to pick up and land drugs, outrunning and outsmarting the coastguard in the process.

It was believed to have been this side of the business that led to a contract being placed on Aronow's life; he was gunned down outside his Cigarette factory on 3 February 1987.

LEFT
Don Aronow.

BELOW
The *Cigarette*, Don Aronow's original raceboat, which became the company's name in 1970.

OPPOSITE and ABOVE
Cigarette 42X powerboat and details.

OPPOSITE and THIS PAGE
Cigarette 45 Maximus offshore racing
powerboat.

OPPOSITE and THIS PAGE
Cigarette 46 Rider TS offshore racing
powerboat.

OPPOSITE and THIS PAGE
Cigarette 46 Rum Runner offshore
racing powerboat and details.

TRADER YACHTS

Trawler yachts, hybrid semi-displacement powerboats that combine the excellent sea-keeping abilities of a deep-sea trawler with the ability to cruise at 20 knots, first emerged in the 1970s with names like Grand Banks, which popularized the building of these conservative craft in the Far East, where traditional hardwoods like teak and mahogany are in plentiful supply. Tarquin Trader is a new name on the U.S. market, but the England-based company has been building these distinctive Trader yachts for more than two decades at a yard at Kaohsiung, Taiwan. Now Tarquin has a sales office in Portland, Maine to market its 44- to 120-ft range to help it to become as popular in the U.S. and the Caribbean as it is in the Mediterranean.

One of the biggest selling points of these custom-built motor yachts is that their interiors can be designed to meet almost any requirement. In many respects, customized boats built around a standard hull offer many advantages over one-off designs, especially at the superyacht end of the

RIGHT
Trader Yacht's 445 Signature motor yacht.

ABOVE RIGHT and OPPOSITE
Trader Yacht's 585 Signature motor yacht.

FAR RIGHT
Dining area.

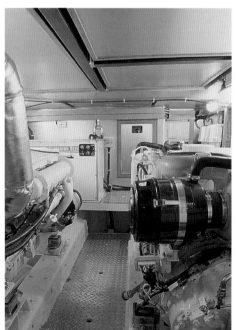

OPPOSITE and ABOVE LEFT
Trader Yacht's 535 Signature motor
yacht.

ABOVE
Saloon.

FAR LEFT
Cockpit and rear view.

LEFT
Engine room.

Trader range. Buyers are invariably high-powered businessmen who, having made a decision, expect fast results. On the other hand, to have a proven production yacht customized to meet individual requirements can cut this time by two-thirds. Even better, the boat will hold no surprises performance or otherwise and the construction and engineering will be already proven. And there are cost savings, too. According to a superyacht designer, 'Modern yachts, built with every labour saving device, have become such complex pieces of engineering these days that they are now closer to a ship than a motor yacht. It can take upwards of a year just to finalize all the installations before a single piece of wood or fibre is laid, so if that development work can be amortized over a number of boats, then the savings are significant.'

Take the interior of the Trader 535 Sunliner as an example. Europeans often favour some separation between the galley and saloon and often have it a few steps away at a lower level forward of the wheelhouse. Americans, however, want to see the galley, either incorporated into the saloon to service the open entertainment areas around the aft deck and flybridge, or have it tucked under the saloon behind the engine room, where there is least motion when under way. Americans and Europeans also have very different requirements when it comes to galley hardware; the U.S. market invariably demands more freezer and fridge space, a bigger cooker and hob and an American-grade dishwasher. Then there is the question of individual cabin layouts. These boats are built for serious passage-making across oceans, and if you plan to do the long legs yourself, rather than have the job done by a delivery crew, then you will appreciate the benefits of a single pilot berth running parallel to the centreline, rather than having several plush king-sized suites with their beds running athwartships. All this can be catered for within the adaptable traditional hulls of a Trader yacht.

These flybridge trawler yachts come in two versions – with or without a structural deck over the stern cockpit, which can add 2–3,000lb (910–1360kg) to their displacement. All have an inside helm position next to a sliding door which opens onto the starboard side deck. They are also fitted with large bow-thrusters to simplify manoeuvrability when docking. Teak-laid decking abounds, from the large raised aft deck right through to the bows and there is a choice of solid maple, cherry or teak furnishings inside, all hand-crafted by English and Taiwanese joiners.

The Trader 445, 505, 535 and 585 models share semi-displacement hulls of similar proportions, with a fine entry to cut through seas, running back to a moderate V single-chine hull form with a long keel that keeps them on track when running through following seas. These boats are renowned for their soft ride, will happily maintain a steady 15–17mph (24–27km/h) over long distances, and have a range of up to 1,700 miles (2736km). The speed estimates given here will vary from one boat to another within each class, in line with the varied specs decided upon at the build stage, which can add as much as 4,000lb (1815kg) to the displacement on the larger boats.

The year 2004 saw the launch of the Trader 64, the first of a new breed of Tarquin trawler yachts designed by Tony Castro. The design was tank-tested extensively before production to prove her performance and sea-keeping qualities, and she carries an extra 1ft 6in of beam over earlier models, which interior designers Redman Whitely Dixon have fully exploited. Her light and spacious saloon benefits from the large panoramic windows and has the galley positioned between the dining area and aft deck. Below deck, the owner's stateroom and private en suite facilities are set aft, facing out through bay windows set in the stern. Two further guest cabins are set forward, together with a private study.

An eye-catching feature is that the observation wings extend out from the flybridge to provide conversational seating and a dining area for guests, which is serviced from a wet bar and galley positioned just ahead of the sunbed area on the coach roof above the stern deck. Steps sweep down from the aft deck to a swim platform, which is large enough to carry a small tender which can be lifted on davits mounted on the deck above.

TRADER 445 SIGNATURE MOTOR YACHT

DIMENSIONS

Length overall:	43ft 05in/13.23m
Beam:	14ft 00in/4.27m
Draft:	4ft 02in/1.27m
Deadrise:	22°
Displacement:	31,360lb/14225kg
Engine Options:	Twin 150 – 400-hp diesels 13–27mph (21–43km/h)
Design:	Tarquin

TRADER 505 SIGNATURE/506 SUNLINER MOTOR YACHT

DIMENSIONS

Length overall:	50ft 06in/15.39m
Beam:	15ft 00in/4.57m
Draft:	4ft 10in/1.47m
Deadrise:	20°
Displacement:	44,800/48,280lb 20321/21900kg
Engine Options:	Twin 225 – 450-hp diesels P. 15–24mph (24–39km/h)
Design:	Tarquin

TRADER 535 SIGNATURE/535 SUNLINER MOTOR YACHT

DIMENSIONS

Length overall:	53ft 06in/16.30m
Beam:	15ft 00in/4.57m
Draft:	5ft 04in/1.62m
Deadrise:	20°
Displacement:	47,000/49,280lb (21319/22353kg)
Engine Options:	Twin 450hp Caterpillar 3126 diesels 25mph/40km/h Twin 500hp Yanmar 6CXM-GTE2 diesels 28mph/45km/h
Design:	Tarquin

LEFT and ABOVE
Trader 48 motor yacht.

TRADER 575 SIGNATURE/575 SUNLINER MOTOR YACHT

DIMENSIONS

Length overall:	57ft 06in/17.53m
Beam:	15ft 00in/4.57m
Draft:	5ft 04in/1.62m
Deadrise:	20°
Displacement:	49,280/53,760lb (22353/24385kg)
Engine Options:	Twin 225–700-hp diesels 450 14–30mph (22.5–48km/h)
Design:	Tarquin

TRADER 585 SIGNATURE MOTOR YACHT

DIMENSIONS

Length overall:	58ft 06in/17.83m
Beam:	15ft 00in/4.57m
Draft:	5ft 04in/1.62m
Deadrise:	20°
Displacement:	54,000lb/24494kg
Engine Options:	Twin Caterpillar 450-hp diesels 24mph (39km/h)
Design:	Tarquin

TRADER 64 SUNLINER MOTOR YACHT

DIMENSIONS

Length overall:	65ft 00in/19.81m
Beam:	17ft 06in/5.33m
Draft:	5ft 03in/1.60m
Deadrise:	20°
Displacement:	100,352lb/45520kg
Engine Options:	Twin Caterpillar C12 700-hp diesels 25mph (40km/h) Twin Caterpillar C18 1,000-hp diesels 30mph/48km/h
Design:	Hull – Tony Castro Interior – Redman Whitely Dixon

TRADER 85 MOTOR YACHT

DIMENSIONS

Length overall:	85ft 00in/25.91m
Beam:	20ft 00in/6.10m
Draft:	5ft 06in/1.68m
Deadrise:	18°
Displacement:	162,000lb/73483kg
Engine Options:	Twin 1500-hp Caterpillar C18 22mph/35km/h
Design:	K.S./Tarquin

www.tradermotoryachts.com

ABOVE
Aft dining area of the Trader 85 motor yacht.

ABOVE LEFT
Trader 85 cockpit.

OPPOSITE
Trader 85 motor yacht.

SUNSEEKER YACHTS

If there are two aspects that have long separated Sunseeker powerboats from others, it has been performance and finish, with a line so distinctive that they are easily spotted in any marina.

Robert Braithwaite launched the company in the mid-1960s under the name of Poole Powerboats to import Scandinavian powerboats to satisfy a growing local market in Dorset, England, for quality day cruisers. In those days, there were simply no builders of any consequence producing sports leisure boats within the U.K., and Braithwaite and his partner, John Macklin, learned all they could before embarking on their own production boats in 1968. In 1972, Poole Powerboats exhibited a new 23-ft (7-m) performance weekender at the London Boat Show, which was the turning point in this story. The man to provide the catalyst was former F1 racing driver Henry Taylor, who was selling boats in the South of France. 'If you could build one in white and put in a full-width sunbed, then I might be interested,' he suggested.

At that time, no one in Britain, which is renowned for its changeable weather

RIGHT
Helm of the Sunseeker Sportsfisher 37, with deck seating.

OPPOSITE
Sunseeker Sportsfisher 37.

patterns, had ever thought of building a boat with a sunbed, or indeed thought much about exporting boats to the Mediterranean. The resulting deep-V Daycab 23 carried 4 berths, a galley and toilet, bathing platform and, of course, a sunbed. Just as important, she had a 41-mph performance and was the first to carry the Sunseeker name.

Compared with the Italian-built Rivas, these boats, which sold well in the U.K. and Northern Europe, were not considered stylish enough for the growing Mediterranean market. But Braithwaite and his crew realized what was needed – a range of boats that could really perform in any weather and with looks to match. They turned to Don Shead, then as now a highly-respected designer of race boats and superyachts. He had never been involved in designing production cruisers, but saw the potential of combining Braithwaite's vision with his own specific skills. The relationship has lasted to this day, and 75 Sunseeker models now bear Shead's distinctive stamp. The current range, which starts with the 37 Sportsfisher, develops through a series of luxury sports and flybridge cruisers to Sunseeker's flagship, the 135 Yacht. They are built in three waterside sites in Poole and produced by a 1,200-strong workforce.

OPPOSITE
Sunseeker Sportsfisher 37.

LEFT
Sportsfisher 37 main cabin.

415

FAR RIGHT
Sunseeker Sportsfisher 37 head.

RIGHT
Galley.

BELOW
Forward Cabin.

OPPOSITE
Sunseeker Sportsfisher 37.

SUNSEEKER SPORTSFISHER 37

Designed around one of Sunseeker's well-proven deep-V hulls, the Sportsfisher is the refined workhorse within the range, specifically suited to fishing and diving. Fitted with a bimini over the forward cockpit and console, she has a wide cockpit with access through transom and side doors. Below decks, she shares the comforts and luxuries of all other Sunseekers, with an open saloon and settee area, a double berth, enclosed head and shower, and a fully-fitted galley. She can be powered either with Volvo inboard/outdrives to give her a speed of 46mph, or rigged with two or three outboards to provide a top speed of 57mph.

SUNSEEKER SPORTSFISHER 37

DIMENSIONS

Length overall:	39ft 08in/12.09m
Beam:	11ft 07in/3.53m
Draft:	2ft 04in/0.71m
Deadrise:	19.8°
Displacement:	17,420/18,300lb (7902/8301kg) (inboard)
Engine Options:	Twin Volvo KAD 300 275-hp inboard/ outdrives 43mph (69km/h) Twin Volvo D6 310-hp inboard/outdrives 46mph/74km/h Triple Yamaha 250-hp outboards 57mph/92km/h
Design:	Don Shead

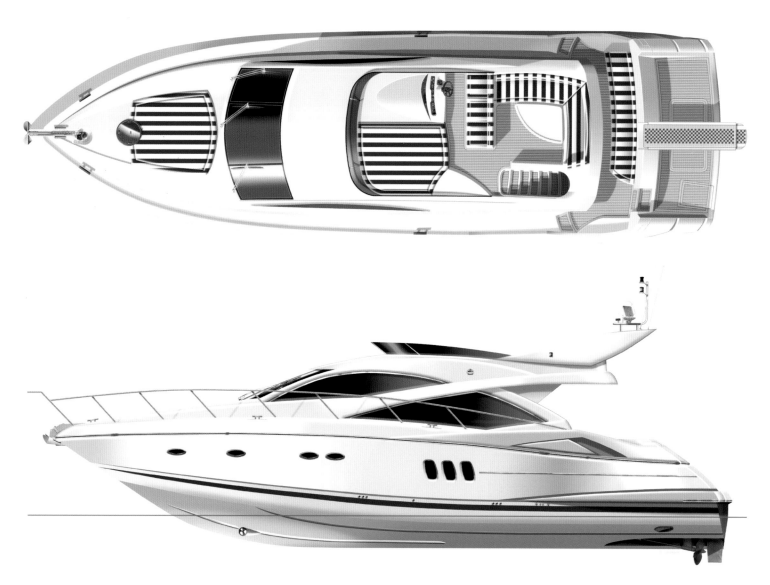

settees and the galley to serve them; the entertainment decks are situated at the aft end of the saloon.

The 64 shares many of the facilities of the 74 but with accommodation for six guests in two staterooms and a twin-bedded cabin. The 56 and 50 (illustrated here) have accommodation for up to six and the option of a separate crew cabin/utility room and lower galley. The swim platform on all models is large enough to accommodate an RIB and the larger models have the option of a garage or self-contained crew accommodation.

ABOVE LEFT
Sunseeker Manhattan 50 deck plan.

LEFT
Side elevation.

OPPOSITE
ABOVE LEFT
Main saloon with seating area, helm, and television on a Sunseeker Manhattan 50.

ABOVE RIGHT
Stateroom.

RIGHT
Forward cabin.

RIGHT CENTRE
Guest cabin.

FAR RIGHT
Stateroom head.

SUNSEEKER MANHATTAN RANGE

The Manhattan flybridge range of family-orientated sports motor yachts starts with the 50-footer and moves upwards in size to include 56-, 64-, and 74-ft models. Each has the flexibility of dual helm options and other all-weather comforts, matched with an imaginative use of interior space and performance.

The 74 has a large flybridge accessed by companionway steps forward down to the saloon and the aft cockpit, and is fitted out with a wet bar behind the helm and co-pilot seating, an L-shaped settee and dining table to port, with a large sunbed area aft. There is a full-width owner's stateroom accessed via a private circular stairway from the saloon, a VIP suite forward and two twin-bedded cabins with a further one aft for crew. The split-level saloon has three entertainment areas with large L-shaped

OPPOSITE
Sunseeker Manhattan 64.

RIGHT
Aft stateroom.

BELOW
Saloon with steps up to the flybridge.

BELOW RIGHT
Galley.

SUNSEEKER MANHATTAN 50

FLYBRIDGE SPORTS CRUISER

DIMENSIONS

Length overall:	52ft 06in/16.00m
Beam:	15ft 01in/4.60m
Draft:	4ft 00in/1.22m
Deadrise:	18.8°
Displacement:	50,600lb/22952kg
Engine Options:	Twin Volvo KAD D1216 690-hp diesels Twin Caterpillar C12 16 710PS 685-hp diesel 36mph/58km/h
Design:	Don Shead

SUNSEEKER MANHATTAN 64
FLYBRIDGE CRUISER
DIMENSIONS

Length overall:	71ft 06in/21.79m
Beam:	17ft 01in/5.21m
Draft:	4ft 08in/1.42m
Deadrise:	20°
Displacement:	42,500lb/19278kg
Engine Options:	Twin Caterpillar
	3406E 16 800-hp
	diesels
	Twin MAN D2840
	V10 1036-hp diesels
	38mph/61km/h
Design:	Don Shead

ABOVE
Sunseeker Manhattan 64 head.

ABOVE LEFT
Forward stateroom.

LEFT
Guest cabin.

OPPOSITE
ABOVE
Sunseeker Porto Fino 53, deck plan.

BELOW
Side elevation.

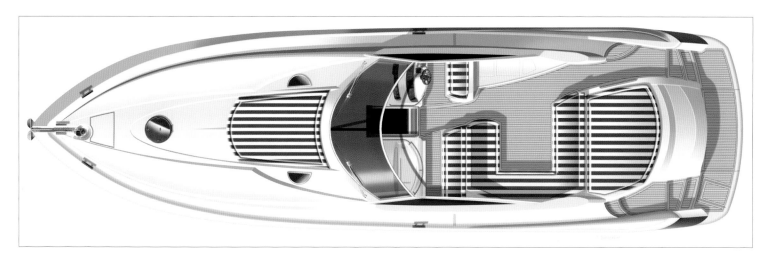

Draft:	3ft 01in/0.94m
Deadrise:	18.8°
Displacement:	42,500lb/19278kg
Engine Options:	Twin Caterpillar C12
	16 710PS diesels
	Twin Volvo D12
	715PS diesels
	41mph/66km/h
Design:	Don Shead

As its name suggests, the Predator range consists of high-performance sports cruisers with the option of twin shaft-tunnel drives or triple Arneson surface props on the 75-, 95- and 108-ft models to provide exhilarating 45-mph plus speeds. Like all Sunseekers, they are luxuriously appointed and have an opening hardtop above the internal steering position, expansive cockpits, garage for the jet skis or tender, and a hydraulic bathing platform.

There are various layout options on all the models, the 68 being available with an upper saloon separated by sliding patio doors from the aft cockpit. Below, a second lavish saloon leads onto two master suites with the central area amidships devoted to a full-width owner's stateroom and two pilot berths amidships, or split into two separate twin-bedded cabins.

SUNSEEKER PORTO FINO RANGE

Sunseeker's Porto Fino offshore sports cruiser range includes 35-, 46-, and 53-ft models that share large open cockpits and sun decks with luxurious interiors as well as impressive speeds and cruising range. The 53 has a dinghy garage built into the stern and sleeps six in three cabins, including an owner's cabin in the bow with a private head and shower room. The two twin-bed cabins share a day head sited amidships close to the companionway steps. There is a large galley fitted to port opposite a shallow V-shaped settee and table.

Available with a choice of 700-hp diesel engines and propeller-shaft options, she has a top speed in excess of 40mph and a cruising range of up to 300 miles.

SUNSEEKER PORTO FINO 53 SPORTS CRUISER

DIMENSIONS

Length overall:	55ft 09in/16.99m
Beam:	15ft 02in/4.62m

SUNSEEKER PREDATOR 68 SPORTS COUPÉ CRUISER

DIMENSIONS

Length overall:	71ft 06in/21.79m
Beam:	17ft 01in/5.21m
Draft:	4ft 08in/1.42m

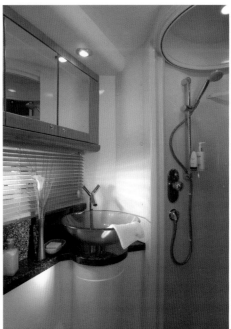

ABOVE
Sunseeker Porto Fino 53 forward cabin.

ABOVE LEFT
Main saloon.

LEFT
Head.

FAR LEFT
Galley.

OPPOSITE
Sunseeker Predator 68.

LEFT
Sunseeker Predator 68 showing
tender garage.

ABOVE
Head.

OPPOSITE
ABOVE LEFT
Saloon.

ABOVE RIGHT
Aft stateroom.

RIGHT
Forward cabin.

FAR RIGHT
Galley.

Deadrise:	18.9°
Displacement:	42,500lb/19278kg
Engine Options:	Twin Caterpillar
	3406E 16 800-hp
	diesels
	Twin MAN D2840
	V10 1036-hp
	diesels
	45mph/72km/h
Design:	Don Shead

Sunseeker's top-of-the-range Yacht flybridge models start with the 82 and move through to the 95, 105 and 135 superyacht levels. These bespoke vessels provide owners with the opportunity to specify almost any interior layout and décor. The Yacht 82 (page 430) has a fully-equipped enclosed helm console repeated on the flybridge, and is large enough to provide a dining area, galley and lounge with two banks of comfortable seating and sliding-door access to the aft sun deck. Accommodation includes an owner's stateroom, two guest cabins and two further single cabins aft for children or crew. Top speed is a respectable 35mph and it has a cruising range of 350 miles.

RIGHT and OPPOSITE
Sunseeker Yacht 82.

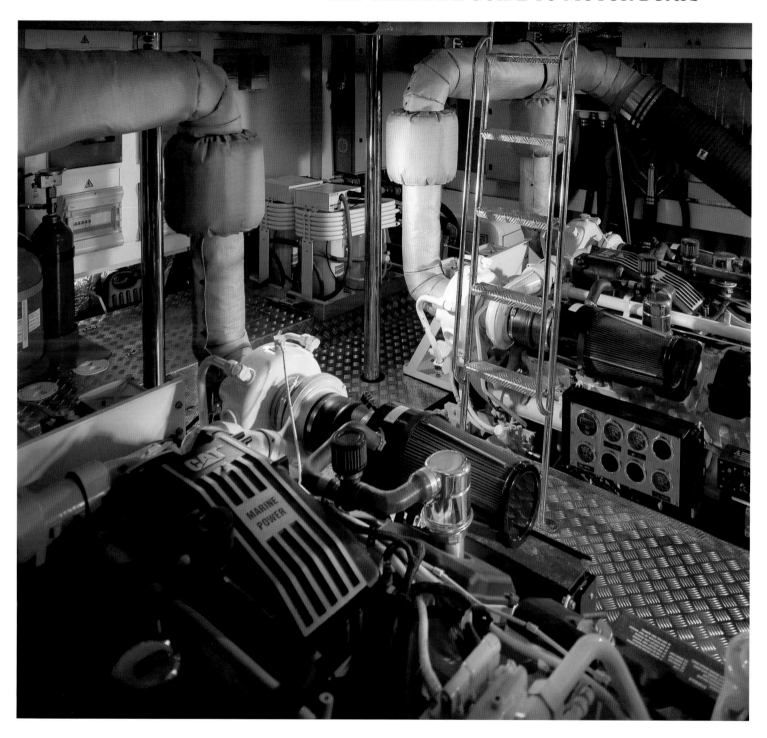

OPPOSITE
Sunseeker Yacht 82, rear and front views.

LEFT
Engine room.

BELOW
Helm.

SUNSEEKER YACHT 82 SPORTS FLYBRIDGE MOTOR CRUISER

DIMENSIONS

Length overall:	82ft 06in/25.15m
Beam:	20ft 03in/6.17m
Draft:	5ft 06in/1.68m
Deadrise:	19.9°
Displacement:	121,300lb/55022kg
Engine Options:	Twin MAN D2842 LE409 1,479-hp diesels
	Twin Caterpillar V12 1,550-hp diesels 35.6mph/57km/h
Design:	Don Shead

www.sunseeker.com

OPPOSITE
Sunseeker Yacht 82.

ABOVE
Sunseeker Yacht 84, dining table.

ABOVE LEFT
Main saloon with seating and dining area.

FAR LEFT
Forward stateroom.

CRUISERS & POWERBOATS

SUPERYACHTS

If the U.S. Government was forced ever again to requisition a fleet of American-owned megayachts for home defence, as happened during the Second World War, then the fleet would dwarf almost every other naval power, both in numbers and performance. Marinas around the cruising grounds of Florida, the Caribbean and the west coast are full to the brim with these 100-ft plus flights of fancy, costing anything from $10–$100 million apiece. Whether or not government officials could ascertain who owns them is another matter. Many fly under flags of convenience for tax purposes, concealing their true ownership in a world where terrorism is now a greater threat to personal security than any foreign power.

All are personal statements of the taste of their first owners, at least, who employ, if not an army, then certainly a squad of stylists and interior designers to produce a vessel to reflect their own personalities and idiosyncracies. Self-publicists, like Donald Trump, can't help themselves when it comes to flaunting their floating assets, but many others remain anonymous to all but a close circle of VIP guests and crew who are sworn to secrecy. The second-hand market can be just as

profitable for the shipyards and design teams, and millions more are spent on changing the décor, just as others have kitchens re-furbished when moving house.

At 413ft (126m), the largest private yacht is the four-tiered *Octopus*, owned by Microsoft co-founder Paul Allen, whose fleet also includes the 301-ft (92-m) *Tatoosh* and the 198-ft (60-m) Feadship *Meduse*. The second largest American-owned private yacht is the diesel electric-powered 315-ft (96-m) *Limitless*, owned by the Limited chain store chief, Leslie Wexner. Then there is the converted ice-

OPPOSITE and ABOVE
The 118-ft *Wallypower*.

breaker *Bart Roberts* at 265-ft (81m) overall whose owner had her converted for a planned five-year cruise to the less accessible parts of the world. Another luxury conversion was made on the 255-ft (78-m) *Lone Ranger* for Peter Lewis, the former CEO of Progressive Auto Insurance, to chart the world during his retirement. Then there is Oracle boss Larry Ellison's 244-ft (74-m) *Katana*. She is among a dozen or more 200-ft plus megayachts, and her gas turbine propulsion systems, which push her up to 36mph (58km/h), means that she can run rings around the others.

There are a further 80 or more American-owned private yachts measuring between 150 and 200ft overall and several hundred more squeeze into the 100-ft plus

superyacht class, but it is usually only when they are put out to charter that the rest of the world gets a glimpse of their splendour.

Every now and then, a multi-millionaire has something built that is outrageously different. In Luca Bassani's case, the Italian superyacht builder is something of a trendsetter anyway, and wanted to show the world what could be achieved by combining Italian minimalistic flare with lightweight state-of-the-art composite engineering and military design know-how. The result is the 118-ft (36-m) *Wallypower* – a prototype triple gas turbine-powered wonder yacht with a turn of speed in excess of 65mph (105km/h. This is the sort of yacht that will quite literally whisk you from Miami to the Bahamas or Monaco to Porto Cervo quicker

than it takes to get to and from the airports.

Scale models were tank-tested extensively in Sweden and in Ferrari's F1 wind-tunnel facility at Marinello, before the Italian warship builder, Intermarine, could build this striking carbon-moulded express motor yacht. She has three en suite staterooms and further accommodation for six crew – one of them being a specialist aero engineer whose prime job is to look after her three TF50 Chinook helicopter engines and two secondary 370-hp Cummins diesels (used for slow-speed manoeuvring), which drive, via common gearboxes, three KaMeWa waterjet units.

The angular, glass-sided deckhouse offers what Luca Bassani calls his 'enclosed open air living space'. This hides a large

CRUISERS & POWERBOATS

saloon with white upholstery, plain wooden features that give the boat a beach-house feel, and a carbon fibre dining table and chairs behind the helm position, providing guests with panoramic views protected from wind and sun. Her tender, another Wally rocket ship, is stowed in an hydraulically-raised garage within the foredeck.

Wallypower's performance is nothing short of spectacular. Her gas turbine engines have a power to weight ration of 3.6hp per lb and producing some 5,600hp

each at an optimum temperature of 50° F, the acceleration is impressive. So is her ride, with those warship bows slicing effortlessly through any chop. She has run the 220-mile (354-km) gauntlet between Monaco and Porto Cervo at an average of 65.5mph (105km/h); Luca Bassani claims that even with the lesser power option of twin 3,650-hp V16 MTU diesels, the boat will still cruise at 46mph. That drop in spec represents an $8 million saving on the $24.83 million tag for the triple-jet version.

WALLY 118 SUPERYACHT

DIMENSIONS

Length overall:	118ft 00in/35.97m
Beam:	26ft 03in/8.00m
Draft:	4ft 01in/1.24m
Deadrise:	22°
Displacement:	undisclosed
Engine Options:	Triple 5,600-hp DDC TF50 gas turbines and twin 370-hp Cummins diesel inboards, driving two

KaMeWa 63 and one KaMeWa 52 waterjets 69mph/111km/h Twin 3,650-hp MTU 16V 4000 diesels driving KaMeWa waterjets 51mph/82km/h

Design:	Wally/Intermarine
Styling:	Interior & exterior Wally/Lazzarini & Pickering

www.wally.com

SQN Motor Yacht

The 126-ft (38-m) Dubois-designed SQN motor yacht, built by Alloy Yachts International in 2003 offers a more traditional insight into the world of modern superyachts. Registered in the Cayman Islands, SQN's rich sycamore and vavona redwood décor was styled by Donald Starkey and includes an owner's stateroom, three guest suites, accommodation for four crew and a double cabin for the captain.

She was designed primarily for cruising in temperate climates and features extensive outdoor areas for relaxing and entertaining guests in a variety of settings, from the al fresco lounging and dining areas on the aft deck and flybridge, where there is also a Jacuzzi, to the more formal banqueting suite and saloon. The accommodation is spread across three decks, with the owner's suite situated on the main deck, comprising a separate study, lounge area, walk-in wardrobe and adjoining 'his and her' bathrooms. Guests are accommodated on the lower deck in three cabins, all with en suite facilities and fully-independent DVD/CD entertainment systems. Two of these cabins are doubles, with the third fitted out with two single beds and a Pullman berth. A fourth cabin

OPPOSITE
Wallypower's saloon (left) and stateroom (right).

BELOW and PAGES 438 and 439
Alloy Yachts' SQN Superyacht, designed by Dubois Naval Architects.

on this deck is equipped as a gymnasium to help guests burn off the calories served up by the cordon bleu chef in a professionally-fitted galley. SQN has a top speed of 16 knots (19mph) and has a range of 4,550 miles when cruising at 10 knots.

SQN MOTOR YACHT
DIMENSIONS

Length overall:	126ft 03in/38.48m
Beam:	27ft 10in/8.48m
Draft:	6ft 02in/1.88m
Displacement:	479,360lb/217438kg
Engines:	Twin 1450-hp Caterpillar diesels 19mph/31km/h
Design:	Dubois Naval Architects/Donald Starkey

www.alloyyachts.com

INDEX